CRICKET
UMPIRING
AND
SCORING

CRICKET UMPIRING

AND

SCORING

THIRD EDITION

Tom Smith MBE

and the Association of Cricket Umpires and Scorers

**With a Foreword by
Sir Colin Cowdrey, CBE**

The official textbook of the Association
of Cricket Umpires and Scorers containing
the M.C.C. Official Laws of Cricket with
interpretations and definitions for
umpires, scorers, players
and spectators

Weidenfeld & Nicolson
LONDON

All communications should be addressed to:
The Association of Cricket Umpires and Scorers
P.O. Box 399, Camberley,
Surrey, GU16 5ZJ

First published by J. M. Dent, 1980
Reprinted 1980, 1981, 1983, 1984, 1986, 1988
2nd edition 1989
Reprinted 1990
3rd edition first published by
Weidenfeld & Nicolson 1993
Reprinted 1994, 1995

This revised edition
first published by Weidenfeld & Nicolson, 1996

Phototypeset in 10 on 11 point Baskerville by
Deltatype, Birkenhead, Merseyside
Printed in Great Britain by Clays Ltd, St Ives plc
Weidenfeld & Nicolson, Orion Publishing Group
5 Upper Saint Martin's Lane, London WC2H 9EA

Contents

Foreword by Sir Colin Cowdrey

The Laws of Cricket have been revised many times since the mid-eighteenth century when the earliest code of the Laws was drawn up – although cricket historians still dispute the actual year. The two most recent major revisions occurred in 1947 and 1980.

Colonel R. S. Rait Kerr, then Secretary of the M.C.C., wrote and published the first edition of *Cricket Umpiring and Scoring* in 1957 to give guidance to umpires in all grades of cricket as to the interpretation of the Laws. During the late 1960s and early 1970s a number of Experimental Laws were introduced, adding greatly to the burden placed upon the umpires. S. C. Griffith, on retiring as Secretary of the M.C.C. in 1974, was requested to undertake the monumental task of revising, and tidying, the Laws; in consultation with Tom Smith the 1980 Code, which reduced the Laws from 47 to 42, was produced. The untidiness, qualifications and notes were removed. Umpires' powers were strengthened and sanction procedures standardized.

To supplement the Code introduced in 1980, Tom Smith rewrote *Cricket Umpiring and Scoring* to include the new Laws and the officially agreed interpretations. After a number of reprints and two revisions the book remained the only authoritative interpretation of the Laws of Cricket accepted by the majority of umpires. Regrettably Tom's failing eyesight prevented him from carrying out any further revision, necessary due to a number of interpretations, promulgated by the Association of Cricket Umpires & Scorers, with the agreement of the M.C.C.

Following limited revision in 1993, the Association's Chairman, Sheila Hill, and Deputy Chairman, Robbie Robins, have combined to produce a new version of *Cricket Umpiring and Scoring* which I am pleased to commend to all whose interest lies in fair play and the upholding of the Laws of the game.

Like most human activities and social behaviour, the game of cricket has changed within the last 50 years. Umpiring is more difficult than it was as decisions are challenged with greater frequency. I do not think I am alone in considering that the game will only flourish if the umpire's decision is accepted without dissent or any show of pique, no matter that occasionally a wrong decision will be made.

Since the Association of Cricket Umpires & Scorers was founded in 1953 its membership has grown to over 6,000 and spans the globe having members in 48 countries outside the United Kingdom. Its interpretation of incidents which occur are sought, and accepted, by numerous correspondents throughout the world. This brotherhood can only be to the benefit of the game which has so much to offer to all who play and enjoy it.

The duties of an umpire do not change. It is still true that an umpire can, alone, ruin a game of cricket. If the two umpires ensure the game is conducted in the correct spirit, enabling all the players to enjoy the match, they rarely will receive thanks for their contribution. Not that they will expect it – nor look for it – but they will be content to have given the players the fullest opportunity to enjoy their sport.

It is vital that umpires fully appreciate their part in ensuring that the game is played fairly. They must not shrink from taking the appropriate action if any instance of unfair play occurs. If the game is to continue to flourish, it is vital that players fully appreciate the umpire's decision must be accepted without question.

It was agreed at the Association's AGM in 1993 to amend the title of the Association to incorporate 'Scorers'. Although a number of scorers had been members of the Association for many years, the change of title recognized the importance of the umpires and scorers forming a 'team'. I am pleased to note that this edition gives added weight to the value of competent scorers as well as offering sound advice as to how they can best carry out their duties.

Cricket Umpiring and Scoring offers clear direction to all umpires and scorers as to how they should conduct themselves as well as offering the latest interpretation of Laws. I am convinced that all who study will benefit from doing so – as will the game of cricket.

Colin Cowdrey

The Author

The late TOM SMITH, after many years as a player, football referee and cricket umpire, founded the Association of Cricket Umpires in 1953; he then served continuously as General Secretary for twenty-five years and upon retirement was appointed a Life Vice President. Well known and respected in every cricket playing country of the world, Tom was recognized internationally as an authority and umpire arbiter on the Laws of the game and the technique of cricket umpiring. For some years he wrote regularly for the *Cricketer* on field umpiring and problems of cricket Law.

During 1956/7 Tom Smith spent many long periods at Lord's assisting the late Col. Rait Kerr with the preparation of the Association's text-book; and in 1961, at the request of the late author, he took over the work of revising the book which he continued until 1979.

The 1980 Code of Laws brought the need for the production of a completely new and up-to-date book.

For services to cricket Tom Smith was awarded an M.B.E. and honoured by the M.C.C. with the election to Honorary Life Membership – a distinction awarded only to a small group of people who have carried out special services for cricket – and in 1980 H.R.H. the Duke of Edinburgh presented him with the National Playing Fields Association's Torch Trophy Award for outstanding service to cricket. He served a term as a member of the Cricket Council, was a member of the Test and County Cricket Board Cricket Committee from its inception, a member of the M.C.C. Laws Committee, and at one time Chairman of the National Cricket Association Cricket Committee. He also served for several years on the National Cricket Association

Management Committee and specialist Working Parties as well as the Surrey County Cricket Association Committee.

During 1974 Tom was appointed by the M.C.C. to assist Mr S. C. Griffith, former M.C.C. Secretary, in revising and redrafting the 1947 Code of Laws at the request of the International Cricket Conference.

During the years between the preparation and framing of a new draft and final presentation to the International Cricket Conference, Cricket Council and other representative bodies, Tom Smith was appointed by the M.C.C. to a special Redrafting Committee set up to produce the final draft of the new code, after giving careful consideration to all suggestions and recommendations from the United Kingdom and overseas.

Tom Smith gave a lifetime of devoted service to umpires and umpiring and, under his leadership and inspiration, the Association of Cricket Umpires, since 1994 the Association of Cricket Umpires and Scorers, has grown from a small beginning to a recognized international Association with over 6000 members and 200 affiliated organizations.

He died on 14 December 1995. His legacy will long be remembered.

Preface to the first Edition

Players, umpires, and all involved know well that cricket is a difficult and complicated game. Although, for well over two centuries, the conduct of the game has been governed by Codes of Laws, these Codes have been, of necessity, subject to revision and change. From 1788 to the present day the M.C.C. has been, and is, recognized internationally as the sole authority for the production, interpretations, and revisions of the Laws.

Although the Codes that have come down to us over the years have shown many changes, it is an astonishing fact that the fundamentals of the game have changed very little since 1744 when the first Laws appeared. The 1947 code, which reduced the number of laws from 55 to 47, has stood the test of 33 years wonderfully well and the work on the 1980 version, which has again reduced the number of laws, from 47 to 42, was mainly concerned with shaping and rearranging rather than with massive changes.

After producing a draft with Mr Griffith, I was privileged to be a member of the M.C.C. Laws Recodification Committee set up to consider and revise the preliminary draft, with a view to producing a final draft for consideration by the I.C.C. and Governing Bodies. Many long days were spent at Lord's on discussion and consideration; and it soon became obvious that to produce every interpretation and modification of the many intricate Laws would be completely impossible. It was already realized that a completely new production of *Cricket Umpiring and Scoring* was necessary, and the Committee asked if I would include in the book some of the extensions and interpretations that we had discussed: I am, of course, happy to do so.

I would emphasize that *Cricket Umpiring and Scoring* is not to be considered in any way a substitute for the official M.C.C. Laws of Cricket. Humbly, I would like the book to be regarded as a back-up or explanatory guide through the Laws, which will assist umpires to extend correct interpretations of the Laws on to the field of play. In that sense I hope that this is very much a practical book.

I hope, too, that the book will be of interest to coaches, players, and in fact all those interested in the game who would like to know a little more about it. If this should happen and young cricketers especially can learn more about the Laws of the game, the more they will understand the umpires' problems of application and the pressures to which they are subjected.

T.S., 1980

NOTE ON THE SECOND EDITION

After six reprints a second edition has become necessary. This has enabled me to include new Laws, to revise and add to the text and to extend some of the definitions. I am most grateful to Len Martin for reading the proofs of this edition.

With official changes in the methods of scoring, Part III has been brought completely up to date, and I am especially grateful to Mrs Pat Cooke and Ian Beveridge, both scorers of the highest quality, for their kind advice and assistance.

Finally, it has been an inspiration and greatly encouraging to receive so many appreciations of the book not only from readers in the U.K. but from other cricketing parts of the world, and I thank the kind people who have corresponded with me and become friends.

T.S., 1988

NOTE ON THE THIRD EDITION

Over the past seven years, a number of queries have been answered and points of Law clarified in consultation with the M.C.C. and T.C.C.B. These points have been incorporated in the rewritten text of Part II, together with changes in the Laws over this period.

The introductory section, Part I, and the scoring section, Part III, have also been altered to a lesser extent. We are grateful to Dennis Cooke, Sally Pitman and Cathy Rawson for their contributions on scoring, throughout Part II as well as in Part III.

S.D.H.; W.T.R., 1996

Acknowledgments

I would like to thank the M.C.C. for their encouragement in the writing of this book and for permission to reprint the new Laws. I am very grateful too for the patience and support of former M.C.C. Secretary Mr S. C. Griffith; the Chairman of M.C.C. Laws Committee Mr F. G. Mann; and former Assistant Secretary M.C.C. Mr J. Lofting, with whom I have spent countless hours in examining, discussing and setting out the many complex problems of the Laws during the long recodification period.

Thanks are also due to friends and colleagues Len Martin, Ian Beveridge, Brian Molloy and Bill Ainsworth for their assistance, and to the late Lewis Trethewey for help with original drawings.

Finally, I am deeply grateful to Mr John Arlott for his charming foreword.

T.S.

Acknowledgments *for the third edition*

In writing this revised edition of Tom Smith's classic book, we must first acknowledge our debt to his text, on which ours is based and from which we have borrowed freely. Lewis Trethewey's drawings are included; they are just as relevant as in the original edition.

We are also grateful to the M.C.C., not only for permission to reprint the Laws, but also for their continuing support in dealing with matters of Law.

Grateful thanks are due to Nigel Plews for his wise advice about some points of Law. Thanks should also go to a number of members who recommended points for inclusion, but particularly to John Isterling and Dick Burden who suggested improvements to the text itself.

We would also like to express our gratitude to our President, Sir Colin Cowdrey, for his generous foreword.

S.D.H.; W.T.R.

Part 1   The Umpires

Although the male gender is used predominantly throughout the text it must be understood that this is purely for brevity. Both men and women are equally welcome either as umpires or as scorers. Nothing in this book is to be taken to imply otherwise.

1 UMPIRES AND UMPIRING

The formation of the Association of Cricket Umpires took place when the author wrote to a number of senior umpires and arranged a meeting in March 1953. The reason for formation was simple: a frank recognition of the fact that umpiring in all grades of cricket was, at that time, at a very low level indeed. It was felt that it was vitally necessary for the future of the game to improve the standard of umpiring by education, training, and examination. Since 1953 the Association has become the internationally recognized parent body for umpires. The qualification of Full Membership can be obtained only by passing stringent written and oral examinations, followed by proof of the highest possible standard of field-work. The same is true of Qualified Scorer Membership, except that there is no oral examination for scorers.

It is said, with justification, that many young players are discouraged and turned away from the game by having to practise and play on bad pitches; it is equally true to say that many promising young players lose interest in the game because of bad umpiring – especially in club, village and school cricket. The game can ill afford to lose young potential and although there has been dramatic improvement in the standard of umpiring over the last four and a half decades, there is still much to be done in maintaining the highest level of field-work.

Internationally, not enough has been done to encourage umpires to become qualified and not enough importance has, as yet, been given to the essentiality of uniformity in control technique and interpretations of Law over the whole cricket world. During 1977, for the first time in the history of cricket, two overseas umpires were seconded by their Boards to the English First Class County Panel. They unquestionably gained valuable experience by officiating throughout an entire English season of seventy days' cricket. England is, of course, the only cricket playing country employing full time professional umpires. If the selected overseas umpires, who have a once-in-a-lifetime opportunity to extend their knowledge and technique, are able to return home and communicate the results of their experience to their colleagues, then some progress towards standard practice must have been achieved. In 1993 support for I.C.C. by the National Grid enabled a panel of umpires to be established to provide independent umpires for international matches. At the same time I.C.C. committed itself to a programme of umpire development particularly in the Associate Member countries. This will undoubtedly make a great contribution towards achieving uniformity of interpretation and practice.

2 NECESSARY QUALIFICATIONS

PHYSICAL QUALIFICATIONS
An umpire must possess first-class eyesight, and spectacles are by no means an impediment. A person who has had modern optical testing with lens prescription is undoubtedly in possession of better eyesight than one who has doubtful vision and has yet to visit an optician.

Standing in the field for long periods is a heavy physical strain, especially so because mental concentration must be maintained throughout these long periods. General good health with well developed hearing is necessary. The ability to concentrate is vital. If there is, as there often is, a shortcoming in this respect, the weakness must be worked on by practice and self-control. It is imperative that the mind be kept clear of all extraneous thoughts: the field action only must dominate.

Complete concentration will mean that the umpire is able to pick up and register the smallest detail of action; and, often, the small details noted will lead to a prediction of what is going to happen. Concentration leads to anticipation and gives just that much more time for correct positioning and judgment. Training by sincere effort and self-discipline (and this also means constant self-criticism), will lead to much improved control of thought, action, and technique. Natural factors for the governing of response to action are: age, health, fatigue, and the effects of alcohol. It behoves umpires to be very wary of alcohol intake on long hot tiring days, when decisions from split second action are often required under heavy pressure.

PERSONAL QUALIFICATIONS

An umpire must be a person of integrity and character. It is by no means easy to remain calm, completely neutral, and unbiased when under pressure. Possession of a judicial mind – one which enjoys quickly weighing up evidence and making sound judgments – is a very helpful quality, but induction training can also help cultivate logical thinking and expression. Absolute impartiality is, of course, essential, as is an even temper, which will enable the game to be controlled firmly, but with good humour. Having to learn to disregard the hasty excited behaviour of players is a very difficult task, especially so when it has, unfortunately, become fashionable in all games and ways of life to denigrate control and authority.

Nevertheless, the umpire must learn to overcome personal sensitivities and remain undisturbed and impartial, fearlessly continuing to control the game according to the Laws. Despite acquisition of knowledge from field training, there will be times when an umpire must make decisions based on action and facts not specifically covered by the Laws. Commonsense and fairness must find an answer and the umpire will find these essential factors in his qualification.

TECHNICAL QUALIFICATIONS

It goes without saying that every umpire must possess a thorough knowledge of the Laws of Cricket. Personal study, training classes; quizzes; and above all, constant discussion and listening will instil knowledge; but there will always be much to learn.

People with trained and retentive memories can easily accumulate academic knowledge of the Laws, and may even pass tests and examinations with flying colours, but this does not necessarily make them good controllers. The real test must come on the field of play where knowledge must be applied to ever-changing situations. Theoretical knowledge is one thing, but the ability to make reasoned decisions in good time when under pressure from split second actions, is quite another. It is a sad fact that many players, at all levels of the game, have only a superficial knowledge of the Laws. An umpire who has played cricket starts with the great advantage of having experienced match atmosphere. Nevertheless it is not necessary to be an ex-player in order to become a top grade umpire.

Players expect, and have a right to expect, the highest standard of umpiring; but like players, and indeed all of us, umpires are not infallible and must occasionally make mistakes. Very seldom are mistakes made through lack of knowledge of the Laws, but rather on the judgment of facts. Players should remember that in these days of instant television playback, telephoto lenses, and large financial rewards, the strain on umpires is heavier now than ever it has been. The spectacle of top players, at times, showing dissent is seen by young cricketers and can very quickly be accepted and imitated as part of the technique of the game. Bad conduct on the field is very harmful to the future spirit and well-being of cricket and as we shall see later, umpires are given powers under the Laws to take appropriate action. Although an umpire should be able to control dissent and bad behaviour by asserting his own personality there will be times when the Laws must be applied.

Trainee umpires must take every available opportunity to stand in at as many matches as possible, regardless of the standard of cricket, or distance of travel. Building up match experience is absolutely vital and it will be impossible to reach the top class of umpiring without really conscientious field practice. As much spare time as possible must be freely sacrificed in order to reach the highest possible standard, bringing a sense of craft and satisfaction at a job well done.

3 THE RECRUITMENT OF UMPIRES

The supply of umpires to the game over the whole cricket world is nowhere near the demand. Although the Association of Cricket Umpires and Scorers has had astonishingly high recruitment figures over the years, it is quite impossible to satisfy the requests for umpires and scorers from Club and League Cricket in the U.K. Overseas Umpire Associations too are always looking for new members. The most promising field for recruitment is undoubtedly cricketers who have retired or are considering retirement. Cricketers will possess some knowledge of the Laws, will have developed powers of concentration, and certainly will have experience of match atmosphere. Many ex-players who are thinking of taking up umpiring say that they are anxious to keep in touch with the game, and umpiring and scoring associations should see to it that every possible encouragement is given.

Another steady source of supply is the large number of men and women who are enthusiastic lovers of the game, but through lack of opportunity, skill, or physical disability have been unable to play. Many of these people possess the strength of character and determination which will lead to qualification and, especially if reasonably young, on to the highest class.

4 THE TRAINING OF UMPIRES AND SCORERS

Many umpiring and some Cricket Associations organize discussions, quizzes, and training lectures for umpires and scorers. Some arrange examinations and grade umpires according to qualifications. Grading of scorers is not undertaken as yet by these Associations.

The Association of Cricket Umpires and Scorers invites umpires and scorers to join as Associate Members. Stringent examinations in written, oral, and field-work are organized over the U.K. and internationally, for entry into Full Membership – a certificated qualification recognized over the cricket world. There is a similar examination structure for entry into Qualified Scorer Membership. Training classes with qualified instructors are also held regularly in various parts of the U.K. both for umpires and for scorers. In some overseas countries there are qualified instructors holding classes. For aspiring umpires not within reach of classes there is an Open Learning Manual. For scorers there are correspondence courses.

It has already been said that the general standard of knowledge of the Laws amongst players at all levels is, at best, superficial. It is, of course, unreasonable to expect players to acquire the detailed knowledge necessary for umpires, but it is essential for the full enjoyment of the game that players have a reasonable understanding of the Laws. Coaches should ensure that knowledge of the Laws forms part of any training curriculum. Every endeavour must be made to establish a good relationship between players and umpires, with mutual respect for each other. Coaches and school officials should impress on young cricketers the importance of the immediate acceptance of the umpire's decision, and the undesirability of putting unnecessary strain on a job which is already difficult enough. At the highest levels of the game, immediate television playbacks of action highlight umpires' decisions for viewers to appraise and, unfortunately, sometimes highlight bad behaviour and players showing dissent. Often, players are seen appealing for LBW decisions when they are in positions from which it is quite impossible to make an assessment of the many considerations that an umpire must apply. Unfortunately the thought in some players' minds is that the louder and more widespread the appeal, the greater is the chance of a favourable decision.

Bad behaviour on the field is harmful to the spirit and the future well-being of the game. Who can blame young cricketers for thinking that such behaviour is correct, when they see their heroes showing petulance and simulated disbelief on the field? Officials at school games carry a heavy responsibility for their pupils' behaviour. Discipline and the spirit of the game must be instilled at this stage.

During coaching sessions for players it is possible for discussions and quizzes on the Laws to be arranged – especially during bad weather when outside work is impossible. Ample material can be found in the official M.C.C. Laws and in this book. The Association of Cricket Umpires and Scorers will also supply quiz questions and answers.

If young cricketers can be taught to grow up with a reasonable knowledge of the Laws as well as their technical skills, they will understand the responsibilities and problems of umpires. This, in turn, will lead to the game becoming more enjoyable for players and officials, and with that, a realization that umpires are not 'enemies', but are there simply to ensure that the game is played according to the Laws. The disciplines involved in playing a game under proper control can only be of benefit to life in general.

Net practice for umpires, especially at the beginning of the season, is invaluable. Club net practice nights are an excellent opportunity for outdoor training – even for experienced umpires – while much more could be done with trainee umpires standing at the nets with instructors. Umpiring Associations should give much more thought to this type of practice and outdoor training in general: it can often easily be organized and arranged with the co-operation of a club.

Under the control of the National Cricket Association, indoor competitive cricket is now being played over the country. Umpires in the U.K. therefore not only find themselves standing all the year round, but having to learn a new technique as well. The pace of the indoor game necessitates the utmost concentration and mobility, and supplementary rules to the general Laws will need to be studied. Verbal instructions to the scorers and a completely new environment is a challenge to umpires that has been accepted, and will be met. Indoor cricket has become very popular and is here to stay. Umpires should make themselves available through their County Cricket Associations for experience and selection. They will find control of the indoor game very enjoyable and rewarding.

5 THE CONDUCT OF UMPIRES

The word 'Umpire', first used in sport as long ago as 1714, is a development of the old middle English word *noumpere*, derived from the old French *nomper* (*non* – not; *per* – equal). One of the most treasured traditions of cricket is, and must always be, the immediate and unqualified acceptance of the umpire's decision.

The office of umpire has always been one of responsibility and dignity. Therefore to maintain their status in the eyes of cricketers and spectators, umpires must never by word or gesture say or do anything to endanger the respect given to them and their colleagues. It is not by any means easy to bear the bad behaviour of players with patience and composure, but even in the extreme cases, disapproval must not be shown by word or gesture. **Law 42** now deals with the conduct of players. Umpires must, when it becomes necessary, courageously follow the procedures laid down.

The power and confidence of a joint appeal may be impressive, but the umpire must make a judgment on the action without hurry, by waiting a second or two to formulate a mental picture of the action before calmly and deliberately giving a decision. On the other hand, an appeal may be individual and quiet, but it must receive exactly the same weight of unhurried consideration as the concerted and noisy bellow.

It is very important that umpires do not offer any form of explanation for a decision, either on or off the field. At the close of play it may be possible to clear up a misunderstanding by drawing attention to a particular Law but, even then, the umpire must be careful to avoid being drawn into an argument. It is also vital to avoid being drawn or led into a discussion around a particular decision of either umpire. Loyalty towards a colleague must be complete and absolute. It has been said, with truth, that many a good decision has been spoilt by a poor explanation and an umpire who so much lacks confidence in himself that he finds it necessary to justify his decision, will never reach the top grade. 'Levelling out' – an attempt to be fair by levelling out a known mistake by deliberately making another – is fatal, and certain to lead to the players losing confidence in the umpire. There will always be some players who will be aware of what is happening and, if a genuine and sincere mistake has been made, the umpire must accept that he, the players, and, in fact, all humans are fallible. Concentration and control must not suffer by emotion or worry over a possible mistake. If it does, it may lead eventually to further mistakes. The whole incident must be put out of mind and this can be done by applying the utmost concentration to the next action in the game.

The umpire must not persist with a decision which he knows, in his heart, was a genuine mistake. It will take considerable courage and cause comment, but the Laws provide for mistakes to be corrected, subject to the correction being made promptly, and the umpire must have the strength of character to put a wrong right. Far from losing face, the umpire who shows a quiet and sincere determination to be scrupulously fair, will gain respect from the players. It is, of course, far better to avoid the whole situation, and such incidents can be kept to an absolute minimum by being unhurried and deliberate in answering appeals. A pause over a decision, followed by a firm and definite answer, is characteristic of the best umpires.

An umpire must not hesitate to consult a colleague who is in a better position to see a point of fact involved in a particular incident. In the past there has been some feeling against consultation, on the grounds that it could appear to indicate weakness or unwillingness to act. The Laws, however, provide for consultation and the official view is that not only may an umpire consult his colleague, but he must regard it as his duty to do so if he knows that his doubt on an essential point can be resolved. Further reference to consultation is made throughout this book. The impossibility of judging a clean catch by the wicket-keeper or close fielder, where the bowler's end umpire's view is obstructed, but the striker's end umpire has a clear view of the action, is a typical example. This is one case, but there are many other incidents where it would be negligent and unjust not to seek assistance or confirmation before an appeal is answered. It must be emphasized that consultation does not mean wasting time by heavy-handed irritating consultations in the middle of the pitch. A series of unobtrusive signals, often merely a glance, can be arranged. There must, however, be no doubt as to either the question being asked or the answer given. If an unobtrusive glance is not enough, an umpire must not hesitate to approach his colleague for a mid-pitch consultation.

Even after consultation, all appeals must be answered by the umpire within whose jurisdiction the responsibility lies. The exception would be the very rare case of an umpire being physically prevented from seeing the action – such as being knocked over by a fieldsman – and in this case the decision could be made and given by the other umpire.

As a body, umpires should regard themselves as part of a guild or fraternity. The great majority will be members of the Association of Cricket Umpires and Scorers, or of a local Association which is affiliated to the ACU & S This will mean that they have the encouragement and support of a strongly based international Association. Scorers too, are eligible for membership of the Association and training and examination for certificated qualification is available. This implies that not only must the two umpires appointed for a match work together from the start on a basis of absolute mutual confidence, but that they will, with the scorers, form a team in which each has a part to play by offering friendship, understanding, and support. Even if the views of the umpires on any particular point may not always agree, this must never be allowed to produce any feeling of constraint or embarrassment, but rather should lead to an increase of respect and loyalty.

6 THE UMPIRE IN THE FIELD

In this section it is intended to deal with a miscellany of points and to give advice on general and technical matters which concern the umpire before and during the match. Most of the material in this section will be outside the scope of Part II, in which the Laws are discussed in detail. Of necessity, there is some repetition and cross reference, especially where some important parts of the pre-match and match duties of the umpires are covered in the text of the Laws.

DRESS
It is a pity that attention to dress has only recently become important. Over the years, the umpire had been seen as a familiar, if rather forlorn figure, usually dressed in grubby long white coat, concertinaed trousers of various hues, cloth capped, and caricatured smothered with players' caps and clothing. Fortunately the picture has changed. Most modern umpires now provide and use their own coats, which they naturally keep clean. Many have loops for the carrying of sweaters, and pockets for their personal requirements. They are a far cry from the 'club' coat which was invariably dirty, often having been used to wipe mud from the ball and bat, and very often buttonless into the bargain. A smart turnout is conducive to confidence and self-assurance. The image of the umpire has now changed very much for the better in the eyes of the cricket watching public and trainee umpires must appreciate the necessity of keeping the highest standard in dress, as well as in field technique. A tie is essential wear. In exceptionally hot weather it is now permissible for the white coat to be discarded, provided that both umpires are dressed alike in white shirts, buttoned to the wrist, with a tie and dark trousers. Where the match is under the administration of a controlling body, the Executives of that body on the ground should be consulted before coats are discarded.

In the past there has been a feeling that sunglasses, especially dark ones, should not be worn. Now, however, there is more general acceptance that some protection for the eyes from strong ultraviolet rays is necessary. In many cases a cap or hat with a good brim will give sufficient shade. If it does not, then it is better to wear sunglasses – particularly if they are tinted or photochromic prescription lenses – than not to be able to see clearly when facing the sun.

7 NECESSARY EQUIPMENT

The amount of equipment carried by umpires must, of necessity, be limited. Some carry a variety of odds and ends, many of which are not used from the beginning of one season to the end of the next. It is much better to keep to the smallest number of items above the absolute essentials.

COUNTERS

If coins, pebbles, etc, are used, it is good practice to carry a spare in an inner pocket. As to the value of counting machines against the use of counters, this is entirely a matter of personal preference. Most umpires hold all the counters in one hand and drop one into a pocket as each ball is delivered. Before an over starts, the number of counters should be checked, and if a wide or no ball is delivered, the counter should be retained in the hand. In the event of a wicket falling, the umpire must have some means of keeping the counters in the hand separate until play restarts.

WATCH

Both umpires should carry a watch. The Law defines that umpires are responsible for the clock or watch to be followed during the match. Even if the ground has a public clock which is to be used, agreement must be reached between the two umpires as to which watch shall take precedence should the clock fail. The Captains and the scorers must be informed.

PENCIL AND PAPER

For the control of modern cricket a pencil and notebook are essential. Limited overs, bowlers limited to a number of overs, and many additional responsibilities under the present Code of Laws make recording more necessary than ever. A printed card is now available for the counting of overs and is a useful aid.

THE LAWS OF CRICKET

The M.C.C. publish the Laws of Cricket in small booklet form convenient for carrying. Umpires will find the hard back copy ideal for this purpose. It is not, of course, suggested that the book be used on the field of play, but it may well be necessary for the settlement of a particular point during an interval, or at the close of play. Again, in order to settle a point of procedure, a copy of the Competition or League regulations will be useful.

BALLS
The balls to be used during the match will be approved by the umpires and captains before the start. If new balls are to be used after a prescribed number of overs, the umpires will, of course, carry new balls. Both umpires should carry at least one spare ball in average condition for replacement where the Laws provide.

BAILS
Bails should be provided by the Ground Authority, but many umpires wisely carry their own set. A spare should always be included for replacement should damage or breakage occur during the match.

BOWLER'S START MARKER
Markers are usually provided by the Ground Authority, but it is as well for one to be carried. Markers must always be collected at the end of play, to avoid the risk of damage to mowers and ground equipment.

DRYING MATERIAL
A piece of towelling or cloth for ball drying is an important piece of equipment which should be carried even on a fine day. Weather can change quickly and no umpire should be without the means of drying a wet ball. As has been pointed out, the amount of equipment an umpire can carry is limited and personal items are best left in the safety of the Ground Authority. On the other hand, the game must not be held up because the umpire is lacking a particular item. To summarize:

Counters (with spare)
Watch
Pencil and Paper
M.C.C. Law Book
Competition or League regulations
Balls (with spares)
Bails (with spares)
Bowler's Start Marker
Drying Material

8 THE UMPIRE'S DUTIES

Although dealt with in detail under the appropriate Laws in Part II, a summary is necessary for guidance in responsibilities before and during the match. It must be emphasized again that the two umpires form a small team of their own (as well as part of a larger team with the scorers) and the striker's end umpire must be very aware of the necessity to be constantly on the alert, not only to cover his own duties, but in readiness at all times to assist and support his busier colleague.

DUTIES BEFORE THE MATCH

Law 3 directs umpires to report on the ground at least thirty minutes before the start of a day's play. In practice it is better to arrive earlier, because there is a good deal to be done before the match starts.

1   Report to Ground Executive, meet partner and together inspect boundaries and sight screens.
2   Inspect pitch and wickets.
3   Check for covers and wet weather equipment – especially sawdust.
4   Obtain bails and used balls for replacements.
5   Meet captains and scorers and check with Ground Authority the procedure for outfield mowing.
6   Check nominations of players.
7   Check toss.
8   Ensure field is cleared of spectators, players and obstructions.
9   Walk out together at least five minutes before the agreed time of start of play and agree upon ends.
10   Check wicket alignment and place bails in position.
11   Check from which end the first over is to be bowled.

Bowler's end umpire
12   Give bowler a marker.
13   Inquire as to bowler's action and inform the striker.
14   If requested, give guard.
15   Assist with directions for sight-screen alignment, if this is necessary.

16 Check that number of fielders does not exceed eleven and that they are ready.
17 Confirm that scorers are in their position and ready.
18 Check that both batsmen and striker's end umpire are ready.
19 Hand the match ball to the bowler.
20 Check with colleague that agreed time for start of play has been reached.
21 Call Play.

DUTIES DURING THE MATCH

Bowler's end umpire

1 Calls Play at the start of each innings, at the start of each day's play and at the end of any interval.
2 Counts the number of balls in the over.
3 Calls and signals to the scorers No balls within his jurisdiction and all Wides.
4 Watches for, calls and signals to the scorers short runs at his end.
5 Signals to the scorers all boundaries, byes and leg byes.
6 Answers appeals for Bowled; Caught; Handled the Ball; Hit the ball Twice; LBW; Obstructing the Field; Timed Out and Run Out at his end.
7 Calls and signals Dead ball when applicable.
8 Calls Over at the stipulated time.
9 Observes position of batsmen with regard to crossing when action indicates possible catch, overthrows, illegal fielding, lost ball or run out at the other end.
10 Watches close fielders for pitch encroachment.
11 Indicates to the scorers when one hour of playing time remains.
12 Watches for all forms of unfair play and initiates action when necessary.
13 Gives consent for fielders leaving and returning to the field and calculates time allowance before permitting returning fielders to bowl.
14 With colleague checks correctness of scores throughout and at the conclusion of the match.
15 Calls Time at cessation of play before intervals, before

interruptions of play, at the end of each day's play and at the conclusion of the match.

Striker's end umpire

1 Counts the number of balls in the over as a check and support to colleague. A signal can be arranged to indicate that the over is completed.
2 Watches for, calls and signals Short runs at his end.
3 Answers appeals for Hit Wicket; Stumped; and Run Out at his end.
4 Observes bowler's action for fairness of delivery.
5 Calls and signals Dead ball when applicable.
6 Checks number of fielders behind the popping crease at instant of bowler's delivery.
7 Calls and signals to the scorers No balls within his jurisdiction.
8 Observes position of batsmen with regard to crossing when the action indicates possible catch, overthrows, illegal fielding, lost ball or run out at the other end.
9 Watches wicket-keeper for positioning.
10 Watches for all forms of unfair play.
11 With colleague checks correctness of scores throughout and at the conclusion of the match.
12 Gives utmost co-operation and assistance to colleague at all times.

BOTH UMPIRES' INTERVAL DUTIES

At the cessation of play before an arranged interval, interruption of play or at the end of a day's play, the bowler's end umpire will call Time and both umpires will then remove the bails. One umpire, by agreement, will be responsible for the safe-keeping of the match ball. A record in writing must be made of:

1 The remaining number of balls to be bowled in the over in progress.
2 Identification of the bowlers bowling the over at each end.
3 The end at which the bowling is to resume.
4 Identification of the batsmen and at which ends they should resume.
5 The time that play ended and, for arranged intervals, the time that play is to resume.
6 The supervision of any permitted rolling.

9 POSITIONING OF THE UMPIRES

Bowler's end umpire

Law 3 directs umpires to stand where they can best see any act upon which their decision may be required. This direction is clear and paramount, but is necessarily qualified by the fact that the bowler's end umpire must stand where he does not interfere with the bowler's run-up and delivery, or the striker's view. Dependent upon the bowler's action the umpire may use his personal judgment. Generally, he will find that standing 4 feet to 6 feet behind the stumps, completely square to the wicket with head over the line of the middle stump, will give a clear view of the bowler's feet and of the popping and return creases, with minimum head movement as the line of sight changes to pick up the trajectory of the ball in the air.

Umpires will often be asked to change position. Instances are: nearer the wicket for round the wicket bowlers who run across and close to the wicket; further back from the wicket by the striker who is unable to see a bowler running up from behind the umpire. Providing the changed position still gives a clear view of any act requiring a decision, the umpire should comply with such a request. But if he considers that the new position would impair, to any extent, his view of the ball and the action, the umpire must quietly, but firmly refuse to move. If a bowler is persistent it might be as well to point out that the new position would certainly be more difficult for judgment of LBW and snick catches behind the wicket. A compromise position is often possible: standing back, and thus enabling the bowler to run between the umpire and the stumps. Standing too close to the stumps can create difficulties with observation of the bowler's back foot and the return crease.

It is worth repeating that head movement must be reduced to a minimum if the trajectory of the ball in flight is to be picked up at the earliest possible moment. Standing square to the wicket enables the umpire to use movement of the eyes rather than movement of the head, as the line of sight moves from the bowler's feet and the creases, to the ball in flight. Whether to bend forward, with eyes looking down the line of the two middle stumps, is preferable to standing upright is purely a personal consideration. Certainly, by bending forward, head movement is reduced and estimation of the amount of lift a rising ball is making off the pitch (very important for LBW judgment) may be easier. The advantages are arguable. Much more important is that the umpire should stand in a comfortable position from where he can concentrate completely, see clearly all the action, and become immediately mobile.

From the moment the bowler commences his run-up, or bowling action, the umpire should remain perfectly still. As the bowler releases the ball, the umpire sweeps his line of sight at once from the bowler's feet and the creases to the ball. Having sighted it in flight, he must watch the ball intently with the utmost concentration until it passes the striker's wicket or is played by the striker.

One of the most important techniques in umpiring is to pick up the ball visually as quickly as possible and, from that moment onwards, to give the ball full and total attention. The trainee and beginner umpire will need considerable self-discipline to train and condition himself, firstly in avoiding spending too much time on judgment of the bowler's feet, especially after the delivery stride, and secondly, in disregarding all extraneous noises and distractions at this vital moment. After long and tiring hours in the field, even the experienced umpire will need effort to maintain the concentration needed. The less experienced man must beware of a gradual and insidious falling off in concentration, which will require considerable self-control to overcome.

The ball, having reached the striker, may be played by him or run into the field. The umpire must now move very quickly into a position for judgment of a fair run or possible run-out. This can be done only from a side-on position. More often than not the movement will be to that side of the wicket to which the ball is struck. From this position a throw-in can be seen without the actual breaking of the wicket being obscured by either a fielder or the bowler. For judgment of the fair breaking of the wicket and the position of the running batsmen in relation to the creases, the umpire should stand well away from the pitch. From here, he will not only be in the best position to see the running batsmen in front of him, but will also be avoiding any interference with a throw-in.

Movement to the side of the wicket to which the ball is struck must not be taken as an article of faith. The experienced umpire may well consider the better observation of a particular piece of action can be made from the opposite side and may change his judgment of positioning accordingly. Sometimes action happens that makes speed of movement the criterion and it is just not possible to move into a particular position without interfering with a batsman or fielder. Experience will bring assessment and reaction so that a fast movement is made into a position in time to be stationary when the wicket is broken.

The ball must be watched with the utmost attention and vigilance until it becomes dead. Swift checking glances will be made at the crease for judgment of short runs. Bowler's end umpire must never allow the bowler to start his run-up, or bowling action, until striker's end umpire is in position; this check is particularly important when the bowler takes only a short run.

Striker's end umpire

Provided that the umpire is almost in line with the popping crease he can use his commonsense in judging the distance he stands from the wicket. Many umpires find that standing approximately the same distance as when at bowler's end (a length of the pitch) gives a clear view of the striker, the wicket, the popping crease, and wicket-keeper, without interfering with the fielding side or wasting too much time in moving in at any time to remake the wicket or to cross to the other side. Some umpires, when in position, stand a little nearer to the line of the stumps if the wicket-keeper is up and a close stumping is possible. The striker's feet in relation to the popping crease may sometimes be seen more easily with a line of sight very slightly behind the action. If the wicket-keeper is standing back, and runs are likely, the umpire should move back to a position directly in line with the popping crease.

Striker's end umpire must be just as attentive and alert as when he is standing at the bowler's end. He must be ready at all times to give support and co-operation to his busier colleague, and be ready to move at speed if his view of the wicket-keeper, wicket, and creases is obstructed by moving fielders. Under the 'Duties during the match' section summarized earlier, it will be seen that there is no time for meditation.

Positioning will also be influenced by the field setting and other factors. Striker's end umpire may, at times, find it necessary to move over and stand on the off side. **Law 3** gives authority for the change over to be made at the umpire's discretion, provided that he informs the Captain of the fielding side and the striker of his intention. He should also inform his colleague. One reason for moving to the off side is that a close fielder is obstructing the umpire's view of the popping crease or wicket. Other situations requiring such a change include: a setting sun making it difficult to see the crease markings; a fielder behind the umpire if there are two other leg-side fielders behind the popping crease; a bowler with a suspect action. When a runner is on the field with the injured batsman striking, the runner should normally be at square leg with the umpire standing on the off side. The techniques of both umpires when a runner is on the field are dealt with in more detail under **Law 2** in Part II of this book.

Each delivery must be scrutinized to ensure that the bowling arm action is fair. Once the ball has been delivered, attention must be switched quickly to the striker and wicket-keeper. The primary duties of watching for stumping, hit wicket and run-out require the umpire to ensure that he is in the best possible position to observe closely the wicket, the wicket-keeper and popping crease. Moreover, when the batsmen are running the umpire must be vigilant for possible short runs. He must be in a position to glance at the popping crease, each time the batsman turns for a further run. He must also watch the progress of the ball and the action on the field, particularly the batsmen crossing.

10 SIGNALS AND SIGNALLING

Law 3 instructs umpires to use a code of signals provided, to enable them to communicate with the scorers. Signals are vitally important for the accurate recording of the match and must be given strictly in accordance with the Law. Scorers are part of the match control team and umpires must co-operate by signalling clearly with the official signal only and in full view of the scorers. The scorers, in return, must co-operate by acknowledging each signal clearly and punctually. Umpires must not allow the game to proceed until the signal is acknowledged. Figure 1 (on page 20) illustrates the official signals:

Figure 1   The umpire's official signals.

Boundary Six	By raising both arms above the head. The hands and arms should be held up firmly and without movement of either.
Bye	By raising an open hand above the head.
Short runs	By bending the arm upwards to touch the nearest shoulder with the tips of the fingers.
No ball	By extending one arm horizontally. If a No ball produces runs, the scorers will need to know whether the runs are to be credited to the striker (if he played the ball), or to extras as No balls. If the runs are extras the umpire will give the No ball signal followed by the bye signal.
Boundary Four	By waving the arm from side to side across the body. A firm clear wave across the body is required. An upward movement of the hand is neither necessary nor desirable.
Dead ball	By crossing and re-crossing both wrists below the waist.
Out	By raising the index finger above the head. It is unnecessary, and undesirable, to qualify a decision by words or any gesture other than the signal. If the batsman appears not to have seen, or to have misunderstood, the umpire must explain.
Wide ball	By extending both arms horizontally.
Leg bye	By touching a raised knee with the hand (do not repeat the bye signal).

SIGNALS WITH CALLS
  Dead ball
  No ball
  Short runs
  Wide ball
The timing of signals and co-ordination with the calls is very important and is dealt with in Part II under the particular Law. As a general rule, umpires should not signal to the scorers while

the ball is in play. It cannot be too often repeated that turning away from the action to signal is fatal. It is a habit that must not be allowed to develop. The calls must be clear with sufficient strength of voice for all the players to hear.

Part II Contents

PART II The Laws of Cricket with Interpretations and Definitions

The Laws are reproduced with the permission of the Marylebone Cricket Club; they are those of the 1980 Code, 2nd edition – 1992. Copies of the Laws in pocket size may be obtained from the Secretary, M.C.C., Lord's Cricket Ground, London, NW8 8QN.

LAW 1 THE PLAYERS

1 NUMBER OF PLAYERS AND CAPTAIN
A match is played between two sides each of eleven Players, one of whom shall be Captain. In the event of the Captain not being available at any time a Deputy shall act for him.

2 NOMINATION OF PLAYERS
Before the toss for innings, the Captain shall nominate his Players who may not thereafter be changed without the consent of the opposing Captain.

Notes

(a) MORE OR LESS THAN ELEVEN PLAYERS A SIDE
A match may be played by agreement between sides of more or less than eleven players but not more than eleven players may field.

Nomination of teams

The names of the eleven players of both sides must be declared before the toss is made. Once the toss has been made a team may not be changed, other than that substitutes may be allowed (see **Law 2.1**), unless the consent of the opposing Captain is obtained. One of the problems confronting umpires is the Special Regulations which apply to some games of high profile which allow the replacement of players called into national squads at very short notice. These may confuse club cricketers as to what the Law allows but, as will be seen, the Laws of Cricket may be amended by the governing bodies (national or league) but such amendments apply only to those matches played under their jurisdiction. The Laws are not changed in any way.

The Captain

The Captain must be one of the nominated players. There will be occasions when the Captain is not available. For instance he may not have arrived in time to make the toss. The Law requires someone to act for him and umpires must insist that this happens. If the Captain of the fielding side has to leave the field, a member of the nominated side must act as captain during his absence. Whilst play is in progress, to avoid time being wasted, the batsmen at the wicket should deputize for the Captain of the batting side.

More than eleven players in a team

It is occasionally agreed, particularly in youth cricket, that there will be more than eleven players in a side. In such cases, the umpires should ensure there are not more than eleven fielders at any one time.

Field Technique

The umpires should ensure that the nomination of both teams precedes the toss. Both umpires should count the number of players on the field before Play is called and check with each other as well as the fielding Captain if there are less (or more) than eleven.

LAW 2 SUBSTITUTES AND RUNNERS: BATSMAN OR FIELDSMAN LEAVING THE FIELD: BATSMAN RETIRING: BATSMAN COMMENCING INNINGS

1 SUBSTITUTES
In normal circumstances, a Substitute shall be allowed to field only for a player who satisfies the Umpires that he has become injured or become ill during the match. However, in very exceptional circumstances, the Umpires may use their discretion to allow a substitute for a player who has to leave the field or does not take the field for other wholly acceptable reasons, subject to consent being given by the opposing Captain. If a player wishes to change his shirt, boots, etc., he may leave the field to do so (no changing on the field) but no Substitute will be allowed.

2 OBJECTION TO SUBSTITUTES
The opposing Captain shall have no right of objection to any player acting as Substitute on the field, nor as to where he shall field; however, no Substitute shall act as Wicket-Keeper.

3 SUBSTITUTE NOT TO BAT OR BOWL
A Substitute shall not be allowed to bat or bowl.

4 A PLAYER FOR WHOM A SUBSTITUTE HAS ACTED
A player may bat, bowl or field even though a Substitute has acted for him.

5 RUNNER
A runner shall be allowed for a Batsman who during the match is incapacitated by illness or injury. The player acting as Runner shall be a member of the batting side and shall, if possible, have already batted in that innings.

6 RUNNER'S EQUIPMENT
The player acting as Runner for an injured Batsman shall wear the same external protective equipment as the injured Batsman.

7 TRANSGRESSION OF THE LAWS BY AN INJURED BATSMAN OR RUNNER

An injured Batsman may be out should his Runner break any one of Laws 33: (Handled the Ball), 37: (Obstructing the Field) or 38: (Run Out). As Striker he remains himself subject to the Laws. Furthermore, should he be out of his ground for any purpose and the wicket at the Wicket-Keeper's end be put down he shall be out under Law 38: (Run Out) or Law 39: (Stumped) irrespective of the position of the other Batsman or the Runner and no runs shall be scored.

When not the Striker, the injured Batsman is out of the game and shall stand where he does not interfere with the play. Should he bring himself into the game in any way then he shall suffer the penalties that any transgression of the Laws demands.

8 FIELDSMAN LEAVING THE FIELD

No Fieldsman shall leave the field or return during a session of play without the consent of the Umpire at the Bowler's end. The Umpire's consent is also necessary if a Substitute is required for a Fieldsman, when his side returns to the field after an interval. If a member of the fielding side leaves the field or fails to return after an interval and is absent from the field for longer than 15 minutes, he shall not be permitted to bowl after his return until he has been on the field for at least that length of playing time for which he was absent. This restriction shall not apply at the start of a new day's play.

9 BATSMAN LEAVING THE FIELD OR RETIRING

A Batsman may leave the field or retire at any time owing to illness, injury or other unavoidable cause, having previously notified the Umpire at the Bowler's end. He may resume his innings at the fall of a wicket, which for the purposes of this Law shall include the retirement of another Batsman.

If he leaves the field or retires for any other reason he may only resume his innings with the consent of the opposing Captain.

When a Batsman has left the field or retired and is

unable to return owing to illness, injury or other unavoidable cause his innings is to be recorded as 'retired, not out'. Otherwise it is to be recorded as 'retired, out'.

10 COMMENCEMENT OF A BATSMAN'S INNINGS
A Batsman shall be considered to have commenced his innings once he has stepped on to the field of play.

Notes

(a) SUBSTITUTES AND RUNNERS
For the purpose of these Laws allowable illnesses or injuries are those which occur at any time after the nomination by the Captains of their teams.

Many Captains and players will not be familiar with the Law governing the use of substitutes and runners. The umpires are responsible for ensuring that the game is conducted strictly in accordance with the Laws and should intervene quietly to advise the Captains if there is any intention shown of infringing the Laws. It is important to understand that the 'duration' of a match is interpreted as commencing with the nomination of the sides and continues until the end of the game including non-playing days as well as other intervals.

Entitlement to a substitute fielder
If, during a match, a player is taken ill, is injured, or suffers a recurrence of an injury, his side is entitled to use a substitute. Once the use of a substitute is agreed (either by right or by permission of the opposing Captain) the opposing Captain has no right of objection to the person acting as the substitute nor to the position in which he may be required to field, other than the substitute may not act as wicket-keeper. A substitute is not allowed to act as Captain; nor is he allowed to bat or bowl.

A player may be unable to play, during a match, not because of injury or illness but for a wholly acceptable reason, for example late arrival at the ground or a doctor on call. In such cases, the umpires have discretionary powers to allow a substitute providing the consent of the opposing Captain is obtained.

The umpires' consent, and possibly that of the opposing

Captain, is required before a substitute is allowed for a player failing to return to the field after an interval.

Player changing shirt or boots

A player must not be allowed to change his shirt or boots on the field of play. Should he leave the field to do so, a substitute is not allowed to field during his absence.

Substituted player allowed to bowl or bat on return

A player for whom a substitute has acted may return to the field at any time and is able to play a full part in the game.

Entitlement to a runner and player who may act as a runner

A runner is allowed for a batsman who is injured, ill or incapacitated during the match and the fielding Captain has, in these circumstances, no right of objection either to the use of a runner nor to the person acting as runner. If an injury has been sustained before the match begins, the batsman does not have an entitlement to a runner; the permission of the fielding Captain would have to be obtained before another player was allowed to act as runner.

The umpires must ensure that the runner is a member of the nominated side and, whenever possible, has already batted in the innings. This will not be possible if either of the two opening batsmen is injured. Although it will save time in this situation for the No. 3 batsman, already padded up, to act as runner, it is desirable that it should be someone from lower in the order. Otherwise, not only may a change of runner be required but an unfair advantage may accrue to the batsman who has the opportunity to get used to the light and to view the bowling immediately before batting. The umpires, however, will not necessarily know the batting order and may not be able enforce this.

Runner's equipment

The runner must wear the same protective equipment as the injured batsman, that is a helmet, if the injured batsman is wearing one, pads and gloves. He must also carry a bat. It is not usual to include a forearm guard, even if not covered by a sleeve.

Positioning of umpires when there is a runner on the field

The presence of a runner on the field poses new problems for the umpires who must keep the runner under observation as well as attend to normal match duties. It is important that the umpires work to a prearranged plan in this situation. When the injured batsman is the striker, the umpire at the striker's end should normally stand on the off side with the runner at square leg (the opposite side of the field). This will enable the striker's end umpire to keep the runner under observation. The bowler's end umpire must change his technique when the batsmen are running or likely to run, moving always to the opposite side of the pitch (normally the off side) to that on which the runner has taken his position. This change from the normal practice of moving to the side to which the ball has been struck is vital to enable the umpire to keep the runner under observation. Moving to the side on which the runner is running will prevent the umpire from being able to adjudicate on short runs or run out as the runner is behind him.

Injured striker to stay in, or regain, his ground

The injured striker passes to his runner the total responsibility to score runs by running and cannot do so himself. The Law requires the injured striker to stay in, or regain his ground, at all times. Many injured batsmen, who have a runner, will instinctively set off for a run, unaware that they should not do so. Should the injured striker be out of his ground, from a fair delivery, and the wicket is put down correctly at the wicket-keeper's end, the injured striker is always out irrespective of the position of the runner and the non-striker. Any runs which have been scored by the runner and non-striker will be disallowed and the non-striker will be required to return to his original (bowler's) end. The bowler's end umpire should always ensure that the scorers are apprised of the situation and that the runs have been disallowed. Should the delivery be a No ball the injured striker would, himself, only be given out if he was attempting a run.

The runner must also stay within his ground, at all times the ball is in play, unless attempting a run. Should he wander to a position in front of the popping crease and the wicket be correctly broken, at that end, the injured striker would be given out, Run Out, on appeal, even if No ball had been called.

The golden rule

If the wicket is broken at the *wicket-keeper's end*, from a fair delivery,

    Consider first the injured striker.

    Is he in his ground?   No – he is out (run out or stumped).

                                    Yes – consider the positions of the non-striker and runner and treat as two normal batsmen.

If the wicket is broken at the *bowler's end*, ignore the injured striker and treat the non-striker and runner as two normal batsmen.

Injured batsman when not the striker

When not the striker the injured batsman is out of the game and should be required to stand, out of the way, alongside the striker's end umpire. He can only be dismissed if he is foolish enough to interfere in any way with the ball or a fieldsman.

Fieldsman leaving and returning to the field

To enable the umpires to keep an accurate record of a fielder's absence from the field, a fielder should obtain permission, from the bowler's end umpire, before leaving the field. The umpires should be advised if a fielder fails to return after an interval or interruption.

Having left the field, or having failed to return after an interval, the fielder may only return with the consent of the bowler's end umpire. This consent should be withheld until the end of an over, or a break in play, to avoid time being wasted. A fielder may bowl immediately after returning providing he has been absent from the field for fifteen minutes or less. Should the length of his absence be more than fifteen minutes, he must be on the field of play for the length of time for which he was absent before being allowed to bowl. This restriction applies to a fielder who has left the field or failed to return after an interval but does not apply to players late for the first day's play. A player late on any other day will be penalized but the time late on one day is not added to time absent of the previous day. Only playing time, that is time while play is actually in progress, counts in assessing the length of either a fielder's absence or the time he is on the field before he can bowl, when he returns.

1) A fielder leaves the field and is off for 20 minutes before play is interrupted by rain for a period of 15 minutes. The fielder returns to the field when play restarts after the interruption. He must wait 20 minutes before being allowed to bowl. The length of any interruption or interval is never taken into account when assessing the time the player was not on the field.
2) A fielder leaves the field and is absent for 24 minutes. He returns 5 minutes before play is interrupted by rain for 20 minutes. He must be on the field, after play has restarted, for 19 minutes before being allowed to bowl. The time that players are off the field, whether for an interruption or interval does not count as 'waiting' time.

A fielder can be absent for less than fifteen minutes without penalty even if he is off the field on more than one occasion, providing each period of absence is less than 15 minutes. The periods of short absence are not added together. On the other hand, if he has more than one period of absence greater than 15 minutes the time he must wait before being allowed to bowl will be the aggregate of the times of these absences.

Example
A fielder leaves the field for 20 minutes for treatment. He returns and is on the field for 10 minutes before having to go off again. He is off for a further 20 minutes. On his return he will not be allowed to bowl until he has been on the field for 30 minutes (20 plus 20 minus 10 minutes).

Batsman leaving the field
The umpires will always be aware that a batsman has left the field because of injury, illness or some other cause. If, however, a batsman is unable to continue his innings after an interval or interruption, the umpires should be advised of the reason. The scorers should be kept informed to enable the correct entry to be made in the score-book. A batsman retiring through injury or illness who is unable to resume his innings, should be recorded as 'Retired not out' whereas a batsman retiring for any other reason and who does not resume his innings should be recorded as 'Retired out'.

If the batsman has retired through injury or illness, or other unavoidable cause, he is allowed to resume his innings at the fall of a subsequent wicket – or the retirement of another batsman. The permission of the opposing Captain for him to be allowed to resume his innings is only required if the reason for his retirement is other than injury or illness.

Start of a batsman's innings

After the fall of a wicket, the incoming batsman's innings starts as soon as he steps on the field of play. This does not apply at the start of an innings until the umpire has called Play. If the two opening batsmen are in position, they will not be considered to have started their innings if play is suspended, due to heavy rain or other cause, before the call is made. If, however, a batsman has walked on to the field of play, after the fall of a wicket, but is unable to start his innings as play is suspended due to the weather, he has started his innings and must continue when play resumes or risk being considered to have retired.

Field Technique

A note must be made of the times at which a fielder leaves and returns to the field. The length of the period of absence must be agreed between the umpires when a fielder returns.

Careful attention should be given to the positioning of the runner and injured batsman when not the striker and to the need for the bowler's end umpire to change his technique when moving to the side of the wicket, when the runner and non-striker are running.

If the runner causes the dismissal of the injured batsman, the scorers may not always be aware of the reason for the dismissal. In such a case the umpires must inform them as well as advising that any runs which have been made prior to an injured striker, himself, being run out are cancelled.

LAW 3 THE UMPIRES

1 APPOINTMENT

Before the toss for innings two Umpires shall be appointed, one for each end, to control the game with absolute impartiality as required by the Laws.

2 CHANGE OF UMPIRE

No Umpire shall be changed during a match without

the consent of both Captains.

3 SPECIAL CONDITIONS

Before the toss for innings, the Umpires shall agree with both Captains on any special conditions affecting the conduct of the match.

4 THE WICKETS

The Umpires shall satisfy themselves before the start of the match that the wickets are properly pitched.

5 CLOCK OR WATCH

The Umpires shall agree between themselves and inform both Captains before the start of the match on the watch or clock to be followed during the match.

6 CONDUCT AND IMPLEMENTS

Before and during a match the Umpires shall ensure that the conduct of the game and the implements used are strictly in accordance with the Laws.

7 FAIR AND UNFAIR PLAY

The Umpires shall be the sole judges of fair and unfair play.

8 FITNESS OF GROUND, WEATHER AND LIGHT

(a) The Umpires shall be the sole judges of the fitness of the ground, weather and light for play.

    (i) However, before deciding to suspend play or not to start play or not to resume play after an interval or stoppage, the Umpires shall establish whether both Captains (the Batsmen at the wicket may deputize for their Captain) wish to commence or to continue in the prevailing conditions; if so, their wishes shall be met.

    (ii) In addition, if during play, the Umpires decide that the light is unfit, only the batting side shall have the option of continuing play. After agreeing to continue to play in unfit light conditions, the Captain of the batting side (or a Batsman at the wicket) may appeal against the light to the Umpires, who shall uphold the appeal only if, in their opinion,

> the light has deteriorated since the agree-
> ment to continue was made.

(b) After any suspension of play, the Umpires, unaccompanied by any of the Players or Officials shall,
on their own initiative, carry out an inspection
immediately the conditions improve and shall
continue to inspect at intervals. Immediately the
Umpires decide that play is possible they shall call
upon the Players to resume the game.

9 EXCEPTIONAL CIRCUMSTANCES

In exceptional circumstances, other than those of
weather, ground or light, the Umpires may decide to
suspend or abandon play. Before making such a
decision the Umpires shall establish, if the circumstances allow, whether both Captains (the Batsmen at
the wicket may deputize for their Captain) wish to
continue in the prevailing conditions: if so their wishes
shall be met.

10 POSITION OF UMPIRES

The Umpires shall stand where they can best see any
act upon which their decision may be required.

Subject to this over-riding consideration the Umpire
at the Bowler's end shall stand where he does not
interfere with either the Bowler's run up or the
Striker's view.

The Umpire at the Striker's end may elect to stand
on the off instead of the leg side of the pitch, provided
he informs the Captain of the fielding side and the
Striker of his intention to do so.

11 UMPIRES CHANGING ENDS

The Umpires shall change ends after each side has
had one innings.

12 DISPUTES

All disputes shall be determined by the Umpires and if
they disagree the actual state of things shall continue.

13 SIGNALS

The following code of signals shall be used by Umpires
who will wait until a signal has been answered by a
Scorer before allowing the game to proceed.

Boundary	by waving the arm from side to side.
Boundary 6	by raising both arms above the head.
Bye	by raising an open hand above the head.
Dead Ball	by crossing and re-crossing the wrists below the waist.
Leg Bye	by touching a raised knee with the hand.
No Ball	by extending one arm horizontally.
Out	by raising the index finger above the head. If not out the Umpire shall call 'not out'.
Short run	by bending the arm upwards and by touching the nearer shoulder with the tips of the fingers.
Wide	by extending both arms horizontally.

14 CORRECTNESS OF SCORES

The Umpires shall be responsible for satisfying themselves on the correctness of the scores throughout and at the conclusion of the match. See Law 21.6 (Correctness of Result).

Notes

(a) ATTENDANCE OF UMPIRES

The Umpires should be present on the ground and report to the Ground Executive or the equivalent at least 30 minutes before the start of a day's play.

(b) CONSULTATION BETWEEN UMPIRES AND SCORERS

Consultation between Umpires and Scorers over doubtful points is essential.

(c) FITNESS OF GROUND

The Umpires shall consider the ground as unfit for play when it is so wet or slippery as to deprive the Bowlers of a reasonable foothold, the Fieldsmen, other than the deep-fielders, of the power of free movement, or the Batsmen the ability to play their strokes or to run between the wickets. Play should not be suspended merely because the grass and the ball are wet and slippery.

(d) FITNESS OF WEATHER AND LIGHT

The Umpires should suspend play when they consider that the *conditions are so bad that it is unreasonable or dangerous to continue.*

Impartiality of umpires

All umpires who take pride in their control of the game will strive to show complete impartiality. This is extremely difficult if the umpire is a member of one of the participating clubs; in such circumstances an umpire has been known to show bias against his own club in an attempt to demonstrate his impartiality. Appeals should be answered without consideration as to which side is batting and in totally neutral tones. Any information imparted, or question answered, should be done with sufficient strength of voice so that members of both sides can hear.

Appointment of umpires

The stipulation that umpires are appointed one for each end indicates that it is incorrect for one umpire to stand at the bowling end throughout an innings or match although Special Regulations may require this if only one appointed umpire is available. Should an umpire be taken ill, or be unable to continue for any reason, the Captains must agree on a replacement.

Discussions with Captains

Both umpires must be clear as to the conditions under which the game is to be played and these must be agreed with both Captains before the toss is made. It is also important that the scorers are fully informed. The following points should be discussed and agreed:

Boundaries

Sight-screens within, or partially within, shall be regarded as boundaries. Agreement must be reached on boundary allowances (see **Law 19**) and whether trees wholly within or overhanging the field of play, or any other obstacles or person, should be regarded as boundaries.

Local customs

Normally, local customs will be observed. These may include 4, instead of 6, runs for hits pitching over the boundary or the ball to be still in play and runs or catches allowed from rebounds off a tree or obstacle within the field of play.

37

Hours of Play and Intervals

The hours of play will almost certainly have been determined in advance. The timing of all intervals, including any drinks intervals, should be agreed and the Captains reminded of the conditions that relate to lunch, tea and drink intervals (see **Law 16**).

Special Regulations

Many Leagues or Competitions have their own Special Regulations which augment or amend the Laws of Cricket.

Match Balls

Agreement and approval must be reached on the balls to be used in the match and, if necessary, the conditions which will determine the use of new balls during an innings.

The clock or watch to be followed

The umpires will agree between themselves and inform the Captains and scorers of the official time piece and the watch which will take precedence if the official time piece should fail.

The number of balls to be bowled in an over

Discussion and agreement would only be necessary in Leagues/Competitions where both 6 and 8 ball overs are bowled.

Nomination of the players

Team lists should be exchanged before the toss for innings takes place.

Scorers

The umpires should make a point of meeting the scorers. This will not only establish a friendly relationship but ensure that all members of the umpires/scorers team are clear about the following important matters:

– The umpires need to know whether the scorers will be working in the score box or in some other place.
– The scorers need to be aware of all the conditions of play stated above.

Signals need to be agreed both for the umpires to check that the scorers are ready at the start of each session and, if appropriate, for the umpires to notify the start of the last hour of play.

Arrival at the ground before the start of play

The Law requires umpires to arrive at the ground at least 30 minutes before the start of play but in view of the formidable list of pre-match checks which each umpire must make it is recommended that umpires arrive up to one hour before play is due to begin. It is essential that the pre-match checks are not hurried, nor overlooked. The umpire's composure may well be disturbed if he is uncertain over a matter which should have been determined before play started.

Umpires working as a team

Umpires derive much greater enjoyment and satisfaction from games in which they consider they have had total support from their colleague. It is essential that the two umpires work together as a team, consult each other on any matter of concern and assist each other at all times. This requires them to have complete confidence in each other which can only be established when both have a complete knowledge of the Laws. Consultation on matters of fact can often be unobtrusive and low key but this should not prevent an umpire, having first called and signalled Dead ball, from moving from his position to consult his colleague. A similar rapport between umpire and scorers will not only contribute towards the smooth running of the game but will also add to the satisfaction enjoyed by the four officials.

Suspension of play due to ground conditions or weather

Once the toss has been made, the umpires are responsible for the use and maintenance of the pitch (Law 7). It is for them to decide whether the ground, weather or light are fit for play. They must distinguish between unsuitable conditions and dangerous conditions.

If conditions are not dangerous but merely unsuitable, both Captains must be consulted. If play is in progress, the batsmen at the wicket will be considered as deputies for their Captain. If both Captains wish to continue, or to start play, their wishes should be met. If one Captain agrees with the umpires' view that conditions are unsuitable for play, then that view will prevail and play will be suspended, or will not be started.

If the umpires agree that the condition of the ground or of the weather is dangerous, then they must suspend play, or not allow it to start.

In deciding whether the ground is fit, the umpires and Captains should not propose to suspend play unless the conditions are unreasonable or dangerous. The fieldsmen must
be able to move safely within 25-30 yards of the pitch and the bowlers must have reasonable footholds. 39
light precipitation ...

minutes before the start of play but in view of the formidable list of pre-match checks which each umpire must make it is recommended that umpires arrive up to one hour before play is due to begin. It is essential that the pre-match checks are not hurried, nor overlooked. The umpire's composure may well be disturbed if he is uncertain over a matter which should have been determined before play started.

Umpires working as a team

Umpires derive much greater enjoyment and satisfaction from games in which they consider they have had total support from their colleague. It is essential that the two umpires work together as a team, consult each other on any matter of concern and assist each other at all times. This requires them to have complete confidence in each other which can only be established when both have a complete knowledge of the Laws. Consultation on matters of fact can often be unobtrusive and low key but this should not prevent an umpire, having first called and signalled Dead ball, from moving from his position to consult his colleague. A similar rapport between umpire and scorers will not only contribute towards the smooth running of the game but will also add to the satisfaction enjoyed by the four officials.

Suspension of play due to ground conditions or weather

Once the toss has been made, the umpires are responsible for the use and maintenance of the pitch (**Law 7**). It is for them to decide whether the ground, weather or light are fit for play.

If, whilst play is in progress, the umpires agree that the ground or weather is no longer fit for play, both Captains must be asked if they wish to continue. The batsmen at the wicket will be considered as deputies for their Captain. The Captains must also be consulted if the umpires decide it is not fit to start play or to resume after an interval. If both Captains wish to continue, or start play, their wishes should be met. If one Captain agrees with the umpires' view that conditions are unfit for play, then that view will prevail and play will be suspended.

In deciding whether the ground is fit, the umpires and Captains should not propose to suspend play unless the conditions are unreasonable or dangerous. The fieldsmen must be able to move about safely within 25–30 yards of the pitch and the bowlers must have reasonable footholds. Light precipitation may cause the surface of the ground and the ball to be wet but this should not be sufficient cause for play to be suspended. The ball can be dried and sawdust used to provide a better foothold for the bowler in his delivery stride.

Small pools of water on the area immediately around the pitch are, however, sufficient cause for play to be suspended. The batsmen must be able to run and play their strokes without fear of slipping on very wet ground.

<u>Suspension of play due to light</u>
If the umpires agree that the light is unfit for play to continue, only the batsmen at the wicket should be consulted. If they wish to go off the field the umpires should suspend play. If the batsmen wish to continue, despite the poor light, the umpires will only subsequently suspend play if, after an appeal by one of the batting side, they consider there has been a deterioration in the light since their original decision that it was unfit for play. This will obtain even if one or more wickets have fallen.

Judgment of light has always brought problems for umpires who will never satisfy the players, officials and spectators. The quality of the light will often be affected by the background of trees and buildings around the ground etc., and will often vary quite considerably from each end of the pitch. Some grounds are notoriously bad for light conditions and the opinion of the players will often be affected by the importance and state of the match. Club cricketers will generally be prepared to continue playing even if, in the opinion of the umpires, the light is extremely poor. It is, therefore, quite impossible to lay down a specific standard. Even the use of a light meter would not enable a specific standard to be laid down although they can be useful in determining the quality of light – and thus offering proof as to whether there has been any deterioration or improvement.

Sight-screens, or the absence of them, will also affect the umpires' judgment on light as well as the type of bowling. If the light is considered just reasonable when a slower bowler is in action, the umpires may well consider that the introduction into the attack of a faster bowler renders the light conditions dangerous for the batsmen.

There have been rare occasions when the batsmen have experienced difficulty in sighting the ball because the light is too bright. If the problem is caused by reflected light it should be possible to cover the offending area; a sun low in the sky is a more difficult problem which can usually be countered by a broad brimmed hat or cap.

<u>Resumption of play</u>
If play has not started or has been suspended due to ground, weather or light conditions the umpires should make frequent inspections to ensure that play can start or be restarted at the earliest possible moment. Ground inspections should be carried out by the umpires unaccompanied by any players or officials. Advice from the players will often be tinged according to the state of the match, a consideration which should have no influence on the umpires' deliberations. The groundsman, however, may well have valuable knowledge on the drying conditions of the ground and the umpires may well consider it wise to consult him, on some occasions. On some public and private grounds, the groundsman may have the final word as to whether play can take place or continue and this, of course, must be accepted.

Once the umpires decide conditions are fit for play, both sides should be called upon to resume play. It is, however, incumbent upon the umpires to ensure both sides clearly understand that play is about to be restarted since failure to resume would constitute a refusal to play. A side which refuses to play forfeits the match.

<u>Suspension of play due to exceptional circumstances</u>
There will be very few occasions when the umpires consider it prudent to suspend play due to exceptional circumstances. They may do so, however, without appeal if there is a likelihood of injury to any of the players – crowd disturbance, pitch invasion or terrorist activity. Whilst it is unlikely that Captains will wish play to continue, they should be consulted before play is suspended. Should both sides wish to continue play their wishes should be met although either has the right to subsequent appeal if they consider the situation has deteriorated.

Once the toss has been made, the Law places the responsibility for deciding if the ground, weather or light are fit for play on the umpires. The Law allows the Captain to agree to continue or to commence play, when the umpires consider the conditions are unfit. Nevertheless, if conditions are so bad as to be obviously dangerous, the umpires should suspend play.

Disputes

The umpires are the final arbiters in deciding disputes on any matter during the match. There should be very few occasions when the two umpires do not agree on how to resolve the dispute; should that occur the status quo will continue whether play is in progress or not.

Umpires changing ends

The umpires should only change ends when both sides have completed one innings. Thus they should remain at the same end throughout a one innings match.

Position of umpires

The over-riding consideration of the position in which the umpires should stand is that they are in the best position to see any act upon which they may be required to adjudicate. They should also take care not to cause any interference to the players.

This is dealt with in detail on page 16 and also on page 30.

Signals

Signals are fully detailed on pages 20, 21. There is also further elaboration under **Law 19** on page 98.

Correctness of scores

The umpires are responsible for satisfying themselves that the scores are correct throughout and particularly at the end of the match. The best way of carrying out this duty is to keep an accurate record of runs scored throughout the match and to check that it agrees with the total shown on the scoreboard. If any discrepancy occurs, the umpires should first check with each other and then, if necessary, resolve any problem with the scorers at the first break in play. Normally the scorebooks and umpires' tally will agree. The umpires, however, should check with the scorers at the end of each innings and at the end of the match, to avoid any dispute.

It follows from this that all umpires should have some

knowledge of scoring and understand the entries which are made on a score-sheet.

LAW 4 THE SCORERS

1 RECORDING RUNS
All runs scored shall be recorded by Scorers appointed for the purpose. Where there are two Scorers they shall frequently check to ensure that the score sheets agree.

2 ACKNOWLEDGING SIGNALS
The Scorers shall accept and immediately acknowledge all instructions and signals given to them by the Umpires.

Umpires and scorers as a team

Whilst umpires consider their contribution to the game is not fully appreciated the lot of scorers is worse. They rarely receive recognition for their labours and yet competent scorers are as essential to a game of cricket as competent umpires. Obviously the number of runs scored by each side is vitally important but that is not enough. Nowadays the points awarded and consequent placings in the League often turn on the intricate details of run rates and the like that scorers record. At higher levels large sums of money may be awarded in prizes to those achieving special feats. The scorers cannot record such matters without the appropriate information from the umpires. Equally the umpires will be unable to satisfy themselves that the scores are correct (**Law 3.14**) if their signals are not acknowledged and correctly interpreted.

It is true to say that in no match can either the umpires or the scorers function adequately without the other. A good rapport between the two sections of this important team is paramount.

During the game there will be occasions when the umpire will need to advise the scorers of the method of dismissal if this is not obvious. Such occasions will include not only the rare dismissals such as Handled the Ball or Obstructing the Field. Equally the scorer watching from behind the boundary may be unable to tell whether the umpire's finger is raised for LBW or for a catch by the wicket keeper. In this case the umpire touching his leg or cupping his hands will tell the scorers what they need to know. Other instances may need more direct communication. Some are detailed under the appropriate Laws.

Before the match the umpires must make a point of meeting the scorers (see also Part III) to ensure that they know what has been agreed in respect of:

Hours of play and intervals

Which watch or clock is to be followed
All four officials should synchronize watches.

Boundaries
If there are any local agreements about the allowance for boundaries. Whether the screens are outside the boundary or not; if any obstacles within the field of play are to be regarded as boundaries. This information will assist the scorers to be ready for the appropriate signal. While the umpire will be responsible for making the correct signals, it is helpful if the scorers are aware of what those signals are likely to be.

Signals
The code of signals is laid down on page 36. If the match is limited by time, there will be need to agree a signal for the start of the last hour.

Umpires have a responsibility to ensure that their signals are clear and visible from wherever the scorers are to be stationed. It should be ascertained where this is, if not in the score box. Scorers must equally ensure that they acknowledge all signals clearly and promptly. Sometimes there is a special light in the score box for this purpose. Often it is necessary to have something light coloured to wave. It is helpful to the umpires to know what method of acknowledgement will be used.

Special Regulations
There may be limitation on the number of overs allowed to one side to bat and one bowler to deliver. The result in a match affected by weather may depend on scores at various points in the game; the scorers must be aware beforehand that they need to record these.

LAW 5 THE BALL

1 WEIGHT AND SIZE
The ball, when new, shall weigh not less than $5\frac{1}{2}$ ounces/155.9g. nor more than $5\frac{3}{4}$ ounces/163g.: and shall measure not less than $8\frac{13}{16}$ inches/22.4cm., nor more than 9 inches/22.9cm. in circumference.

2 APPROVAL OF BALLS
All balls used in matches shall be approved by the Umpires and Captains before the start of the match.

3 NEW BALL
Subject to agreement to the contrary, having been made before the toss, either Captain may demand a new ball at the start of each innings.

4 NEW BALL IN MATCH OF 3 OR MORE DAYS' DURATION
In a match of 3 or more days' duration, the Captain of the fielding side may demand a new ball after the prescribed number of overs has been bowled with the old one. The Governing Body for cricket in the country concerned shall decide the number of overs applicable in that country which shall be not less than 75 6-ball overs (55 8-ball overs).

5 BALL LOST OR BECOMING UNFIT FOR PLAY
In the event of a ball during play being lost or, in the opinion of the Umpires, becoming unfit for play, the Umpires shall allow it to be replaced by one, that in their opinion, has had a similar amount of wear. If a ball is to be replaced, the Umpires shall inform the Batsmen.

Notes

(a) SPECIFICATIONS
The specifications as described in 1 above shall apply to top-grade balls only. The following degrees of tolerance will be acceptable for other grades of ball.

    (i) MEN'S GRADES 2–4
        Weight: $5\frac{5}{16}$ ounces/150g. to $5\frac{13}{16}$ ounces/165g.
        Size: $8\frac{11}{16}$ inches/22.0cm. to $9\frac{1}{16}$ inches/23.0cm.

      Weight: $4\frac{15}{16}$ ounces/140g. to $5\frac{5}{16}$ ounces/150g.
      Size: $8\frac{1}{4}$ inches/21.0cm. to $8\frac{7}{8}$ inches/22.5cm.

(iii) JUNIOR
      Weight: $4\frac{5}{16}$ ounces/133g. to $5\frac{1}{16}$ ounces/143g.
      Size: $8\frac{1}{16}$ inches/20.5cm. to $8\frac{11}{16}$ inches/22.0cm.

___

Approval before the start of the match

The Law has been framed to allow as much flexibility as possible with regard to the use of new balls during a match. Whilst there will be agreement for many matches that each side bowls with a new ball, this is not obligatory. Due to the high cost of cricket balls, it may be agreed to use one ball only during the match which may give a significant advantage to the side fielding first. Agreement must be reached before the toss is made. The umpires must then take possession of the ball or balls to be used during the match, to ensure that there is no breach of this agreement.

Weight and size

Although ball gauges, consisting of two measuring rings are available and used in the higher grades of cricket, club and League umpires will rarely need to check either the weight or size of a new ball since the reputable manufacturers can be depended upon to carry out their own quality checks. The specifications contained in the Law relate to top grade balls only; other grades of balls are subject to greater tolerances.

Replacement of ball lost or unfit for play

Unless there is a hazard near the ground, a river perhaps, there is little likelihood of a ball being lost – but it is a possibility. Balls do become unfit for play, either by losing their shape or by the seam opening up. Either is particularly likely if the ball is struck against a wall or other hard surface. The decision as to whether the ball should be replaced rests with the two umpires, after jointly inspecting the ball. Bowlers will sometimes suggest that the ball be changed, hoping to obtain more assistance from another ball. Umpires must deal as expeditiously as possible with any complaint by the fielding side to ensure time is not wasted and should only agree to the ball being changed when, in their opinion, it is no longer fit for play. The replacement ball should be, as far as is possible, one which has had a similar amount of wear to that which was being used although a wet ball which has become unfit for use will be replaced by a dry ball.

Should it be agreed to change the ball, the umpires are required to notify the batsmen that a replacement ball is to be used.

LAW 6 THE BAT

1 WIDTH AND LENGTH

The bat overall shall not be more than 38 inches/ 96.5cm. in length; the blade of the bat shall be made of wood and shall not exceed $4\frac{1}{4}$ inches/10.8cm. at the widest part.

Notes

(a) *The blade of the bat may be covered with material for protection, strengthening or repair. Such material shall not exceed $\frac{1}{16}$ inch/1.56mm. in thickness.*

All reputable bat manufacturers can be depended upon to produce to the limits laid down by Law. Only the overall length and width of the bat are limited; there is no restriction as to the weight or shape.

As with the size and weight of cricket balls, umpires need not be over anxious about bat measurements. Yet there have been recent complaints about the width of bats and umpires should not hesitate to check measurements if a discrepancy is suspected. They must ensure that all the implements used are strictly in accordance with the Laws.

The Law specifies that the blade shall be made of wood and allows for it to be protected, strengthened or repaired by the use of other material. Any material used to cover the blade should not exceed $\frac{1}{16}$ inch in thickness at any one point. The width of the bat should be checked if there is a suspicion that binding used exceeds that measurement; should this be confirmed the umpires should not allow the bat to be used unless binding is removed to bring it within the stated limits.

47

LAW 7 THE PITCH

**The pitch is the area between the bowling creases –
see Law 9: (The Bowling and Popping Creases). It shall
measure 5 feet/1.52m. in width on either side of a line
joining the centre of the middle stumps of the wickets
– see Law 8: (The Wickets).**

2 SELECTION AND PREPARATION
**Before the toss for innings, the Executive of the
Ground shall be responsible for the selection and
preparation of the pitch; thereafter the Umpires shall
control its use and maintenance.**

3 CHANGING PITCH
**The pitch shall not be changed during a match unless
it becomes unfit for play and then only with the
consent of both Captains.**

4 NON-TURF PITCHES
**In the event of a non-turf pitch being used, the
following shall apply:**
(a) *Length*
   **That of the playing surface to a minimum of 58
   feet (17.68m).**
(b) *Width*
   **That of the playing surface to a minimum of 6 feet
   (1.83m).**
**See Law 10: (Rolling, Sweeping, Mowing, Watering the
Pitch and Re-marking of Creases) Note (a).**

Note that the area of ground defined in this Law is the pitch, not
the wicket, which is the stumps and bails. In cricket jargon,
'wicket' is commonly used both for the pitch and for the wicket
itself. Umpires must be clear as to the difference between them.

Selection, preparation and maintenance of the pitch
The umpires do not select the pitch. Before the toss, the whole
responsibility for the pitch lies with the ground staff. After the
toss the umpires are to control the use of the pitch and supervise
any work of maintenance such as mowing, sweeping, rolling and

so on. (See **Laws 10 and 11.**)

<u>Measurements</u>
Although control of the pitch does not pass to them until after the toss has taken place, umpires should inspect the pitch before the match, to check that it conforms to the Law. (See Pre-match duties of the umpires.)

The width is important for the application of **Law 41.3** (Position of Fieldsman). It is to be 10 feet – more specifically 5 feet either side of the line of centre-stump to centre-stump. This means that it extends 8 inches beyond the line of the return crease and its forward extension. This will be a more reliable guide than the strip mown by the groundsman, which in some cases may not be exactly of the required width.

The 22 yard length is measured between the back edges of the bowling crease markings. It is not necessary to measure this length, although there are cases on record of its being found to be incorrect after a match has started. With experience, the umpire will develop the ability to make a good visual assessment. After a few matches in a season, old marks on neighbouring pitches may be a guide. If it is suspected that the length may not be correct, then proper measurement should be made. Pacing it out is too inaccurate to be of value. Errors should be corrected if at all possible. If it is not possible then both Captains should be made fully aware of the situation.

<u>Changing the pitch during the match</u>
It is necessary first that the umpires decide that it is unfit for play, and then that both Captains agree to play on a new pitch – if one is available. There may, for instance be a non-turf pitch which could be used. If such agreement is reached, the game continues on the new pitch. It is not re-started.

If the Captains do not agree to the use of another pitch, this does not constitute a refusal to play (**Law 21**). In that case, play will be postponed until either conditions are fit to resume on the original one, or it is decided that no further play is possible that day.

<u>Non-turf pitches</u>
Umpires should be aware of the different measurements that apply.

LAW 8 THE WICKETS

1 WIDTH AND PITCHING

Two sets of wickets, each 9 inches/22.86cm. wide, and consisting of three wooden stumps with two wooden bails upon the top, shall be pitched opposite and parallel to each other at a distance of 22 yards/20.12m. between the centres of the two middle stumps.

2 SIZE OF STUMPS

The stumps shall be of equal and sufficient size to prevent the ball from passing between them. Their tops shall be 28 inches/71.1cm. above the ground, and shall be domeshaped except for the bail grooves.

3 SIZE OF BAILS

The bails shall be each $4\frac{3}{8}$ inches/11.1cm. in length and when in position on the top of the stumps shall not project more than $\frac{1}{2}$ inch/1.3cm. above them.

Notes

(a) DISPENSING WITH BAILS
In a high wind the Umpires may decide to dispense with the use of bails.

(b) JUNIOR CRICKET
For Junior Cricket, as defined by the local Governing Body, the following measurements for the Wickets shall apply:

Width	*8 inches/20.32cm.*
Pitched	*21 yards/19.20m.*
Height	*27 inches/68.58cm.*
Bails	*each $3\frac{7}{8}$ inches/9.84cm. in length and should not project more than $\frac{1}{2}$ inch/1.3cm. above them.*

Pre-match inspection

An important pre-match duty of the umpires is to inspect the wickets to ensure they have been pitched correctly. It can be assumed that the stumps are the correct size. It is important that they have been set into the ground correctly. Whilst the diameter of each stump is not specified, the wicket should measure nine inches in width and the ball should not be able to pass between the stumps without dislodging a bail. The umpires must check, well before play starts, that the gap between the stumps is less than the diameter of the ball. It is also important to check the wickets from end to end.

The stumps and bails

All the stumps and bails should be made of wood. The bails should fit snugly into the grooves at the top of the stumps and must not project more than half an inch above the top of the stumps.

The stumps should be driven firmly into the ground, parallel with each other, and the bails placed perfectly level on the top. In dry weather the stump holes should be filled with water well before play starts to prevent them from crumbling and providing insufficient support. Additional firmness will also be obtained if the stump holes are watered if the pitch is being used for a second or third time. As detailed in **Law 9** the stumps should be set with their centre on the bowling crease – the back edge of the marking.

Both umpires should carry a spare bail to be used if a bail is broken during play. Should this happen it may well prove extremely difficult to obtain a replacement from the pavilion; an irritating delay can be avoided if the umpire has a spare available. It is often difficult to find a matching pair before the match let alone a third bail during the match. Most umpires carry three or more bails in their match accessories and this is a practice that is strongly recommended.

Providing the grooves at the top of the stumps are of sufficient depth, there should be few occasions when the bails are disturbed by high winds. The bails, however, may be blown off by sharp gusts of wind particularly on grounds that are very exposed. Should a bail, or both bails, be blown off, at the striker's end, before he has received a delivery, the umpire must be quick to call and signal Dead ball to avoid the possible complications which might ensue. No action need be taken if the dislodgement occurs after the ball has been played by the striker, or passed his wicket, or if the bails are dislodged from the non-striker's end.

Dispensing with bails

The continual dislodgement of the bails by a high wind will

prove irritating to the players and umpires. Should this happen the umpires may decide to dispense with the bails until the wind has abated but this decision is one for the umpires to take without reference to the players. The added difficulty of determining when the wicket is put down (see **Law 28**) suggests that umpires should not take this decision lightly and that the bails should be replaced, as soon as it proves possible to do so.

LAW 9 THE BOWLING, POPPING AND RETURN CREASES

1 THE BOWLING CREASE

The bowling crease shall be marked in line with the stumps at each end and shall be 8 feet 8 inches/2.64m. in length, with the stumps in the centre.

2 THE POPPING CREASE

The popping crease, which is the back edge of the crease marking, shall be in front of and parallel with the bowling crease. It shall have the back edge of the crease marking 4 feet/1.22m. from the centre of the stumps and shall extend to a minimum of 6 feet/ 1.83m. on either side of the line of the wicket.

The popping crease shall be considered to be unlimited in length.

3 THE RETURN CREASE

The return crease marking, of which the inside edge is the crease, shall be at each end of the bowling crease and at right angles to it. The return crease shall be marked to a minimum of 4 feet/1.22m. behind the wicket and shall be considered to be unlimited in length. A forward extension shall be marked to the popping crease.

The ability to gauge distances and measurements varies greatly from person to person and all umpires would benefit from close study of a correctly marked out pitch. They must be able to make a correct assessment before each match as to whether or

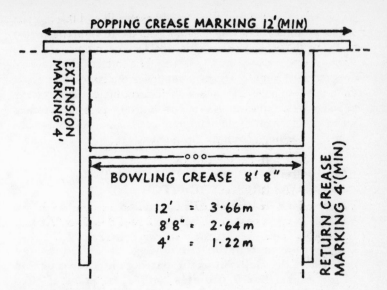

POPPING CREASE MARKING 12'(MIN)

EXTENSION MARKING 4'

BOWLING CREASE 8'8"

12' = 3·66m
8'8" = 2·64m
4' = 1·22m

RETURN CREASE MARKING 4'(MIN)

Figure 2

not the creases are marked correctly. Even the most experienced groundsmen have been known to make errors in both measurement and alignment; there is value in checking both carefully.

Creases and crease markings

The Law makes the clear distinction between 'crease markings' and the 'creases'. The lines painted on the ground are the 'crease markings' and the back or inside edges of the lines are the 'creases'. The width of the painted strip is immaterial although it is aesthetically pleasing, and a matter of pride to some groundsmen, to see the bowling, popping and return crease markings neatly and correctly drawn.

Appreciation that the white line is not the crease is of particular importance to the understanding of **Law 24** (No Ball) and **Law 29** (Batsman Out of His Ground).

Bowling crease

Although the bowling crease is now redundant for bowling

53

purposes, the back edge of the marking should run through the centre of the wicket which should be set 22 yards from the wicket at the other end.

<u>Popping and Return creases unlimited in length</u>
Figure 2 (on page 53) shows the minimum marking of the popping crease and return creases both of which are deemed unlimited in length. Note that the return creases extend forward from the bowling crease to the popping crease.

LAW 10 ROLLING, SWEEPING, MOWING, WATERING THE PITCH AND RE-MARKING OF CREASES

1 ROLLING
During the match the pitch may *before the toss* be rolled at the request of the Captain of the batting side, for a period of not more than 7 minutes before the start of each innings, other than the first innings of the match, and before the start of each day's play. In addition, if, after the toss and before the first innings of the match, the start is delayed, the Captain of the batting side may request to have the pitch rolled for not more than 7 minutes. However, if in the opinion of the Umpires, the delay has had no significant effect upon the state of the pitch, they shall refuse any request for the rolling of the pitch.

The pitch shall not otherwise be rolled during the match.

The 7 minutes rolling permitted before the start of a day's play shall take place not earlier than half an hour before the start of play and the Captain of the batting side may delay such rolling until 10 minutes before the start of play should he so desire.

If a Captain declares an innings closed less than 15 minutes before the resumption of play, and the other Captain is thereby prevented from exercising his option of 7 minutes rolling or if he is so prevented for any other reason, the time for rolling shall be taken out of the normal playing time.

2 SWEEPING
Such sweeping of the pitch as is necessary during the match shall be done so that the 7 minutes allowed for rolling the pitch provided for in 1, above, is not affected.

3 MOWING
(a) *Responsibilities of Ground Authority and of Umpires*
All mowings which are carried out before the toss for innings shall be the responsibility of the Ground Authority. Thereafter they shall be carried out under the supervision of the Umpires, see Law 7.2: (Selection and Preparation).

(b) *Initial Mowing*
The pitch shall be mown before play begins on the day the match is scheduled to start or in the case of a delayed start on the day the match is expected to start. See 3(a) above (Responsibilities of Ground Authority and of Umpires).

(c) *Subsequent Mowings in a Match of 2 or More Days' Duration*
In a match of two or more days' duration, the pitch shall be mown daily before play begins. Should this mowing not take place because of weather conditions, rest days or other reasons the pitch shall be mown on the first day on which the match is resumed.

(d) *Mowing of the Outfield in a Match of 2 or More Days' Duration*
In order to ensure that conditions are as similar as possible for both sides, the outfield shall normally be mown before the commencement of play on each day of the match, if ground and weather conditions allow. See Note (b) to this Law.

4 WATERING
The pitch shall not be watered during a match.

5 RE-MARKING CREASES
Whenever possible the creases shall be re-marked.

6 MAINTENANCE OF FOOT HOLES
In wet weather, the Umpires shall ensure that the holes made by the Bowlers and Batsmen are cleaned out and dried whenever necessary to facilitate play. In

matches of 2 or more days' duration, the Umpires shall allow, if necessary, the re-turfing of foot holes made by the Bowler in his delivery stride, or the use of quick-setting fillings for the same purpose, before the start of each day's play.

7 SECURING OF FOOTHOLDS AND MAINTENANCE OF PITCH
During play, the Umpires shall allow either Batsman to beat the pitch with his bat and players to secure their footholds by the use of sawdust, provided that no damage to the pitch is so caused, and Law 42: (Unfair Play) is not contravened.

Notes

(a) NON-TURF PITCHES
The above **Law 10** *applies to turf pitches.*

The game is played on non-turf pitches in many countries at various levels. Whilst the conduct of the game on these surfaces should always be in accordance with the Laws of Cricket, it is recognized that it may sometimes be necessary for Governing Bodies to lay down special playing conditions to suit the type of non-turf pitch used in their country.

In matches played against Touring Teams, any special playing conditions should be agreed in advance by both parties.

(b) MOWING OF THE OUTFIELD IN A MATCH OF 2 OR MORE DAYS' DURATION
If, for reasons other than ground and weather conditions, daily and complete mowing is not possible, the Ground Authority shall notify the Captains and Umpires, before the toss for innings, of the procedure to be adopted for such mowing during the match.

(c) CHOICE OF ROLLER
If there is more than one roller available the Captain of the batting side shall have a choice.

The complexities of this Law are rarely completely understood by players and therefore merit careful study by all umpires. There may occasionally be Special Regulations, particularly with regard to rolling the pitch, which must be taken into account.

Umpires responsible for maintenance after the toss
The Ground Authority is responsible for the production of a properly cut and rolled pitch ready for play on the first day of the match. **Law 7** (The Pitch) places the responsibility of controlling the use and maintenance of the pitch on to the umpires once the toss has been made. All rolling and sweeping of the pitch must be timed and supervised by the umpires. The Captain of the side batting first may not have the pitch rolled before the start of the match, unless, after the toss, the start is delayed and then only if the umpires consider the delay has had a significant effect on the state of the pitch. It is not possible to indicate a specific length of delay which would result in a significant effect on the state of the pitch; much will depend upon the weather. The rolling, if granted, will be limited to a period of no more than 7 minutes.

Rolling before play starts
The rolling before the start of each day's play, other than the first day, is permitted only if carried out during the half hour period before play begins. 'Before play begins' means that if the agreed starting time is delayed, the rolling may be delayed so as to take place during the half hour period before play actually starts. The Captain may, of course, delay the rolling until 10 minutes before the start of play; if this happens the umpires must make certain that the rolling is completed so as to allow play to start at the agreed time.

Late declaration during an interval
The Law gives the Captain of the batting side the right to have the pitch rolled prior to the start of the second or subsequent innings. If a late declaration, during an interval, prevents this from happening, the umpires should allow the full 7 minutes' rolling, if required, even though playing time is lost (see **Law 14**).

Maximum time allowed for rolling – 7 minutes
The 7 minutes allowed is the maximum time for rolling; a Captain may opt for a shorter period if he so wishes. He may not, however, designate that only certain portions of the pitch should be rolled or mowed. Umpires must check that the whole

of the pitch is treated. No indication is given to the time allowed for sweeping the pitch but any such attention must not interfere with the 7 minutes allowed for rolling.

No restrictions are placed on the size or weight of the roller; if there is more than one available, the Captain of the batting side may choose the one he considers most suitable for the prevailing conditions.

Mowing the pitch and outfield
The mowing of the pitch and ground before play begins will be the responsibility of the Ground Authority. The umpires' responsibility and supervision of mowing will begin only after the toss. The pitch will be mown daily during a match of two or more days under the supervision of the umpires. It is not necessary for the umpires to supervise the mowing of the outfield, except to check that the mowing is completed before the start of play and in accordance with any procedure agreed before the toss.

Re-marking of creases
The obliteration of part of the popping crease by some bowlers can make it extremely difficult for the umpire to judge the fairness of a delivery. The loss of the marking can cause a delay in the umpire making his decision at a time when he can ill afford it. It is important that creases, particularly the popping crease, are re-marked during every interval.

Drying and cleaning footholds
It is likely that rolling, sweeping the pitch and the re-marking of the creases will fully occupy the members of ground staff during the interval of a club or League match so that the task of drying and cleaning the footholds of bowlers and batsmen will not be attempted. Umpires should be aware that this should be done and, if necessary, they should call upon the executive of the ground to attempt an improvement. Both bowlers and batsmen may use sawdust to enable them to obtain better purchase; umpires should ensure that any sawdust put down by the bowler does not create a hazard for the striker. One of the important pre-match duties of the umpires is to make sure that sawdust is available.

Damage to the pitch

The Law permits batsmen to beat the pitch with their bats; unfortunately some batsmen abuse this concession either by attempting to damage the pitch or by deliberately wasting time. Umpires should be prepared to take the necessary action if they consider the batsmen guilty of unfair play. Particular care should be taken to monitor the batsmen towards the end of an innings. Attempts may be made to damage the pitch both by prodding with the bat as well as deliberately running onto the danger area.

Fieldsmen too may cause damage, either innocently or deliberately. Umpires must be alert and ready to intervene at once if they consider the action by members of either side is causing damage which may be detrimental to their opponents at a later stage. Damage to the pitch whether by a batsman, fielder or bowler is fully dealt with under **Law 42** which sets out the procedures which umpires must follow whether the damage is accidental or deliberate. Delay by the umpires may result in damage to the pitch which cannot be repaired.

LAW 11 COVERING THE PITCH

1 BEFORE THE START OF A MATCH
Before the start of a match complete covering of the pitch shall be allowed.

2 DURING A MATCH
The pitch shall not be completely covered during a match unless prior arrangement or regulations so provide.

3 COVERING BOWLERS' RUN-UP
Whenever possible, the Bowlers' run-up shall be covered, but the covers so used shall not extend further than 4 feet/1.22m. in front of the popping crease.

Notes

(a) REMOVAL OF COVERS
The covers should be removed as promptly as possible whenever the weather permits.

Agreement on the use of covers

At one time, covers were rarely available on grounds other than those used for highest grades of cricket but covering is now available on many club grounds. Many Leagues insist that member clubs have some form of covering to be used during inclement weather and often insist that full covering is provided during any interruption. There are many Special Regulations relating to covering, particularly for First Class cricket. Such Regulations have been drawn up in an attempt to ensure the least possible loss of playing time and may insist on the complete covering overnight, throughout any rest day and as soon as play is abandoned for the day. Umpires should clarify, in the pre-match discussion, any agreement relating to the covering of the pitch and ensure that such agreement conforms to Regulations applicable to that match.

If full covering is not agreed, it is essential that the bowlers' run-ups be protected. Covering so used must not be allowed to project more than 4 feet in front of each popping crease. There is no limit to the distance behind the bowling crease which can be covered.

Umpires must check that any covering is removed as early as possible when the weather permits.

LAW 12 INNINGS

1 NUMBER OF INNINGS
A match shall be of one or two innings of each side according to agreement reached before the start of play.

2 ALTERNATE INNINGS
In a two innings match each side shall take their innings alternately except in the case provided for in Law 13: (The Follow-On).

3 THE TOSS
The Captains shall toss for the choice of innings on the field of play not later than 15 minutes before the time scheduled for the match to start, or before the time agreed upon for play to start.

4 CHOICE OF INNINGS

The winner of the toss shall notify his decision to bat or to field to the opposing Captain not later than 10 minutes before the time scheduled for the match to start, or before the time agreed upon for play to start. The decision shall not thereafter be altered.

5 CONTINUATION AFTER ONE INNINGS OF EACH SIDE

Despite the terms of 1 above, in a one-innings match, when a result has been reached on the first innings the Captains may agree to the continuation of play if, in their opinion, there is a prospect of carrying the game to a further issue in the time left. See Law 21: (Result).

Notes

(a) LIMITED INNINGS – ONE-INNINGS MATCH

In a one-innings match, each innings may, by agreement, be limited by a number of overs or by a period of time.

(b) LIMITED INNINGS – TWO-INNINGS MATCH

In a two-innings match, the first innings of each side may, by agreement, be limited to a number of overs or by a period of time.

Importance of the toss being made on time

One of the pre-match duties of the umpires is to ensure that the toss is made, on the field of play, not later than 15 minutes before the scheduled starting time, or the time agreed upon for play to start. The 'agreed' starting time is the time agreed for play to start should conditions delay the scheduled start. The toss can be made at a much earlier time, should the Captains so wish, but the umpires should do whatever is necessary to make certain that the toss is made in good time to enable a prompt start to the match. The non-arrival of a Captain should not be allowed to delay the toss. Unless the players promptly arrange a deputy Captain, the umpires should draw the players' attention to **Law 1** which requires a deputy to act for the Captain should he not be available.

Notification of decision to bat or field

The toss having been made, a Captain may delay his decision as to whether his side will bat or field providing his notification to the opposing Captain is made not later than 10 minutes before the scheduled or agreed time for the start of play. Once the Captain has notified his decision, he cannot under any circumstance, reverse it.

Continuation after one innings

Most club games are limited to one innings per side and this may be one of the Special Regulations relating to a particular match. The Law, however, allows for the continuation of a game if sufficient time remains for a second innings when a result has been achieved on the first innings (see **Law 21**). This is a matter for the Captains to agree upon; the umpires may advise them of the condition of the Law which is aimed at providing as much play as possible within the time allowed for the match.

Limited overs or time

It is important that umpires discuss with Captains, before the toss, any Special Regulations which apply. The Captains and umpires do need to have a clear understanding of any limitations which may be placed upon the number of overs or time allowed for an innings. Such Regulations may state that any overs or time not taken up by the side batting first will be added to the number of overs or time allowed for the side batting second. There are many other possible complications which may result in dispute. The Captains should be tactfully reminded of any of the Regulations which the umpires consider may not be fully understood by the players.

LAW 13 THE FOLLOW-ON

1 LEAD ON FIRST INNINGS

In a two-innings match the side which bats first and leads by 200 runs in a match of five days or more, by 150 runs in a three-day or four-day match, by 100 runs in a two-day match, or by 75 runs in a one-day match, shall have the option of requiring the other side to follow their innings.

If no play takes place on the first day of a match of 2 or more days' duration, 1 above shall apply in accordance with the number of days' play remaining from the actual start of the match.

The lead required

The lead must be, in each case, at least the number stated. A follow-on, however, is not obligatory. If his side has the necessary lead, the Captain is to decide whether or not to require the opposition to follow-on. The normal allowance of 10 minutes between innings will apply.

Umpires may need to give guidance to captains as to the provisions of the Law. This may be especially the case if there has been loss of time for adverse weather or light conditions.

The duration of the match

Only if the match starts a whole day (or more) late will it be considered as being of shorter duration. If there is any play at all on the first day, the match will be considered as consisting of its original number of days. Play will have taken place as soon as the opening bowler starts his over. Normally this will be by delivering a ball, even if it is one that is not to count as one of the balls of the over. Exceptionally, it may be by attempting to run out the non-striker before delivering the first ball.

LAW 14 DECLARATIONS

1 TIME OF DECLARATION

The Captain of the batting side may declare an innings closed at any time during a match irrespective of its duration.

2 FORFEITURE OF SECOND INNINGS

A Captain may forfeit his second innings, provided his decision to do so is notified to the opposing Captain and Umpires in sufficient time to allow 7 minutes rolling of the pitch. See Law 10: (Rolling, Sweeping, Mowing, Watering the Pitch and Re-Marking of

Creases). The normal 10 minute interval between innings shall be applied.

Declaration

Whether to declare, and at what time, is entirely for the Captain of the batting side to decide. If, however, he declares when less than 15 minutes of an interval remain, the provisions of **Law 10.1** (final paragraph) will apply.

The opposing Captain is entitled, as usual, to a maximum of 7 minutes rolling of the pitch. Any necessary sweeping is not to interfere with this nor should any re-marking of the creases. It may not be possible, therefore, to complete the rolling before the time scheduled for resumption. The interval should then be extended by the minimum length of time required, and the playing time reduced by this amount; there will be no overall extension of the time for the match. Although the Captain may himself decide to waive part or all of his permitted rolling time, he should not be forced to do so in order to resume play at the originally scheduled time.

In the case of a declaration very late in an interval, it may be necessary to allow a reasonable time for players padding up etc, even if no rolling is required, but there is no mandate in Law for adding the 10 minutes between innings. Play should be resumed with the minimum delay. Playing time will be reduced by the length of the delay.

Forfeiture

A Captain may decide to forfeit his second innings. This means that the side batting second will have their two innings consecutively. The normal 10 minutes between innings will apply.

As in the case of a late declaration, it is necessary that there is sufficient time for the opposing Captain to exercise his right to 7 minutes' rolling, if he so wishes. If it is not possible to complete the rolling in time, then the same conditions would apply as set out above for a declaration late in an interval.

LAW 15 START OF PLAY

1 CALL OF PLAY
At the start of each innings and of each day's play and

on the resumption of play after any interval or interruption the Umpire at the Bowler's end shall call 'play'.

2 PRACTICE ON THE FIELD
At no time on any day of the match shall there be any bowling or batting practice on the pitch.

No practice may take place on the field if, in the opinion of the Umpires, it could result in a waste of time.

3 TRIAL RUN-UP
No Bowler shall have a trial run-up after 'play' has been called in any session of play, except at the fall of a wicket when an Umpire may allow such a trial run-up if he is satisfied that it will not cause any waste of time. *or retirement of batsman*

<u>When to call Play</u>
The bowler's end umpire must call Play whenever play is to resume having not previously been in progress. The Law specifically cites four occasions. The start of each innings; the start of each day's play; the resumption of play after any interval; the resumption of play after any interruption.

The first two require no explanation. 'Re-starting after an interval' means after all arranged intervals. Consequently this will include re-starting play not only after the lunch or tea interval, but also after an interval for drinks. The gap between one day and the next is, of course, also an arranged interval. The fact that there is a separate statement about 'the start of each day's play', however, leaves no room for doubt and also emphasizes that there are situations in which the overnight interval is treated differently from other intervals – see **Law 2.8**.

Umpires should remember that re-starting after an interruption also requires the call of Play. In this context an interruption may include an investigation by the umpires under **Law 31** (Timed Out), as well as suspensions of play for reasons of ground, weather or light. It will also include an interruption of play for exceptional circumstances – see **Law 3.9**.

Significance of calling Play

There are very many circumstances in which the call of Play is important. At the beginning of a match, it confirms that the match has begun, although no play will have taken place until there is some incident. Normally this will be the opening bowler delivering his first ball, even if it is a No ball or a Wide ball. There will be exceptional occasions, however, when he does not achieve the delivery of this first ball. These are dealt with under **Laws 13 and 22**. The call of Play at the start of an innings is also the necessary signal that the opening batsmen's innings have commenced – see **Law 2.10**.

Umpires should note the two particular restrictions – on fielding practice and trial run-up for bowlers – laid on the players by the call of Play. Practice on the outfield before commencement of play is commonplace, but once Play has been called, it can be allowed only if the umpires are satisfied that there is no consequent waste of time. Players will frequently use the gap between the fall of a wicket and the arrival of the incoming batsman for this purpose. They may even do so during the adjustment of a sight-screen. This can be allowed, but umpires must be ready to stop it if they consider that time is being lost. They must use their common sense, without being officious, in dealing with such fielding practice – as indeed they must in many other situations.

Again, no bowler is allowed a trial run-up once Play has been called, except at the fall of a wicket, and then only if the umpire is satisfied that there will be no waste of time. Some bowlers may take a run-up, either through ignorance of the Law or in a deliberate attempt to overcome this restriction. Umpires must be on their guard against this. Once it has happened, nothing can be done except to remonstrate quietly with the bowler. It is recommended that at any time when it is necessary to prevent the bowler from starting his run-up, the bowler's end umpire should stand to the side of the wicket in the bowler's path. This is better than standing in the normal position behind the stumps, with an outstretched arm.

Practising batting or bowling on the pitch itself is forbidden at any time during the match. This applies even during intervals or interruptions; one aim of this restriction is of course to prevent damage to the pitch. During play, umpires must be on the alert for players attempting to practise on the pitch, particularly at the fall of a wicket, and must be ready to stop it at once. There are Special Regulations which equally forbid bowling practice on any part of the square, or even on strips which may be outside the square but adjacent to the pitch in use. This is to prevent an advantage being gained by the bowling side which is not available to the batsmen. At present this restriction applies only in the First Class game, except where it may be specially stated in the regulations governing matches in a particular competition.

Field Technique

Before the start of the match, the umpires, having checked that the field is cleared of spectators, players and obstructions, will walk out 5 minutes before the time agreed for play to start (see 'Umpire's duties before the match' page 13). On some grounds there is a bell which can be rung 5 minutes before play is due to begin. Where there is no '5-minute bell', umpires should ensure in some other way that both Captains know that they are going out.

Having agreed at which ends they will stand, the umpires will re-check the alignment of the stumps and place the bails in position before the fielding side arrives. When it is clear from which end the bowling is to begin, the umpire at that end must enquire the bowler's mode of delivery, i.e. right- or left-handed, from over or round the wicket. This is a suitable point for the umpire to give the bowler a marker if required.

When the batsmen arrive at the pitch, the bowler's end umpire must notify the bowler's action and will be required to give guard to the striker. The sight-screen may need moving. If so it is helpful for the bowler's end umpire to stand with the appropriate arm upraised in the approximate place from which the bowler will deliver the ball. He must then check all the following:

that the number of fielders does not exceed eleven;
that the fielding Captain has finished setting his field;
that the scorers are in position and ready;
that both batsmen are ready.

He will then hand the match ball to the bowler.

The bowler's end umpire will then check that his colleague is ready. The experienced striker's end umpire will be ready and looking for the enquiry, having already checked that the field setting does not involve more than two on-side fielders behind the line of the popping crease – see **Law 41**. The two umpires will agree that the time scheduled for start of play has been reached. Then the bowler's end umpire will call Play. The call must be made clearly so that the fielding side and both batsmen are aware that the match has started and play is to begin.

All these checks are important. Probably the one most often neglected by inexperienced umpires is satisfying themselves that the scorers are ready. To start play without any recording facilities would be a serious lapse by the umpire/scorer team. If there has been proper discussion at the pre-match meeting with the scorers, there should be no risk of this. A frequently used signal is to raise one arm high above the head until an acknowledgment is received from the score box that all is in order.

In general the routine described above will be necessary at each call of Play. There will be small exceptions. For example, after an interval for drinks the umpires and players will already be on the field of play. After an interruption, and also after drinks, there will be no specific time agreed for start of play. It will begin as soon as all the checks reveal that everyone is ready.

LAW 16 INTERVALS

1 LENGTH
The Umpire shall allow such intervals as have been agreed upon for meals, and 10 minutes between each innings.

2 LUNCHEON INTERVAL – INNINGS ENDING OR STOPPAGE WITHIN 10 MINUTES OF INTERVAL
If an innings ends or there is a stoppage caused by weather or bad light within 10 minutes of the agreed time for the luncheon interval, the interval shall be taken immediately.

The time remaining in the session of play shall be added to the agreed length of the interval but no extra allowance shall be made for the 10 minutes interval between innings.

3 TEA INTERVAL – INNINGS ENDING OR STOPPAGE WITHIN 30 MINUTES OF INTERVAL

If an innings ends or there is a stoppage caused by weather or bad light within 30 minutes of the agreed time for the tea interval, the interval shall be taken immediately.

The interval shall be of the agreed length and, if applicable, shall include the 10 minute interval between innings.

4 TEA INTERVAL – CONTINUATION OF PLAY

If at the agreed time for the tea interval, nine wickets are down, play shall continue for a period not exceeding 30 minutes or until the innings is concluded.

5 TEA INTERVAL – AGREEMENT TO FOREGO

At any time during the match, the Captains may agree to forego a tea interval.

6 INTERVALS FOR DRINKS

If both Captains agree before the start of a match that intervals for drinks may be taken, the option to take such intervals shall be available to either side. These intervals shall be restricted to one per session, shall be kept as short as possible, shall not be taken in the last hour of the match and in any case shall not exceed 5 minutes.

The agreed times for these intervals shall be strictly adhered to except that if a wicket falls within 5 minutes of the agreed time then drinks shall be taken out immediately.

If an innings ends or there is a stoppage caused by weather or bad light within 30 minutes of the agreed time for a drinks interval, there will be no interval for drinks in that session.

At any time during the match the Captains may agree to forego any such drinks interval.

Notes

(a) TEA INTERVAL – ONE-DAY MATCH

In a one-day match, a specific time for the tea interval need not necessarily be arranged, and it may be agreed to take this interval between the innings of a one-innings match.

(b) CHANGING THE AGREED TIME OF INTERVALS

In the event of the ground, weather or light conditions causing a suspension of play, the Umpires, after consultation with the Captains, may decide in the interest of time-saving, to bring forward the time of the luncheon or tea interval.

Agreeing the intervals

This Law assumes that before the toss proper agreement was made, under **Law 3.3**, as to hours of play, the timing and length of intervals for meals, and drinks intervals, if any. No flexibility is allowed on the interval between innings. That will be 10 minutes, and cannot be altered. Note (a) to the Law does, however, allow for the tea interval in a one-day match to be agreed as between innings, rather than at a specified time. This means that the 10 minutes between innings will be saved.

Alterations to the agreed intervals – general

Having first stated that the umpires are required to see that the arrangements are observed – 'the umpires shall allow such intervals' – this Law goes on to give details of when these arrangements **must** be changed and when they **may** be changed. Umpires must have a clear understanding of these variations. Moreover, in many competitions the Special Regulations lay down particular procedures both for what the intervals should be and how they are to be changed in given circumstances. Umpires must be fully conversant with the provisions of any such regulations governing the match, and how they interact with the Law. The umpires have a responsibility to see that changes to the pre-match agreed intervals are only those required or permitted by Law, or by Special Regulations.

Stoppages for ground weather or light

Note (b) to the Law gives general guidance on stoppages for ground weather or light. If there is a suspension of play for such adverse conditions, it is clearly sensible to try to have as much time for play as possible, by bringing forward lunch (or tea if appropriate) so that the interval is taken, if possible, during the stoppage. It is, however, necessary that both Captains agree to such a change. The two umpires will have already agreed between themselves before approaching the Captains. It would be surprising if either Captain did not see the wisdom of the move and agree to the change. Nevertheless, if either of them does not agree, the umpires are not empowered to enforce it. In any case, it is prudent to seek the cooperation of the catering service, before making such changes.

Changing the lunch interval

Apart from the general observations above, the Law provides for changing the time of lunch in two specific situations: – if an innings ends within 10 minutes of the agreed time; or if a stoppage for adverse conditions of ground weather or light starts within 10 minutes of the agreed time. Suppose that lunch has been arranged for 1–30 p.m. to 2–10 p.m. If the last wicket falls at 1–25 p.m., 5 minutes before the agreed time, lunch will be taken at once. There will be no allowance for the 10 minutes between innings, but the extra 5 minutes will be added to the time allowed for lunch, making it 45 minutes. Play will be resumed at the originally agreed time of 2–10 p.m.

Similarly, if conditions of ground weather or light mean that play has to be suspended at say 1–22 p.m., 8 minutes before the agreed time, again lunch will be taken at once. The extra 8 minutes will be added on to the time allowed for lunch. Play will be resumed, if conditions permit, at 2–10 as originally agreed.

If, however, the innings ends, or a stoppage for ground weather or light begins, at or before 10 minutes ahead of the time agreed, lunch will be taken at the pre-match agreed time. For a stoppage, of course, it would be possible to use the flexibility given by Note (b) to bring it forward, if the umpires thought it advisable, and providing the Captains agree.

Changing the tea interval

There are three ways in which the tea interval can be altered from the pre-match agreed time. It may be taken early, postponed or cancelled altogether. This Law lays down the conditions for each of these possibilities.

Dispensing with the tea interval

The most straightforward of these is that the Captains, not the umpires, can agree to dispense with it. They can do this at any time during the match. In a match of more than one day's duration, the agreement may be made separately for each day.

If they come to such an agreement, then there will be no tea interval on that day, notwithstanding that it had been agreed before the toss. The umpires have to accept the Captains' decision. It would be helpful to ensure that the scorers were aware of it, too.

Bringing the tea interval forward

In addition to the general provision under Note (b) for taking tea early by agreement, the tea interval must be taken earlier than agreed if an innings ends, or there is a stoppage caused by ground weather or light, within 30 minutes of the agreed time. Although this is similar to changes for the lunch interval, there are significant differences. The period ahead of the agreed time is 30 minutes, not 10 minutes. The extra time is not added on to the length of the interval; that is to remain at the agreed length. The one point that is the same as for lunch is that if the change is occasioned by the end of an innings, there will be no allowance for the 10 minutes between innings.

Suppose for example that tea is scheduled for 20 minutes starting at 4–30 p.m. An innings ends at 4–15. Tea will be taken immediately and will last for 20 minutes. Play will resume at 4–35 p.m., with the start of the new innings. If, however, the innings had ended at 3–55 p.m., more than 30 minutes before the scheduled time, the 10 minute interval would be taken and the new innings would start at 4–05 p.m.

If a stoppage for conditions of ground weather or light starts within 30 minutes of the time agreed for tea, then it is treated in exactly the same way as an innings ending. If, for example, with the times agreed as above, an interruption for rain starts at 4–05 p.m., tea will be taken immediately. If conditions permit, play will resume at 4–25. A stoppage may however have begun earlier and already be in progress at 30 minutes before the agreed time. For instance in the example above, if the stoppage had begun at 3–55 p.m., so that at 4 p.m. it was already in progress, tea would be taken at 4 p.m., instead of at 4–30. Play would resume at 4–20 or as soon thereafter as conditions permitted.

It is perhaps helpful to remember that while the lunch interval will end at the previously agreed time, so that it is extended by the few minutes gained by taking it early, the tea interval will always be the agreed length. In both cases no extra allowance is to be made for 10 minutes between innings.

Postponing the tea interval
If when the agreed time for tea has been reached, the batting side has lost 9 wickets, tea must be postponed. The postponement will be up to a maximum of 30 minutes. Assuming that there is no interruption for conditions of ground weather or light, play will continue for half an hour or until the innings ends, should this happen before the half-hour has expired. Tea will then be taken, unless the Captains have agreed to forego it.

In any of these situations where intervals are to be different from those agreed before the toss, it is important to remember that the scorers may not be aware of the changes. Umpires should ensure that they are informed, especially but not solely if the change is one made by agreement and not one of those laid down as obligatory in this Law.

Drinks Intervals
Whether intervals for drinks are to be permitted at all must be agreed before the toss, as well as when they are to occur. The Law restricts the times which can be agreed.
- only one interval for drinks is permitted in each session;
- no drinks are permitted in the last hour of a match;
- if there is a stoppage for conditions of ground weather or light within 30 minutes of the agreed time for the next interval the drinks interval will be cancelled for that session.

Many competitions also lay down strictures on the frequency and timing of drinks intervals. The umpires will have ensured that the pre-toss agreement is within the Law as modified, if applicable, by any Special Regulations.

Although intervals for drinks may have been agreed before the match, each one remains an option. If both Captains agree, any one of them may be cancelled. The Law, however, makes it clear that this must be an agreement by both Captains. If either Captain wishes to retain a drinks interval, then it cannot be cancelled, except in the case of a stoppage as outlined above. Umpires are responsible for seeing that the agreed times are strictly observed. The only variation, apart from the right of the Captains to agree to forego an interval, is that if a wicket falls within 5 minutes of the agreed time, then drinks will be taken immediately.

It is also important that an interval for drinks takes no more time than is absolutely necessary. In **Law 42** it is made clear that time-wasting is unfair. Consequently, time-saving is something that umpires and Captains alike must take seriously. The various provisions of this Law for moving previously agreed intervals in different circumstances are all designed for that purpose. As far as drinks are concerned, the permitted length of 5 minutes is a maximum. Umpires should make every effort to see that less time than this is taken if possible.

More generally, umpires must use every endeavour to see that play starts punctually, both at the beginning of the game and at the resumption after every break, whether it be interval or interruption. Players will sometimes need reminding of the necessity for such punctuality. The co-operation of the Captains will be needed both in ensuring this and in maximizing the time available by agreeing to the bringing forward of lunch or tea as permitted by Note (b).

Field Technique

The routine which umpires must follow at the start of any interval, and the written record they should make of the state of play and the times involved, are all dealt with fully under the next Law. It must be appreciated, however, that an interval for drinks is no different in this respect from any other. The same routine should be employed as for other intervals.

LAW 17 CESSATION OF PLAY

1 CALL OF TIME

The Umpire at the Bowler's end shall call 'time' on the cessation of play before any interval or interruption of play, at the end of each day's play, and at the conclusion of the match. See Law 27: (Appeals).

2 REMOVAL OF BAILS

After the call of 'time', the Umpires shall remove the bails from both wickets.

3 STARTING A LAST OVER

The last over before an interval or the close of play shall be started provided the Umpire, after walking at his normal pace, has arrived at his position behind the

stumps at the Bowler's end before time has been reached.

4 COMPLETION OF THE LAST OVER OF A SESSION

The last over before an interval or the close of play shall be completed unless a Batsman is out or retires during that over within 2 minutes of the interval or the close of play or unless the Players have occasion to leave the field.

5 COMPLETION OF THE LAST OVER OF A MATCH

An over in progress at the close of play on the final day of a match shall be completed at the request of either Captain even if a wicket falls after time has been reached.

If during the last over the Players have occasion to leave the field the Umpires shall call 'time' and there shall be no resumption of play and the match shall be at an end.

6 LAST HOUR OF MATCH – NUMBER OF OVERS

The Umpires shall indicate when one hour of playing time of the match remains according to the agreed hours of play. The next over after that moment shall be the first of a minimum of 20 6-ball overs (15 8-ball overs), provided a result is not reached earlier, or there is no interval or interruption of play.

7 LAST HOUR OF MATCH – INTERVALS BETWEEN INNINGS AND INTERRUPTIONS OF PLAY

If, at the commencement of the last hour of the match, an interval or interruption of play is in progress or if, during the last hour, there is an interval between innings or an interruption of play, the minimum number of overs to be bowled on the resumption of play shall be reduced in proportion to the duration, within the last hour of the match, of any such interval or interruption.

The minimum number of overs to be bowled after a resumption of play shall be calculated as follows:
(a) In the case of an interval or interruption of play being in progress at the commencement of the last hour of the match, or in the case of a first interval

or interruption a deduction shall be made from the minimum of 20 6-ball overs (or 15 8-ball overs).

(b) If there is a later interval or interruption a further deduction shall be made from the minimum number of overs which should have been bowled following the last resumption of play.

(c) These deductions shall be based on the following factors:

   (i) the number of overs already bowled in the last hour of the match or, in the case of a later interval or interruption in the last session of play.

   (ii) the number of overs lost as a result of the interval or interruption allowing one 6-ball over for every full three minutes (or one 8-ball over for every full four minutes) of interval or interruption.

   (iii) any over left uncompleted at the end of an innings to be excluded from these calculations.

   (iv) any over of the minimum number to be played which is left uncompleted at the start of an interruption of play shall be completed when play is resumed and to count as one over bowled.

   (v) an interval to start with the end of an innings and to end 10 minutes later; an interruption to start on the call of 'time' and to end on the call of 'play'.

(d) In the event of an innings being completed and a new innings commencing during the last hour of the match, the number of overs to be bowled in the new innings shall be calculated on the basis of one 6-ball over for every three minutes or part thereof remaining for play (or one 8-ball over for every four minutes or part thereof remaining for play); or alternatively on the basis that sufficient overs be bowled to enable the full minimum quota of overs to be completed under circumstances governed by (a), (b) and (c) above. In all such cases the

alternative which allows the greater number of overs shall be employed.

8 BOWLER UNABLE TO COMPLETE AN OVER DURING LAST HOUR OF THE MATCH
If, for any reason, a Bowler is unable to complete an over during the period of play referred to in 6 above, Law 22.7: (Bowler Incapacitated or Suspended during an Over) shall apply.

The occasions when Time is to be called
Just as under **Law 15** the umpire at the bowler's end must call Play to begin a session of play, so he must call Time whenever play is in progress and is to cease. Again, this Law gives four specific instances: on the cessation of play before any interval; on the cessation of play before any interruption; at the end of each day's play; at the conclusion of the match. Just as with the call of Play, these four instances overlap each other.

'At the end of each day's play' is obvious enough. 'At the conclusion of the match' means at the conclusion whatever form that may take. A match will end when a result is reached; that is, the side batting last has no more wickets to fall, or reaches the total necessary to win. It may also end prematurely, if conditions of ground weather or light make continuance of play impossible. There are also other less normal ways in which a match can end, discussed under **Law 21** (The Result). Even if one side achieves victory before the expiry of time, Time must still be called at the end of the match.

'Before any interval' means before any arranged interval. Therefore, as well as lunch and tea, this includes any drinks interval. The inexperienced umpire may not appreciate that Time should also be called on the cessation of play at the start of any interruption. However rapid departure from the field of play may be, in the case of a sudden torrential downpour, the bowler's end umpire must remember, among other things, to call Time. He must do this, even if there has been no play, if the downpour comes after Play has been called, but before any play takes place.

The significance of calling Time
The call of Time is not only the signal that this session of play is

at an end. It means the complete cessation of play for the time being. The only actions thereafter, by any of the players, that can have any significance are those which are allowed, or forbidden, 'at any time during the match'. For example the batting Captain may declare after Time has been called, but it is only actions of this nature which can have any relevance to the match.

The ball is automatically dead on the call of Time. There are plenty of other occasions when the ball becomes dead; these are dealt with under **Law 23** (Dead Ball). The call of Time, however, is a final termination. No appeal can be made thereafter, even if the incident took place before Time – see **Law 27**. The ball cannot come into play again until the umpire calls Play at the start of the next session, if there is one.

This Law requires the umpires to remove both sets of bails after calling Time. Physically, this cannot be done immediately, certainly by the striker's end umpire and probably not by the bowler's end umpire unless he is for some reason very close to the stumps. The cessation of play, however, comes into effect at the call of Time; it does not have to wait until the bails are removed.

The time when Time is to be called

The beginning of a session, for calling Play, is an obvious moment; the end of a session, the moment for calling Time, may not be so obvious. At the exact time when it has been agreed that the interval should begin, the ball is very nearly always in play. Clearly the call must at least be delayed until the events significant to that delivery are completed. More than this, normally the over in progress will be completed, before Time is called. The Law lays down specific guidelines,

  on whether an over should be completed, or even started;
  on the time for close of play at the end of the match;
  on calling Time prematurely in various circumstances.
Each situation is discussed under its own heading.

The last hour of a match

Among the times agreed before the toss, will be a time for close of play at the end of the match. Section 6 of this Law requires that the umpires shall notify the players and scorers when one hour remains before this time. Thereafter a minimum of 20 6-ball overs (15 8-ball overs) must be bowled, unless the match comes to a conclusion sooner. This requirement is modified if an interval occurs, or if time is lost for suspensions of play.

It must be emphasized that the 20 overs are a minimum. If they are completed before the agreed time for close of play is reached, then play will continue until that finishing time, or even beyond if necessary to complete an over as discussed later. If the overs are not completed by the agreed time, play will continue until they are. This period of play is variously referred to as 'the last hour' or the 'last 20 overs'. Neither of these descriptions is necessarily correct. Play will often last much longer than an hour in order to achieve the minimum number of overs. Sometimes more than 20 overs will be bowled before time is reached. Nevertheless 'last hour' is a readily understood description.

Calculations for the minimum number of overs

Should there be an interval or interruption during the 'last hour', the system for calculating a revised minimum number of overs may appear complicated at first sight, but in fact is straightforward once the main principle is grasped. This is that when time is lost, overs are deleted from the minimum at the rate of one over for every full 3 minutes lost (4 minutes for 8-ball overs). The details also look complicated, and there are many of them, but each will be found to be logical on working through. The list is set out below to make a complete record, but only a few will apply to any one situation. As 8-ball overs are now rare, only the calculations for 6-ball overs are stated.

1. Every **full** 3 minutes lost means one over to be deducted from the minimum that must be bowled. Ignore any odd 1 or 2 minutes.
2. If there is more than one interruption, each is to be treated separately.
3. If an interruption is in progress at the start of the 'last hour', the time lost is counted from the time when the 'last hour' should begin until the actual resumption of play.
4. If an interruption is in progress at the start of the 'last hour', any part over completed on resumption will not count as one of the minimum 20.
5. If an *interruption* occurs part way through an over, the over

Example 1

1. Close of play is agreed for 6–30. **2.** The first over of the minimum 20 begins at 5–32. **3.** At 5–39, 2.2 overs (2 overs and 2 balls) have been bowled. **4.** There is then an interruption of 5 minutes for rain. **5.** Play is resumed at 5–44.

1.	5–30		one hour remains		
2.	5–32		minimum 20 overs start		Minimum of **20** overs remain
3.	5–39	**2.2**	overs have been bowled		Minimum of **17.4** overs remain
4.			**Interruption** of 5 minutes	Lose **1** over	
5.	5–44		Play resumes		Minimum of **16.4** overs remain
6.		**0.4**	bowled to complete broken over		Minimum of **16** overs remain

Notice that although the 'last hour' does not start until 5–32, this has no effect on any calculation.

Notice that in column 2, the 2.2 overs and 0.4 overs together make a total of 3 overs achieved, partly before the interruption, the rest by the completion of the broken over after the interruption

Notice that in column 4 only 1 over is lost. The 5 minute interruption is only one **complete** period of 3 minutes. The remaining 2 minutes are ignored.

The achieving of 3 overs shown in column 2 and the loss of 1 over shown in column 4 tallies with the final statement that 16 must still be bowled.

Example 2 – exactly as above, but now with a second interruption

1. Close of play is agreed for 6–30. **2.** The first over of the minimum 20 begins at 5–32. **3.** At 5–39, 2.2 overs (2 overs and 2 balls) have been bowled. **4.** There is then an interruption of 5 minutes for rain. **5.** Play is resumed at 5–44. **6.** The broken over is completed and **7.** a further 5.1 overs bowled. **8.** There is then a second interruption of 10 minutes.

1.	5–30		one hour remains		
2.	5–32		minimum 20 overs start		Minimum of **20** overs remain
3.	5–39	**2.2**	overs have been bowled		Minimum of **17.4** overs remain
4.			**Interruption** of 5 minutes	Lose **1** over	
5.	5–44		Play resumes		Minimum of **16.4** overs remain
6.		**0.4**	bowled to complete broken over		Minimum of **16** overs remain
7.		**5.1**	further overs bowled		Minimum of **10.5** overs remain
8.			**Interruption** of 10 minutes	Lose **3** overs	
			Play resumes		Minimum of **7.5** overs remain
		0.5	bowled to complete broken over		Minimum of **7** overs remain

In column 2, a total of 9 overs are shown as bowled (2.2 + 0.4 = 3; 5.1 + 0.5 = 6; total 9). In column 4, 4 overs (1, then 3) have been lost. These total 13. The minimum number remaining out of 20 is thus 7. Notice that the two interruptions are not aggregated to make 15 minutes. They are treated separately.

Example 3 – An interruption is already in progress when the 'last hour' is reached

1. Close of play is agreed for 6–30. **2.** At 5–10 rain holds up play, with 2 balls of an over still to be bowled. **3.** Play resumes at 5–38.

OVERS calculation

2.	5–10	Interruption starts		
1.	5–30	One hour remains		Minimum of **20** overs remain
3.	5–38	Play resumes		
		8 minutes lost	Lose **2** overs	
	0.2	over bowled		
5–40		(not part of minimum number)		Minimum of **18** overs remain

The irregular numbering on the left is intentional. It corresponds with the events, which are described in logical sequence.

Notice here that although the interruption lasted for 28 minutes, only 8 minutes came after 5–30. Consequently, only 8 minutes of the 'last hour' have been lost. As this is only 2 **complete** periods of 3 minutes, only 2 overs are deducted.

Notice also that although the over in progress at the start of the interruption must be completed on resumption, it does not form part of the minimum 20 overs.

Example 4 – as in example 3 but additionally an innings ends and a new one begins during the 'last hour'.

1. Close of play is agreed for 6–30. **2.** At 5–10 rain holds up play, with 2 balls of an over still to be bowled. **3.** Play resumes at 5–38. **4.** The remaining 2 balls of the over are completed by 5–40. **5.** After 1.5 further overs the innings closes at 5–45. The calculation is for the minimum number of overs for the next innings.

OVERS calculation

2.		5–10	Interruption starts		
1.		5–30	One hour remains		Minimum of **20** overs remain
3.		5–38	Play resumes	Lose **2** overs	
			8 minutes lost		
4.	**0.2**	5–40	over bowled		Minimum of **18** overs remain
			(not part of minimum number)		Minimum of **16.1** overs remain
5.	**1.5**	5–45	overs bowled		Minimum of **17** overs remain
			Innings ends; ignore part over		
			Interval = 10 minutes	Lose **3** overs	
6.		5–55	**New innings starts**		Minimum of **14** overs remain

TIME calculation

5–45	**Innings ends**	45 minutes remain
	Interval = 10 minutes	35 minutes remain = 12 overs
5–55	**New innings starts**	Allocate minimum of **12** overs.

The larger number is 14. A minimum of **14** overs to be bowled.

Notice that the 5 balls of an over at the end of the innings are ignored.

Notice that 33 minutes gives 11 overs. An extra over is added for the other 2 minutes of the 35.

will be completed on resumption; the two parts count together as one over.

6. If an *interval* between innings occurs during the 'last hour',
   (a) a part over at the end of the innings will be ignored in the calculation.
   (b) the interval counts as 10 minutes and hence as 3 overs.
   (c) two calculations must be made, one on overs achieved, the other on time remaining. The overs calculation is as set out above. In the time calculation, one over is to be allowed for every full 3 minutes of time remaining before the agreed close of play. If the time is not exactly divisible by 3, an extra over is allowed for the final incomplete 3 minutes.

   The larger number resulting from the two calculations is the minimum number to be bowled.

These points are demonstrated in examples 1 to 4.

Notice that the interval is always to be counted as 10 minutes. Sometimes the players may be slow to start – perhaps a sight-screen has to be moved, or there is some other reason. The calculation will still be based on an interval of 10 minutes, even though play may not start until 12 minutes have elapsed. If, of course, the start of the new innings is held up by conditions of ground weather or light, then this counts as an interruption and the calculation will be made accordingly.

After an interruption, the calculation for the minimum number of overs remaining to be bowled clearly cannot be made at the precise moment when Play is called for the resumption. The umpires must make a prior calculation, based upon an agreed time for restart, on exactly the same principle as counting the interval between innings as 10 minutes, even if circumstances mean that the actual start varies slightly from this agreed time.

In all cases of re-calculation, it is imperative that the scorers know the new minimum number of overs to be achieved.

Bowler unable to complete an over
If a bowler is unable to complete an over, either because he is incapacitated, or because he is suspended, another bowler will complete the over (**Law 22**). The incapacity or suspension of the bowler may occur during the 'last hour' of a match. In this case,

the same provisions apply. The umpire calls and signals Dead ball. Another bowler must complete the over. He must not have bowled the previous over, nor may he bowl the following one.

Completing the over in progress

During the match
Except in the last session of play, the over in progress will be completed, unless a batsman is out with less than 2 minutes remaining until the agreed time for the interval. In that case, the bowler's end umpire will call Time on the fall of the wicket, even though the over is not complete. It may be that a wicket falls on the last ball of an over, with less than 2 minutes remaining. Again, Time will be called, even though if the wicket had not fallen, it might have been possible to start another over.

At the end of the match
In the last session of play, the over in progress will always be completed (except as detailed in the next paragraph) if either Captain requests it, even though a wicket might fall during this over but after the agreed time for close of play. An umpire can reasonably assume that at least one Captain will want to complete the over, if there is the slightest chance of a definite result. In competition matches limited by the number of overs, there will always be a result and the final over should always be completed, unless the match has reached an earlier conclusion. This will also apply to the statutory minimum number of overs in the last hour of a timed match, if time has been reached before the minimum is achieved.

If, however, the players leave the field for any reason during the last over of the match, they will not return to the field to complete it.

Starting another over

1 *During the normal course of play − not at the fall of a wicket*
When it is getting near time for the end of a session, the umpires will check with each other as to the time remaining. If at the end of an over, time has already been reached, then Time will be called. If, however, there is even a short time remaining, the umpires will walk to their positions for the next over. This must be done 'at their normal pace'. It therefore follows that a

'normal pace' must have been established during the course of the match. When the umpire who was at the striker's end reaches his position behind the stumps, a further check on the time is made. If time has still not been reached, then another over will be started. There may be delay in starting it for a number of reasons. For example, the Captain might decide on a bowling change, necessitating considerable changes in the field placing. Such delay will have no bearing on the start of the over. The only criterion is the arrival at the stumps of the umpire.

2 *At the end of the match*

Even if the match is one limited by time, during the 'last hour' the number of overs becomes the deciding factor. Unless the match comes to a premature conclusion, the minimum number of overs as calculated must be bowled and no question of time or of starting another over can arise. Once the minimum number is achieved, then exactly the same routine will be applied as described in 1. The first time check will be at the end of the last over of the minimum number required. Now, however, the fall of a wicket, either during the course of an over, or on the last ball of an over, will not affect the decision as to whether another over will be started. It will be started if time has not been reached when the umpire arrives at his position behind the stumps.

If of course the whole match is limited by the number of overs, then the match will continue until those have been completed, unless a conclusion is reached earlier.

Field Technique

Calling Time

The way to make the decision when to call Time has already been described. When Time is called, the umpires remove both sets of bails. Unless it is the end of the match, it is important to ensure that when play resumes it does so as if there had been no break. The umpires must therefore note, and make a written record,

    which batsmen are at which ends;

    who is bowling and at which ends;

    if there are balls remaining in the over, and if so how many;

    the time at which the break in play began.

The scorers will also make a note of these details – see Part III **Laws 16 and 17** on page 205.

It may also be helpful, for an arranged interval, to note the time for resumption, although it will in fact be determined by the time of start of the break.

They must also take charge of the ball; it is sensible for the umpire from whose end the bowling is to resume to take it.

The Last Hour

The decision when this is to start is made by checking between the umpires in precisely the same way as for a call of Time before an arranged interval, since it too is a question of agreeing that the correct time has been reached. The exact time may well be when the ball is in play. The announcement is therefore normally made at the end of the over in progress at that time. The scorers certainly need to know when the 'last hour' is starting. There is no official signal. The umpires and scorers must arrange a suitable one in pre-match discussions.

Although the scorers will record the passage of the 20 overs, the umpires must be in control. Both umpires must keep a written record of the overs as they are bowled, to ensure that the minimum is achieved. As a check, it is helpful for an umpire to note that if the first over of the minimum 20 is bowled from his end, then all the odd overs – 3rd, 5th, etc. – will be from his end; otherwise he will have all the even ones.

LAW 18 SCORING

1 A RUN

The score shall be reckoned by runs. A run is scored –

(a) **So often as the Batsmen, after a hit or at any time while the ball is in play, shall have crossed and made good their ground from end to end.**

(b) **When a boundary is scored. See Law 19: (Boundaries).**

(c) **When penalty runs are awarded. See 6 below.**

2 SHORT RUNS

(a) **If either Batsman runs a short run, the Umpire shall call and signal 'one short' as soon as the ball becomes dead and that run shall not be scored. A run is short if a Batsman fails to make good his ground on turning for a further run.**

(b) **Although a short run shortens the succeeding one, the latter, if completed shall count.**

(c) **If either or both Batsmen deliberately run short the Umpire shall, as soon as he sees that the fielding side have no chance of dismissing either Batsman, call and signal 'dead ball' and disallow any runs attempted or previously scored. The Batsmen shall return to their original ends.**

(d) **If both Batsmen run short in one and the same run, only one run shall be deducted.**

(e) **Only if 3 or more runs are attempted can more than one be short and then, subject to (c) and (d) above, all runs so called shall be disallowed. If there has been more than one short run the Umpires shall instruct the Scorers as to the number of runs disallowed.**

3 STRIKER CAUGHT
If the Striker is Caught, no run shall be scored.

4 BATSMAN RUN OUT
If a Batsman is Run Out, only that run which was being attempted shall not be scored. If, however, an injured Striker himself is run out no runs shall be scored. See Law 2.7: (Transgression of the Laws by an Injured Batsman or Runner).

5 BATSMAN OBSTRUCTING THE FIELD
If a Batsman is out Obstructing the Field, any runs completed before the obstruction occurs shall be scored unless such obstruction prevents a catch being made in which case no runs shall be scored.

6 RUNS SCORED FOR PENALTIES
Runs shall be scored for penalties under Laws 20: (Lost Ball), 24: (No Ball), 25: (Wide Ball), 41.1: (Fielding the Ball) and for boundary allowances under Law 19: (Boundaries).

7 BATSMAN RETURNING TO WICKET HE HAS LEFT
If, while the ball is in play, the Batsmen have crossed in running, neither shall return to the wicket he has left even though a short run has been called or no run has been scored as in the case of a catch. Batsmen,

however, shall return to the wickets they originally left, in the cases of a boundary and of any disallowance of runs and of an injured Batsman being, himself, run out. See Law 2.7: (Transgression by an Injured Batsman or Runner).

Notes

(a) SHORT RUN
A Striker taking stance in front of his popping crease may run from that point without penalty.

This Law explains how the batsmen can score a run, and how they can fail to score a run. It includes several of the cases when the runs they make are not to be allowed. It also summarizes what runs, if any, are to be allowed if a batsman is dismissed. It is therefore at the very heart of the game of cricket.

There are three distinct ways in which runs are scored. The batsmen run, runs are awarded for boundary hits, runs are awarded as penalties against the fielding side.

When the batsmen score a run by running

The Law makes it clear that a run is not scored until both batsmen have run, have crossed and have each made good their ground from end to end. This means each must have arrived behind his new popping crease; each must have grounded some part of his person, or of his bat in hand, behind that crease – that is, behind the back edge of the popping crease marking. It is this grounding behind the line that is essential for the completion of the run. Grounding on the marking is not sufficient, nor is being behind the line but not grounded. Whenever the batsmen run, each umpire must be in position to watch that every run is properly completed. For the bowler's end umpire, this entails moving away from the wicket to a position where he can observe the creases and the wicket from the side.

The words 'after a hit or at any time while the ball is in play' emphasize that, except in the case of illegal leg byes (**Law 26**), the batsmen can run whether or not the striker has hit the ball with his bat. The ball of course comes into play as soon as the bowler starts his run-up (or action, if he has no run-up). While the striker may, and very often will, leave his crease before the ball is delivered, the batsmen must not attempt to score a run before the ball is delivered. This situation is dealt with under the laws on No ball and unfair play (**Laws 24 and 42**).

Short runs

The definition of a short run is not difficult to understand if it is appreciated that it is failure to *complete* a run, as set out above, *when turning* for the next one that makes it short. If either batsman starts a run from a position in front of the popping crease, that run will not be considered short. The next run after a short run, provided it is properly completed, will be scored as a run. Of course, if one of the batsmen is run out on the next run, then it has not been properly completed. In that case, neither the short run, nor the next one will be allowed. If there are short runs, the call and signal are not made until the ball is dead.

If the batsmen run only one, then they have not turned for a further run and so there can be no short run. If they have run two, they have turned only once; only the first run can be short. Consequently, if both umpires call and signal One short, it must be for that first run. Only one run will be deducted since the call has been for the same run. If the batsmen run three, or more, and both umpires call and signal One short, then they will need to confer, to discover whether one or two runs are to be deducted. It may be of course that only one umpire calls and signals, but two of the three runs are to be deducted because on two occasions the run was not completed at that end.

The scorers must be left in no doubt as to how many are to be recorded. This is a particular case of the need for close cooperation between the two halves of the team of officials. There will be occasions when the number of runs to be disallowed as short will not be obvious to the scorers. In such circumstances, it is incumbent upon the umpires to give the scorers the necessary help and information.

Deliberate short running

The umpire may form the opinion that the failure to complete a run at his end was deliberate. Such deliberate short running is unfair. Now, instead of waiting till the ball is dead, the umpire will call and signal Dead ball as soon as he is satisfied that the fielding side have no immediate chance of dismissing either batsman. Not only the short run but any previously completed runs from that delivery will also be disallowed. The umpire will need to ensure that the scorers know that all runs are to be cancelled. The batsmen must be returned to their original ends.

Scoring of runs if batsman is dismissed
The umpires should note here the various provisions for runs allowed or not allowed, if one of the batsmen is dismissed. No runs will be allowed if the striker is Caught, or if an obstruction prevents an attempted catch. All runs previously completed will be allowed for other obstructions, or if either batsman is run out. The one exception is that no runs are allowed in the case of an injured striker being himself run out, rather than because his runner is. These also appear in the various Laws relating to these dismissals.

Runs scored for boundary hits
These are fully dealt with in **Law 19**. In this Law, Boundaries appear in section 6, under the heading of Penalties. They are separated from penalties in the wording of the text, making it clear that a boundary is not in any way a penalty.

Runs scored for penalties
These are each dealt with under their respective Laws, enumerated in the text of section 6 to this Law. It should be noted here, however, that the runs awarded for a call of Lost Ball (**Law 20**) are not penalties, notwithstanding that they are included in the list of penalties here. The significance of this distinction is dealt with under **Law 20**.

Batsmen crossing
In general, understanding what is meant by 'the batsmen have crossed' is simple enough, but there can be difficulties. A concept allied to that of the batsmen crossing is that of '*his ground*'. If one batsman is grounded behind the popping crease at one end, then that is *his ground*. Except in the case of an injured striker with a runner, if neither batsmen is within a ground, then whichever of them is the one who is nearer to a particular end, must count that end as *his ground*. If both batsmen are within the same ground, then whichever of them grounded behind the popping crease first, claims it as *his ground*. It ceases to

be *his ground*, however, if he subsequently leaves it and the other batsman remains within it.

It therefore follows that the batsmen exchange ends every time they cross. It is important to realize that the batsmen cannot be considered to have crossed unless each of them is out of his ground. If one batsman is within his ground and is joined there by the other, then no crossing has taken place, even though physically one may have passed the other. If two batsmen are within the same ground, however, then, as stated in the previous paragraph, whichever leaves it first surrenders his claim to that ground as his.

It should also be noted that being level, shoulder to shoulder, counts as not having crossed.

Another point which can cause confusion is that the Law talks of 'the wicket he has left'. In the case of a short run, a batsman will not have made good his ground at one end. He may have been very far short of doing so, if the short running was deliberate, or there was a misunderstanding between the batsmen. Nevertheless, he is still to be regarded as having left that end, if it is *his* end, even if he never reached it. It will have become *his end* when the batsmen last crossed, even though he has not reached it and may never do so.

In the case of an injured striker, with a runner, it should be noted that *his end* is always the wicket keeper's end; it is never the bowler's end, no matter where the injured striker is in relation to the non-striker and runner.

Batsmen returning to their original ends

This Law governs the three circumstances in which the batsmen will be returned to their original ends, even though they have crossed, and might have expected to be at the opposite ends. These are

- for a boundary hit;
- all cases of disallowance of runs, including deliberate short running and illegal leg byes (although these are not the only two instances);
- if an injured striker is himself run out.

In these cases, returning them to their *original* ends is to imply the ends at which they were before the ball came into play. They will not be returned to their original ends, in that sense, in any other cases. It may, however, be necessary in other situations to direct them to particular ends. Each will go *his end*; that is if they have crossed they continue on; if they have not crossed they are to go back. Each of the possible situations is discussed in conjunction with the appropriate Law.

If a catch is taken, it will be necessary to know whether or not they had crossed, to determine the ends to which the not out batsman and the new batsman should go. In the case of a run out, whether or not they have crossed will determine which of the batsmen is out. It will also be significant in determining the number of runs to be awarded in certain cases which are discussed in the later Laws.

The ends at which the batsmen resume may have a considerable effect on the scoring of runs. It is therefore incumbent upon the umpires to see that these ends are the correct ones in Law. Both in the case of a catch, and if there is a run out, the not out batsman will go to *his* end. That is, if they have crossed he will continue on; if they have not crossed he will go back.

Field Technique

The umpires must watch most carefully both the position of the batsmen when running and the progress of the ball. They must then see that each run is properly completed. They must also know whether or not the batsmen had crossed at the appropriate moment. The 'appropriate moment' may be the completion of a catch, the breaking of the wicket for a successful run out, the fielder's throw in the case of boundary overthrows, or the ball crossing the boundary. An umpire must be able to adjudicate on any action at his end, such as an attempted run out, and to assist his colleague with information on other events. He will need to establish a rhythm in order to watch what is happening in the field, to glance back at the crease to check for short running and to see the batsmen cross. He must not allow his attention to be focused on any of these to the exclusion of the other(s).

LAW 19 BOUNDARIES

1 THE BOUNDARY OF THE PLAYING AREA

Before the toss for innings, the Umpires shall agree with both Captains on the boundary of the playing area. The boundary shall, if possible, be marked by a

white line, a rope laid on the ground, or a fence. If flags or posts only are used to mark a boundary, the imaginary line joining such points shall be regarded as the boundary. An obstacle, or person, within the playing area shall not be regarded as a boundary unless so decided by the Umpires before the toss for innings. Sight-screens within, or partially within, the playing area shall be regarded as the boundary and when the ball strikes or passes within or under or directly over any part of the screen, a boundary shall be scored.

2 RUNS SCORED FOR BOUNDARIES

Before the toss for innings, the Umpires shall agree with both Captains the runs to be allowed for boundaries, and in deciding the allowance for them, the Umpires and Captains shall be guided by the prevailing custom of the ground. The allowance for a boundary shall normally be 4 runs, and 6 runs for all hits pitching over and clear of the boundary line or fence, even though the ball has been previously touched by a Fieldsman. 6 runs shall also be scored if a Fieldsman, after catching a ball, carries it over the boundary. See Law 32: (Caught) Note (a). 6 runs shall not be scored when a ball struck by the Striker hits a sight-screen full pitch if the screen is within, or partially within, the playing area, but if the ball is struck directly over a sight-screen so situated, 6 runs shall be scored.

3 A BOUNDARY

A boundary shall be scored and signalled by the Umpire at the Bowler's end whenever, in his opinion –
(a) A ball in play touches or crosses the boundary, however marked.
(b) A Fieldsman with ball in hand touches or grounds any part of his person on or over a boundary line.
(c) A Fieldsman with ball in hand grounds any part of his person over a boundary fence or board. This allows the Fieldsman to touch or lean on or over a boundary fence or board in preventing a boundary.

any part of fielder's person

94

4 RUNS EXCEEDING BOUNDARY ALLOWANCE

The runs completed at the instant the ball reaches the boundary shall count if they exceed the boundary allowance.

5 OVERTHROWS OR WILFUL ACT OF A FIELDSMAN

If the boundary results from an overthrow or from the wilful act of a Fieldsman, any runs already completed and the allowance shall be added to the score. The run in progress shall count provided that the Batsmen have crossed at the instant of the throw or act.

Notes

(a) POSITION OF SIGHT-SCREENS

Sight-screens should, if possible, be positioned wholly outside the playing area, as near as possible to the boundary line.

Agreeing the boundaries

This Law lays upon the umpires the duty of agreeing with the Captains both what the boundary of the playing area is and what runs shall be allowed for boundary hits. This agreement is to be made at the meeting with the Captains before the toss takes place (**Law 3**). One of the most important pre-match duties of both umpires is therefore to inspect the boundaries and sight-screens. They must observe how the boundary is marked, where there are trees overhanging the playing area or even within it. They must note the positions of the sight-screens and of any other possible obstacles. A sight-screen within, or even partially within, the playing area must be regarded as the boundary, but the umpires are to decide before the toss whether or not other obstacles inside the playing area are to be boundaries. In general it is desirable that they should be. It will eliminate any misunderstanding should a spectator pick up and throw in a ball before it reaches the boundary. It will avoid any complications such as a dog running on to the field after the ball. The umpires will then inform the captains of these decisions when agreeing with them the boundary of the playing area and the boundary allowances. Once agreement is made, the scorers must be informed of these allowances.

Boundary allowances

The Law states the normal allowances for boundaries, but on some grounds – especially if they are situated adjacent to houses, shops or busy roads – the boundary 6 is reduced to 4 runs by local custom. The umpires and captains must respect such local customs. There are two important points to note. The first is that the 6 run allowance is to be made even if a fielder touches the ball before it pitches over the boundary, or if he catches it and carries it over the boundary. The second is that the 6 run allowance is awarded only for balls which are struck by the bat, and pitch over and clear of the boundary. There is a widespread belief that it is possible to award 6 wides, or 6 byes, for a ball that pitches over the boundary directly from the bowler's hand. This is a misconception.

Scoring a boundary

Although the boundary may be delineated in a number of different ways, these ways can be divided into no more than two categories. One is a rope or line. Anything that is laid along the ground is a 'rope'. The other category is a fence. Anything that is fixed so as to stand upright – a hedge, a wall etc – is a 'fence'. As soon as the ball in play touches either variety, a boundary 4 is scored. If the ball has been hit by the bat and lands over and clear of the boundary then a boundary 6 is scored.

If, however, the fielder is in contact with the ball, then he may touch or lean against a fence without penalty, as long as the ball does not touch it. If he touches a boundary which is a rope, then a boundary 4 is scored. The special case of 6 runs being scored when a catch is attempted is dealt with more fully under **Law 32** (Caught). Where white lines, or posts and imaginary lines mark the boundary, the umpires will, of necessity have to depend upon the fielder's honesty in indicating a boundary. If a rope is used, usually it is possible to see if the ball hits it, but it may not be possible to see if the fielder touches it. In some cases the striker's end umpire may be better placed to see whether a boundary is scored, and whether or not it is a boundary 6. He should always be ready to assist his colleague with this information if he can.

If the batsmen have completed any runs before the ball reaches the boundary, these will not count if they are fewer than the boundary allowance. The batsmen should return to their original ends. The batsmen may at times, however, complete 5 or more runs before the instant that the ball reaches the boundary. If this happens the runs completed will be scored, but not the boundary allowance. Completed runs are scored when the batsmen have crossed and made good their ground from end to end.

Sight-screens within, or partially within the playing area

If any part of a sight-screen, even just one of the wheels, is within the playing area, then the whole screen is to become the boundary. It may be that although the wheels are inside, the blade of the screen is outside the original line. Nevertheless, the outline of the screen together with the blade will replace the original boundary line there. The note to the Law urges that, wherever possible, sight-screens should be positioned wholly outside the playing area. It is becoming increasingly common to have a rope or bar across the front wheels and to agree that this shall be the boundary line at that place, putting the whole screen outside the boundary. This is by far the most satisfactory arrangement.

If such an arrangement is not made, then the area of grass between the wheels is still part of the field of play, irrespective of where the original boundary line ran. The blade has the status of a fence. The wheel struts count as rope. To pass within the screen, the ball has to pass between the various struts and bars that screens have. If the ball strikes the blade full pitch, then it has not pitched over and clear of the boundary and only 4 runs will be awarded. If, however, the ball passes directly over the sight-screen, 6 runs will be scored. The ball then becomes dead and therefore cannot be legally fielded or caught behind a sight-screen which is within or partially within the playing area. Passing over a strut is not passing directly over the screen.

Boundaries resulting from overthrows or from the wilful act of a fielder

Boundary overthrows differ from ordinary boundaries, in that the boundary allowance is added to runs made by the batsmen.

A boundary may result from the wilful act of a fielder. Such acts are usually attempts to keep the non-striker from the wicket keeper's end. If the fielder deliberately throws, kicks, or assists the ball to the boundary, then the act will be penalized by treating the boundary as boundary overthrows. He may, without penalty however, deliberately allow the ball to run on to the boundary under its own impetus.

If after gathering the ball the fielder's throw goes awry, so that the batsmen can continue running, such runs are overthrows. They are no different from other runs, unless the misfired throw subsequently crosses the boundary or hits an obstacle (such as a tree) agreed as a boundary. Then boundary overthrows are scored.

In either of these circumstances, when the ball crosses the boundary, a boundary four will be signalled, irrespective of the point at which the ball crossed the boundary, or whether this was an accidental mis-throw or a deliberate act by the fielder. The boundary allowance will be added to the runs made. The Law defines the moment from which the umpires will count the runs made. At the instant of the throw, or act, the position of the batsmen is noted and the run in progress counted or discounted, according to whether the batsmen have crossed or not. All runs completed prior to this also count. The total is added to the boundary allowance. Thus, if the batsmen have crossed on their first run when the ball is thrown, 5 will be added to the total, and the batsmen should have changed ends – the striker should finish at the bowler's end. If they have completed two runs and not yet crossed on the third at the moment of the throw, 6 runs will be scored and they should be at their original ends. Although the batsmen may continue running after the throw or act, and apparently complete further runs, such further runs will not be counted. However, they may possibly be at the wrong ends by the time the ball reaches the boundary. They should then be directed to the correct ends on this odd and even principle, according to the number of runs to be scored. For an even number of runs, the striker should be at his original end; for an odd number of runs he should be at the opposite end.

Signalling to the scorers

Of course boundaries are not signalled until the ball is dead. When the signal is made, there may be other signals to be given as well. Each signal should be made separately, and separate acknowledgments received. The last one should be the boundary 4 or boundary 6.

For a fair delivery, if only the boundary 4 is signalled, the scorers will assume that the ball came off the striker's bat and the runs are to be credited to him. If the striker does not hit the ball, the bye signal (or leg bye signal if appropriate) should precede the boundary 4 signal. For a boundary 6, of course, the ball must have come off the striker's bat. It is not necessary to give the Bye signal if the delivery was a Wide ball, since by definition the ball cannot have touched the striker's bat or person and runs scored must be extras.

If No ball is called, this signal should precede any others. Notice too that in the case of a No ball, the leg bye signal should never be used. Any runs are to be scored either as No balls from the bat or as No ball extras. These two cases are covered respectively by:

No ball, directly followed by the boundary signal;

No ball, then bye, followed by the boundary signal.

By the umpires maintaining a recognized order in this way, the scorers will know when the signalling is complete.

LAW 20 LOST BALL

1 RUNS SCORED

If a ball in play cannot be found or recovered any fieldsman may call 'lost ball' when 6 runs shall be added to the score; but if more than 6 have been run before 'lost ball' is called, as many runs as have been completed shall be scored. The run in progress shall count provided that the Batsmen have crossed at the instant of the call of 'lost ball'.

2 HOW SCORED

The runs shall be added to the score of the Striker if the ball has been struck, but otherwise to the score of byes, leg-byes, no-balls or wides as the case may be.

In the period before 1809 the game was played without boundaries and outfields were often very rough with long grass requiring a Law to cover the possibility of the ball being lost. Lost ball is not likely to be called during the cricket lifetime of most umpires, nowadays, but isolated cases when the ball has been lost, or more likely become irrecoverable, are on record.

Runs scored

Whilst the ball is in play, the fielding side may call Lost ball at any time the ball cannot be found or recovered. Once a member of the fielding side has called Lost ball 6 runs are awarded at once, even if the ball is recovered immediately afterwards.

It is virtually certain that the batsmen will be running prior to the call of Lost ball. The number of runs they have already completed, plus the one in progress if they have crossed at the moment of the call, will be the number of runs scored if it is more than 6. Otherwise 6 runs will be awarded. It may be useful to note that the number of runs completed plus the one in progress, if they crossed, is the number of times they have crossed altogether providing there has been no short running.

How the runs are scored

If the striker has played the ball with his bat, or hand holding the bat, the 6 or more runs are added to his score. If not played with the bat the runs will be scored as they would normally have been scored (byes; leg byes; no balls or wides). The umpire must inform the scorers of the number of runs to be added as well as making any appropriate signal.

End at which batsmen should resume

Note that if the batsmen have crossed for an odd number of times they should not return to their original ends even though 6 runs are awarded. In practice, if the fielding side are alert, continued efforts will be made to recover the ball until the batsmen have crossed on the 6th run resulting in 6 runs only being scored.

Award of runs is not a penalty

Although **Law 23** states that the ball is dead on the award of a penalty under **Law 20**, it has already been noted in **Law 18** that Lost ball is not strictly a penalty. Therefore, should the delivery have been called either a No ball or Wide ball the one run penalty is not added to the award of 6 runs or the number of runs scored.

Field Technique

If it is not possible to recover the ball, another one, which has a similar amount of wear to the lost ball, must be taken into use (**Law 5**).

LAW 21 THE RESULT

1 A WIN – TWO-INNINGS MATCHES

The side which has scored a total of runs in excess of that scored by the opposing side in its two completed innings shall be the winners.

2 A WIN – ONE-INNINGS MATCHES

(a) **One-innings matches, unless played out as in 1 above, shall be decided on the first innings, but see Law 12.5: (Continuation After One Innings of Each Side).**

(b) **If the Captains agree to continue play after the completion of one innings of each side in accordance with Law 12.5: (Continuation After One Innings of Each Side) and a result is not achieved on the second innings, the first innings result shall stand.**

3 UMPIRES AWARDING A MATCH

(a) **A match shall be lost by a side which, during the match,**
    (i) **refuses to play, or**
    (ii) **concedes defeat,**
    and the Umpires shall award the match to the other side.

(b) **Should both Batsmen at the wickets or the fielding side leave the field at any time without the agreement of the Umpires, this shall constitute a refusal to play, and, on appeal, the Umpires shall award the match to the other side in accordance with (a) above.**

4 A TIE

The result of a match shall be a tie when the scores are equal at the conclusion of play, but only if the side batting last has completed its innings.

    If the scores of the completed first innings of a one-

day match are equal, it shall be a tie but only if the match has not been played out to a further conclusion.

5 A DRAW

A match not determined in any of the ways as in 1, 2, 3 and 4 above shall count as a draw.

6 CORRECTNESS OF RESULT

Any decision as to the correctness of the scores shall be the responsibility of the Umpires. See Law 3.14: (Correctness of Scores).

If, after the Umpires and Players have left the field, in the belief that the match has been concluded, the Umpires decide that a mistake in scoring has occurred, which affects the result, and provided time has not been reached, they shall order play to resume and to continue until the agreed finishing time unless a result is reached earlier.

If the Umpires decide that a mistake has occurred and time has been reached, the Umpires shall immediately inform both Captains of the necessary corrections to the scores and, if applicable, to the result.

7 ACCEPTANCE OF RESULT

In accepting the scores as notified by the scorers and agreed by the Umpires, the Captains of both sides thereby accept the result.

Notes

(a) STATEMENT OF RESULTS
The result of a finished match is stated as a win by runs, except in the case of a win by the side batting last when it is by the number of wickets still then to fall.

(b) WINNING HIT OR EXTRAS
As soon as the side has won, see 1 and 2 above, the Umpire shall call 'time', the match is finished, and nothing that happens thereafter other than as a result of a mistake in scoring, see 6 above, shall be regarded as part of the match.

However, if a boundary constitutes the winning hit — or extras — and the boundary allowance exceeds the number of runs required to win the match, such runs scored shall be credited to the side's total and, in the case of a hit, to the Striker's score.

Umpires responsible for correctness of scores

Law 3 places the responsibility with the umpires to satisfy themselves on the correctness of the scores throughout and at the conclusion of the match. **Law 21** requires the umpires to check the scores, as notified by the scorers, and to agree the result of the match.

Umpires can assist the accuracy of the scorers by observing a high standard of clarity of signals as well as suspending play if necessary until the scorers have acknowledged any signal. If signals and their acknowledgment have been clear and the score books have been correctly kept throughout the match, there should seldom be any complications, providing the umpires have taken care to advise the scorers, where there may be any doubt, of the number of runs to be recorded – for example in the case of overthrows, short runs etc. Umpires must check the result with the scorers as any decision regarding the correctness of the scores, during and at the conclusion of the match, rests with them.

One-innings match may be continued

As explained under **Law 12**, the umpires may remind the Captains that play may continue in a one-innings match, even though a result on the first innings has been reached, unless Special Regulations do not so permit. If play is continued to a second innings and no result emerges, the result of the match will be that which was reached on the first innings.

Mistake in score books discovered

If at the end of a match the umpires, having left the field, find that a mistake in scoring has been made which affects the result, providing time has not been reached, they must instruct Captains to resume play until the pre-match agreed finishing time or an earlier result is reached. In a match governed by time, the players may have left the field during the last hour. Play would be resumed if any of the minimum of 20 overs remained to be bowled.

The same principle will apply to matches in which the

number of overs per innings is limited. If a mistake is made in scoring, which affects the result of a limited overs match and the agreed number of overs have not been bowled the umpires will instruct the Captains to resume play until the prescribed number of overs have been bowled, or an earlier result reached. It will be appreciated that the mistake which has been discovered would normally require the batting side to make only a small number of runs – or the fielding side to bowl their opponents out.

If, however, a mistake is discovered after time has been reached the mistake must be corrected; if it affects the result the Captains must accept the corrected result as it then stands. After both Captains have accepted the result, checked and agreed by the umpires, it cannot be changed at any later stage. Cases are on record where attempts have been made to have the result of a match changed. The Law does not allow any committee or arbitrating body to do so.

Result of a match

If the side batting last have not scored more runs than their opponents, even if the scores are level, the result is a draw unless the side batting last has completed its innings, in which case the result is a tie.

As soon as a side has won the match, bowler's end umpire should call Time. The ball is dead and the match completed. If the scores are level and the batsmen complete one run, the batting side have won. Any further action by either side will be discounted. The same is true if the scores are level and either No ball or Wide ball is called. Time should be called and the match is at an end. The Law, however, makes the exception for a boundary either from a hit or extras. Should the ball cross the boundary the umpire will award a boundary 4 or 6 which will be signalled and recorded as appropriate.

Completion of an innings

The side batting last will have lost the match if its score is less than its opponent's providing the last innings of the match is completed, that is to say if there are no further batsmen to come in. As explained above, if the scores are level and the side batting last has completed its innings the result is a tie.

In determining whether the side batting last has indeed completed its innings, complications are caused by the retirement of a batsman who is unable to resume.

Suppose a batsman had retired early in the innings and during further play the 9th wicket falls. If the 9th wicket falls off the last ball of the match, the question as to whether the retired batsman is fit to return does not arise and the innings has not been completed. If, however, the 9th wicket falls before the last ball of the match, with the retired batsman unable to resume, the batting side have completed their innings. This would also apply in the case of more than one batsman having retired and being unable to resume.

If 9 wickets are down and one of the last pair at the wicket is forced to retire, the same principle will be observed. If the retirement is on the last ball of the match, the match is finished and whether or not the batsman would have been able to remain at the wicket is irrelevant. If the injury occurs before the last ball of the match and the batsman is forced to leave the field, he will be unable to resume his innings as there are no further wickets to fall. The innings is now completed.

Umpires awarding a match

Regrettably, instances have occurred where one side has refused to continue to play. Such action places the umpires in a most difficult situation but they should together advise the Captain of the only possible action available to them. It is emphasized that the umpires must act in concert. If both batsmen, or the fielding side leave the field without the agreement of the umpires, this must be regarded as a refusal to play and, on appeal, the match should be awarded to the other side. Equally this will apply if a side refuses to come out on to the field; the umpires must make it clear to both sides that play is to start, or restart, and together take the appropriate action if either side refuses to play.

It is possible for a Captain to concede defeat at any time during the match. Instances of this happening are rare but the Captain's decision can only be accepted and the umpires must award the match to the other side.

Scoring – the result in the case of a Win

Although there may be provisions in the rules of a competition for the case of the teams finishing with the scores level, if the result is a Draw or a Tie the Law does not require the scorers to state anything else but that. Note (a) to the Law sets out how a result is to be stated in the case when one side wins.

If the side batting last wins, this will be by overtaking the total score of the opposing team. In most cases the match will end as soon as the score reaches one run more than the other side scored. If the batsmen run three when only two are required to win, only the two are to be entered. Under Note (b) to the Law, however, if it is a boundary that takes the score past the required total, then all 4 (or 6) runs will count. This will not, however, affect the statement of the result. That is to be recorded as a win by the number of wickets that have not fallen.

If the side batting last completes its innings with its score less than that of the other team, then the opposing team has won. In this case the result is stated as a win by a number of runs. This number will be the difference between the two total scores. If side A scores 236, side B needs 237 to win. If side B makes only 230, side A wins by 6 runs, not 7.

LAW 22 THE OVER

1 NUMBER OF BALLS
The ball shall be bowled from each wicket alternately in overs of either 6 or 8 balls according to agreement before the match.

2 CALL OF 'OVER'
When the agreed number of balls has been bowled, and as the ball becomes dead or when it becomes clear to the Umpire at the Bowler's end that both the fielding side and the Batsmen at the wicket have ceased to regard the ball as in play, the Umpire shall call 'over' before leaving the wicket.

3 NO BALL OR WIDE BALL
Neither a no ball nor a wide ball shall be reckoned as one of the over.

4 UMPIRE MISCOUNTING
If an Umpire miscounts the number of balls, the over as counted by the Umpire shall stand.

5 BOWLER CHANGING ENDS
A Bowler shall be allowed to change ends as often as desired provided only that he does not bowl two overs consecutively in an innings.

6 THE BOWLER FINISHING AN OVER

A Bowler shall finish an over in progress unless he be incapacitated or be suspended under Law 42.8: (The Bowling of Fast Short Pitched Balls), 42.9: (The Bowling of Fast High Full Pitches), 42.10: (Time Wasting) and 42.11: (Players Damaging the Pitch). If an over is left incomplete for any reason at the start of an interval or interruption of play, it shall be finished on the resumption of play.

7 BOWLER INCAPACITATED OR SUSPENDED DURING AN OVER

If, for any reason, a Bowler is incapacitated while running up to bowl the first ball of an over, or is incapacitated or suspended during an over, the Umpire shall call and signal 'dead ball' and another Bowler shall be allowed to bowl or complete the over from the same end, provided only that he shall not bowl two overs, or part thereof, consecutively in one innings.

8 POSITION OF NON-STRIKER

The Batsman at the Bowler's end shall normally stand on the opposite side of the wicket to that from which the ball is being delivered, unless a request to do otherwise is granted by the Umpire.

Number of balls in an over
It is now rare for an over to consist of 8 balls although a small number of limited over competitions prefer 8 ball overs as a means of shortening the time for the agreed number of overs.

Counting balls in the over
The umpire at the bowler's end counts the balls in the over. As explained under 'Necessary Equipment' (page 11) a system of counting should be rigidly adopted and strictly adhered to until it becomes a habit. Unless some form of counting machine is used, coins, pebbles or other suitable objects should be held in one hand and one counter dropped into a pocket as each ball is

bowled. Some umpires prefer to wait until the ball becomes dead before dropping a counter into the pocket. The umpire would be wise to check he has the correct number of counters in his hand before the over begins. If a No ball or Wide ball is bowled the counter should be retained in the hand. When a wicket falls, the umpire should make mental note of the number of balls left in the over since it will not always be possible to retain the counters in the hand – e.g. when remaking a wicket.

The striker's end umpire, being part of the team of umpires and scorers, should also count the balls in the over as back-up and support for his colleague. A quiet signal may well be arranged between umpires, to be used when the last ball of the over is due.

Umpire miscounting

Although the experienced umpire will rarely lose count, it can happen; a check with the striker's end umpire is much more professional than a shouted request to the scorers. If umpires give each other this assistance, it should be very rare that an umpire will miscount the number of balls and call Over when only five (or more than six) balls have been delivered. One cause of miscounting is the umpire counting a No ball or a Wide ball as one of the six balls, whereas the Law makes it clear that neither of these deliveries counts as one of the balls in the over. Should the umpire miscount, the over stands as a complete over, whether fewer or more than 6 balls.

Number of balls left in the over

The laws do not instruct the umpires to inform an incoming batsman of the number of balls left in the over in progress. It is, nevertheless, reasonable for a batsman or any member of the fielding side – usually the bowler – to ask for this information at any time. Umpires should answer in such a way that **both** sides are aware of the number of balls left to be bowled.

Call of Over

The call of Over should not be made in a hurry but should be made when the ball is dead or when it is clear that the batsmen do not intend to run and the fielding side no longer regard the ball as being in play. The call should be made before leaving the wicket. It should be loud and clear so that both the batsmen and the fielding side are aware that the ball is dead. There is a tendency for some umpires to be careless with the call of Over, using such expressions as 'Andover' or 'Hold it', often while walking away from the wicket. This is to be discouraged. Some umpires give a verbal indication to both sides such as 'Left hander facing' after calling Over, and leaving the wicket at the bowler's end. This action is purely personal and impartial, with the intention of saving time.

Over must be completed

A bowler must complete an over unless he is incapacitated or is suspended for unfair play. If the bowler becomes incapacitated during his run-up for the delivery of the first ball of an over, the umpire must call and signal Dead ball, as the ball is in play. The umpire will then request the Captain of the fielding side to assign a member of his side to bowl the complete over from the same end. If a bowler is suspended, or unable to continue bowling at any time during an over, the umpire will call and signal Dead ball and request the Captain to provide another bowler to complete the over. Umpires must be particularly careful in ensuring that the fielder who is appointed to bowl a complete or partial over for a suspended or incapacitated bowler did not bowl the previous over and does not bowl the next over from the other end.

Except at the end of an innings, an over which has not been completed at the start of any interval or interruption of play must be finished on the resumption of play, by the same bowler from the same end. Umpires should keep a written record of the remaining number of balls to be bowled in the over in progress; the identification of the bowlers **at each end**; the end at which the bowling is to resume and the identity of the two batsmen, including which of them is to take strike. (See the interval duties of both umpires – page 15 and **Law 17**).

Bowler changing ends

A bowler must not be allowed to bowl two consecutive overs, or any part of each of two consecutive overs, in an innings. He is, however, allowed to change ends as often as his Captain dictates.

Position of non-striker

The non-striker normally stands on the opposite side of the

wicket to that from which the ball is delivered. If either side wishes the non-striker to stand on the same side of the wicket as that from which the ball is being delivered, the request must be made to the umpire at the bowler's end, who will grant the request if he satisfied that neither side is gaining an unfair advantage from the abnormal position.

Limitation of number of overs bowler may bowl

Umpires are reminded of the importance of carefully studying all Special Regulations of competition matches in which they may be officiating, especially with regard to the limitation of the number of overs to be bowled in an innings (see **Law 12**) and by each bowler. It is normal for any part over (even one ball) to count as a full over against any bowler's quota.

LAW 23 DEAD BALL

1 THE BALL BECOMES DEAD, WHEN:

(a) **It is finally settled in the hands of the Wicket-Keeper or the Bowler.**
(b) **It reaches or pitches over the boundary.**
(c) **A Batsman is out.**
(d) **Whether played or not, it lodges in the clothing or equipment of a Batsman or the clothing of an Umpire.**
(e) **A ball lodges in a protective helmet worn by a member of the fielding side.**
(f) **A penalty is awarded under Law 20: (Lost Ball) or Law 41.1: (Fielding the Ball).**
(g) **The Umpire calls 'over' or 'time'.**

2 EITHER UMPIRE SHALL CALL AND SIGNAL 'DEAD BALL', WHEN:

(a) **He intervenes in a case of unfair play.**
(b) **A serious injury to a Player or Umpire occurs.**
(c) **He is satisfied that, for an adequate reason, the Striker is not ready to receive the ball and makes no attempt to play it.**
(d) **The Bowler drops the ball accidentally before delivery, or the ball does not leave his hand for any reason, other than in an attempt to run out the**

Non-Striker (see Law 24.5 – Bowler Attempting to Run Out the Non-Striker Before Delivery).

(e) One or both bails fall from the Striker's wicket before he receives delivery.

(f) He leaves his normal position for consultation.

(g) He is required to do so under Laws 26.3: (Disallowance of Leg Byes), etc.

3 THE BALL CEASES TO BE DEAD, WHEN:

(a) The Bowler starts his run up or bowling action.

4 THE BALL IS NOT DEAD, WHEN:

(a) It strikes an Umpire (unless it lodges in his dress).

(b) The wicket is broken or struck down (unless a Batsman is out thereby).

(c) An unsuccessful appeal is made.

(d) The wicket is broken accidentally either by the Bowler during his delivery or by a Batsman in running.

(e) The Umpire has called 'no ball' or 'wide'.

Notes

(a) BALL FINALLY SETTLED

Whether the ball is finally settled or not – see 1(a) above – must be a question for the Umpires alone to decide.

(b) ACTION ON CALL OF 'DEAD BALL'

(i) *If 'dead ball' is called prior to the Striker receiving a delivery the Bowler shall be allowed an additional ball.*

(ii) *If 'dead ball' is called after the Striker receives a delivery the Bowler shall not be allowed an additional ball, unless a 'no ball' or 'wide' has been called.*

It is important to understand what is meant by the ball being 'dead'. A better description is that the ball is no longer in play which means that the batsmen are unable to score runs and the fielding side cannot dismiss either batsman. The ball is deemed to be in play at the moment a bowler starts his run up or, in the very rare circumstance of his having no run up, bowling action. From that moment, until the ball becomes dead, runs may be scored and the batsmen's wickets are in peril.

<u>Ball automatically dead</u>

There are seven instances listed when the ball is automatically considered to be no longer in play. Six of these are matters of fact but the question as to when the ball is finally settled in the hands of either the bowler or wicket-keeper requires judgment on the part of the umpire. If there is a reasonable opportunity for the fielding side to attempt to take a wicket, it would be wrong to regard the ball as being finally settled. Certainly, even though the ball may be in possession of the wicket keeper the ball could not be considered as dead if either batsman was attempting a run. The wicket-keeper, having taken a delivery, may transfer the ball to one of the slip fielders, considering that the slip fielder is the more likely to be able to hit the wicket and run out the striker. On the other hand, he may transfer the ball in such a way that it is clear he has no intention that an attempt should be made to dismiss the striker even if he is out of his ground. In this case, the ball should be considered to be finally settled and automatically dead. Should the ball be transferred from the wicket-keeper to a close fielder and then on to mid-off, or any other fielder, it would be clear that the fielding side have no intention to attempt to effect a dismissal.

The ball becoming finally settled in the hands of the bowler is less likely to pose problems for the umpires, who will judge on the facts as they see them. If the ball is thrown quickly to the bowler, the umpire should anticipate that an attempt to run out the non-striker may be made. If the bowler receives the ball and immediately begins to walk back to the start of his run-up, the ball is clearly no longer in play.

There are occasions when the ball, whether played or not, lodges in the top of the striker's pads. The ball becomes automatically dead when this occurs, or indeed if it lodges (unusually) in any other part of his dress or of his, or the non-striker's, helmet. Less common is the ball lodging in a fielder's helmet, but it would obviously be wrong for the fielding side to benefit from such a happening. Again the ball immediately becomes dead as it would if it lodged in any clothing worn by the umpire. There should be little difficulty in determining if the ball has 'lodged' even if the ball is quickly shaken or plucked from the clothing or helmet.

The call of Over or Time will render the ball dead. Mention

has been made in **Law 22** that umpires should not be over-anxious to make the call, particularly if there is an opportunity for the fielding side to dismiss either batsman.

Although the ball is automatically dead on the call of Lost ball, or when there is an instance of illegal fielding, it is recommended that the umpire at the bowler's end should call and signal Dead ball, so that both sides are aware that the ball is no longer in play.

Either umpire required to call Dead ball

The ball is in play when the bowler starts his run-up, or delivery action, but there are occasions when the Law requires the umpire to intervene before the striker has received the delivery. Either umpire should call and signal Dead ball if:
- the bowler drops the ball or fails to deliver it, for any reason other than an attempt to run out the non-striker;
- one or both bails fall from the striker's wicket;
- the striker is not ready, for an adequate reason, and does not attempt to play the ball.

Other reasons for the umpire's intervention are less likely before the striker has received a delivery but the call and signal should be made if:
- he intervenes if there is an incident of unfair play;
- a serious injury to a player or umpire occurs;
- he leaves his normal position, while the ball is in play, to consult his colleague;
- the striker has illegally deflected a delivery and the ball crosses the boundary, the batsmen attempt to score a run or remain in their ground.

In most cases bowler's end umpire will make the call and signal of Dead ball but, certainly if a bail is dislodged from the striker's wicket, it is the striker's end umpire who is most likely to be first aware of this.

If the non-striker does not remain within his ground until the ball has been delivered, the bowler is entitled to attempt to run him out. This is dealt with in detail under **Law 38**.

For the striker to be given out if his wicket is broken, a bail must be completely removed from the top of the stumps. Should the umpire fail to intervene by calling and signalling Dead ball if one or both bails have fallen off, before the striker receives a delivery, a possible embarrassing situation could develop.

Should the ball hit the stumps from which the bails had already been dislodged, the umpire would be unable to give the striker out Bowled.

The striker will usually indicate that he was not ready to receive a delivery by pulling away from his guard position, perhaps with one hand raised. One problem for the umpire is that his attention will be focused on the area in which the bowler's feet are likely to land. It may be after the front foot has landed before he is aware that the striker has pulled away. Providing he is so aware and the batsman makes no attempt to play at the ball, Dead ball should be called and signalled. Should the striker, having withdrawn, attempt to hit the ball he will be deemed to have accepted the delivery.

If Dead ball is called before the striker has received the delivery, the ball is considered to be dead from the moment it last came into play. Whether the ball has been delivered or not it does not count in the over. If the striker has received it the ball will count, providing it is not a No ball or Wide ball.

Umpires must not hesitate to call and signal Dead ball if they decide to intervene because of unfair play. The same action should be taken immediately should serious injury occur to a player or umpire. The responsibility resting upon the umpire to determine whether a player or colleague is seriously injured is considerable; the reaction of other players may prove the best guide. Should the ball be in the air and a catch possible the umpire's intervention should be delayed for that tiny length of time until the catch is completed or the ball has made contact with the ground. Whether the bowler will be allowed another delivery will depend upon the general principle of whether the call is made before or after the striker has received the delivery.

The calling and signalling of Dead ball will primarily be a duty of the bowler's end umpire but the Law empowers either umpire to do so. The striker's end umpire may well intervene under certain circumstances such as unfair play taking place, the bails falling from the striker's wicket before he has received a delivery, or serious injury to a player or his colleague.

Ball is not dead
The ball is not dead when an unsuccessful appeal is made nor when a wicket is struck down or accidentally broken, nor when the ball hits a helmet **worn** by one of the players. (For further comment see **Laws 32 and 38**).

Scoring

Scorers must be aware of the principle which governs whether the delivery counts in the over. Providing it is not a No ball or Wide ball, any delivery which the umpire considers has been received by the striker will count as one of the balls in the over – even if the ball has not reached the striker (see **Law 25**). If the umpire calls and signals Dead ball *before* the striker has received a delivery, it will not count in the over.

Umpire leaving his position to consult colleague

It is possible that an umpire will need to leave his normal position to consult his partner, the players or the scorers. If the ball is still in play he must call and signal Dead ball before leaving his position.

LAW 24 NO BALL

1 MODE OF DELIVERY

The Umpire shall indicate to the Striker whether the Bowler intends to bowl over or round the wicket, overarm or underarm, or right- or left-handed. Failure on the part of the Bowler to indicate in advance a change in his mode of delivery is unfair and the Umpire shall call and signal 'no ball'.

2 FAIR DELIVERY – THE ARM

For a delivery to be fair the ball must be bowled not thrown – see Note (a) below. If either Umpire is not entirely satisfied with the absolute fairness of a delivery in this respect he shall call and signal 'no ball' instantly upon delivery.

3 FAIR DELIVERY – THE FEET

The Umpire at the bowler's wicket shall call and signal 'no ball' if he is not satisfied that in the delivery stride:
(a) the Bowler's back foot has landed within and not touching the return crease or its forward extension or
(b) some part of the front foot whether grounded or raised was behind the popping crease.

4 BOWLER THROWING AT STRIKER'S WICKET BEFORE DELIVERY

If the Bowler, before delivering the ball, throws it at the Striker's wicket in an attempt to run him out, the Umpire shall call and signal 'no ball'. See Law 42.12: (Batsman Unfairly Stealing a Run) and Law 38: (Run Out).

5 BOWLER ATTEMPTING TO RUN OUT NON-STRIKER BEFORE DELIVERY

If the Bowler, before delivering the ball, attempts to run out the non-Striker, any runs which result shall be allowed and shall be scored as no balls. Such an attempt shall not count as a ball in the over. The Umpire shall not call 'no ball'. See Law 42.12: (Batsman Unfairly Stealing a Run).

6 INFRINGEMENT OF LAWS BY A WICKET-KEEPER OR A FIELDSMAN

The Umpire shall call and signal 'no ball' in the event of the Wicket-Keeper infringing Law 40.1: (Position of Wicket-Keeper) or a Fieldsman infringing Law 41.2: (Limitation of On-side Fieldsmen) or Law 41.3: (Position of Fieldsmen).

7 REVOKING A CALL

An Umpire shall revoke the call 'no ball' if the ball does not leave the Bowler's hand for any reason. See Law 23.2: (Either Umpire Shall Call and Signal 'Dead Ball').

8 PENALTY

A penalty of one run for a no ball shall be scored if no runs are made otherwise.

9 RUNS FROM A NO BALL

The Striker may hit a no ball and whatever runs result shall be added to his score. Runs made otherwise from a no ball shall be scored no balls.

10 OUT FROM A NO BALL

The Striker shall be out from a no ball if he breaks Law 34: (Hit the Ball Twice) and either Batsman may be Run Out or shall be given out if either breaks Law

33: (Handled the Ball) or Law 37: (Obstructing the Field).

11 BATSMEN GIVEN OUT OFF A NO BALL
Should a Batsman be given out off a no ball the penalty for bowling it shall stand unless runs are otherwise scored.

Notes

(a) DEFINITION OF A THROW
A ball shall be deemed to have been thrown if, in the opinion of either Umpire, the process of straightening the bowling arm, whether it be partial or complete, takes place during that part of the delivery swing which directly precedes the ball leaving the hand. This definition shall not debar a Bowler from the use of the wrist in the delivery swing.

(b) NO BALL NOT COUNTING IN OVER
A no ball shall not be reckoned as one of the over. See **Law 22.3**: *(No Ball or Wide Ball).*

Mode of delivery
At the start of the match and when the bowling is changed from his end, bowler's end umpire must enquire from the bowler the style of bowling which he will use and the side of the wicket from which the delivery will be made. The bowler should not be allowed to start bowling until this information has been conveyed to the batsmen. Should the bowler change his mode of delivery without advising his intention, the umpire at the bowler's end must call and signal No ball.

A bowler who suddenly, without advising the umpire, bowls from a markedly different point, even though his run-up was normal, will be considered to have changed his mode of delivery if his back foot lands on the other side of the line of the centre stump from that on which he ran up.

Throwing
Over the history of the game, throwing has been the cause of much bitterness and acrimony – particularly at the highest levels. Although much unpleasantness may be engendered this

should not deter the umpires from taking action if they are not entirely satisfied with the absolute fairness of the delivery. The definition of a throw clearly states that it is the straightening of the bowling arm at the elbow, immediately before the ball is delivered, which makes the delivery an unfair one. The use of the wrist in the bowling action does not constitute a throw, nor does bowling with a bent arm, although there may be difficulty in determining that a bent arm does not straighten a little during the last part of the delivery swing. In view of the repercussions, the responsibility of dealing with suspect bowling is a demanding one but this should not prevent the umpire from ensuring that the game is played within the Laws. No ball should be called and signalled if there is the slightest doubt about the fairness of the delivery.

Umpires, especially those officiating in youth cricket, must not allow young bowlers with suspect actions to continue and go on to higher grades of cricket. If umpires shirk their duty at this early stage, their colleagues will eventually have to take action. The attendant unpleasantness in dealing with bowling that should have been judged as unfair long before, is an irritating and unfair burden of responsibility that will have been passed from one umpire to another. Fortunately, suspect throwing actions are now rare but, unquestionably, a substantial burden of responsibility still rests upon umpires to continue to eliminate throwing. Captains, administrators and officials must also play their part by backing and supporting the umpires, and by being firm in non-selection of bowlers not satisfying umpires as to the fairness of their bowling action.

Fair delivery – the feet

Inexperienced umpires will quickly appreciate the difficulty of determining whether a bowler's feet placement – particularly a fast bowler – conforms to the Law. The umpire has but a split second in which to make a judgment of the delivery stride. The requirements of the Law limit the delivery point both by width and by length.

Back foot

The landing of the back foot begins the delivery stride. It must **land** within and must not touch the return crease or its forward extension. The return crease is the inside edge of the marking;

should any part of the back foot land outside or on the marking the delivery is unfair. Any movement of the back foot after it has landed should be ignored. The return crease is unlimited in length. Should the bowler deliver the ball some distance behind the bowling crease the umpire must be satisfied that the bowler's back foot landed within the imaginary extension of the return crease. Should he not be completely satisfied, No ball must be called and signalled. This does not mean that every delivery bowled from behind the umpire is necessarily unfair. The line of the delivery may be sufficient to persuade the umpire that the delivery point conformed to the Law but if he is not certain that it was a fair delivery, No ball must be called and signalled. Once the back foot has landed the umpire should very quickly change his line of sight to the front foot.

Front foot
The delivery stride is completed when the front foot **lands**. For the landing of the front foot to be fair, some part, on landing, whether grounded or raised, must be behind the popping crease, which is the back edge of the marking. It is not a No ball if the front foot lands on or outside the forward extension of the return crease providing some part of the foot is behind the popping crease. As with the back foot any subsequent movement should be ignored.

Once the front foot has landed the umpire must as quickly as possible look down the pitch. It is most important that he should not allow his gaze to dwell on the point at which the front foot landed but should pick up the flight of the ball as soon as possible. Throughout this sequence of events, the umpire should try to keep head movements to an absolute minimum.

The call and signal of No ball should be made the instant any infringement, by either foot, is noted. To make the call it is necessary for the lungs to be full of air as the bowler enters his delivery stride. Umpires should control their breathing to ensure the call can be made as early as possible.

Recording No balls
Having made the call and signal, umpires must concentrate on what is happening on the field until the ball becomes dead. Only then should the umpire turn to the scorebox to repeat the signal and obtain an acknowledgment. Competent scorers will under-

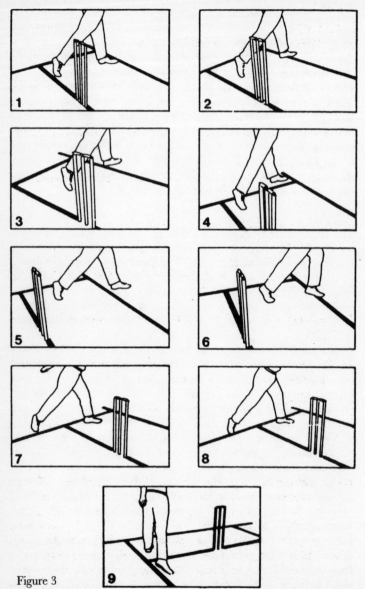

Figure 3

Figure 3

1 *A fair delivery*
The Bowler's front foot is behind the popping crease and the back foot is within, but not touching, the return crease.

2 *A fair delivery*
Part of the front foot is behind the popping crease and the back foot is correctly placed.

3 *A no ball*
No part of the front foot, whether grounded or raised, is behind the popping crease.

4 *A fair delivery*
The front foot is outside the forward extension of the return crease but this does not constitute a no ball.

5 *A no ball*
The front foot is clear beyond the popping crease.

6 *A fair delivery*
The Bowler has landed on the ball of his foot beyond the popping crease and with the heel raised. If some part of the raised heel is behind the popping crease the delivery is fair.

7 *A no ball*
The back foot has not landed within the return crease or its forward extension.

8 *A no ball*
The front foot is behind the popping crease but the back foot has landed on the return crease.

9 *A fair delivery*
The Bowler's heel is raised but clear of the return crease.

stand that the first signal is not intended for them but will wait for the signal to be repeated. If the striker has played the ball with his bat any runs will be credited to him and no further signal, unless a boundary has been scored, is necessary. However, if the striker has not played the ball with his bat, even if the ball has hit part of his person or equipment, any runs will be scored as No ball extras. To indicate this the umpire will give the bye signal immediately after receiving acknowledgement for the No ball signal. The boundary signal will follow if 4 no ball extras are to be recorded (see also **Law 19**).

Bowler attempting to run out striker or non-striker before delivery

As soon as the bowler starts his run-up (or bowling action) the ball is in play and either batsman may be dismissed. Should either batsman be out of his ground before the ball is delivered, the bowler may attempt to run him out. If the *striker* advances up the pitch the bowler may throw at the striker's wicket. The Law requires either umpire to call and signal No ball as the ball has been thrown; the striker would not be given out Run Out unless he was attempting a run (see **Law 38**) and could not be Stumped (**Law 39**).

The bowler will normally attempt to run out the *non-striker* with ball in hand although he is entitled to throw at the wicket. If he throws at the wicket No ball should not be called. Should he throw at the wicket but fail to dismiss the non-striker, as the ball is in play, the batsmen could score runs. Any runs taken have to be scored as No balls, even though no call is made. It would be essential for the umpire to inform the scorers that the runs should be scored as No ball extras (see **Law 38**).

Infringement by wicket-keeper or fielders

Law 40.1, Law 42.2 and **Law 42.3** deal in detail with possible infringements by the wicket-keeper or members of the fielding side. Should an infringement occur, one of the umpires should call and signal No ball at the instant of delivery or, if the infringement occurs after the ball has been delivered, as soon as it is possible to do so.

Revoking call of No ball

The umpire will give his full concentration to the position of the bowler's feet, in the delivery stride, and will call and signal No ball as soon as a foot lands outside the prescribed limits. The bowler may realize that he has overstepped the popping crease and not deliver the ball. Having called and signalled Dead ball in such circumstances the umpire should make certain that the scorers understand that the call of No ball has been revoked and no penalty should be recorded.

One run penalty

Providing no other runs are scored, a penalty of one run will be awarded to the batting side, even if a batsman is out. Should there be an act of illegal fielding, after No ball is called, a further penalty of 5 runs will be incurred. The 5 runs are added to any runs scored. If no other runs accrue, the two penalties are both added to the score. The entries to be made in the score book are discussed below.

If a No ball is bowled when the scores are level the one run penalty is sufficient for the batting side to win the match. Any further action by either side will be discounted and the umpire will follow the call of No ball by calling Time and removing the bails.

Out off a no ball

Striker can be dismissed	Either batsman can be out
Hit the ball twice	Handled the ball
	Obstructing the field
	**Run out

**Striker can only be Run Out if he is attempting a run. He would be deemed to be attempting a run if he remains out of his ground and the non-striker runs past him.

Should either batsman be given out off a No ball the penalty of one run is awarded to the batting side providing no other runs have been made from that delivery.

Field Technique

A No ball does not count in the over. As mentioned in **Law 22** umpires must make the necessary adjustment to the method which they use for counting the balls in the over – e.g. by retaining the counter in their hand.

Although the Law requires umpires to call and signal No ball when aware of an infringement, the signal must be repeated to the scorers when the ball is dead. The sequence for two or three signals for the same delivery is important. The repeated No ball signal should precede any other. If required it should be followed by the Bye signal to indicate that any runs are to recorded as No ball extras. If a boundary has been scored this should be the final signal to the scorers. An acknowledgment for each signal should be received.

Striker's end umpire is required, on occasions, to call and signal No Ball. Should bowler's end umpire also be required to make a signal to the scorers when that delivery is no longer in play, bowler's end umpire should signal No ball to the scorers. If both umpires are signalling at the same time, it will not be possible to be certain as to which signal the scorers are acknowledging.

Scoring

Full details of the entries to be made in the score book when No ball is signalled are included in Part III on pages 213–15.

The bowler does not receive credit for any dismissal off a No ball.

A No ball does not count as one of the balls in the over.

If the fielding side is penalized for an act of illegal fielding the 5 penalty runs will be added to any runs scored or, if no runs are scored, to the one run penalty for the No ball. There are three possible ways for the runs to be recorded in the score book:

– The striker plays the ball, with his bat, and the batsmen cross in an attempted run, before the illegal act takes place. All 6 penalty runs are credited to the striker.
– The striker does not play the ball. The 6 runs are all No ball extras.
– The striker plays the ball, with his bat, but no run is attempted. The runs are to be recorded as 1 No ball extra and 5 runs to the striker. The same would apply if a run was attempted but the batsmen had not crossed.

LAW 25 WIDE BALL

1 JUDGING A WIDE

If the Bowler bowls the ball so high over or so wide of the wicket that, in the opinion of the Umpire, it passes out of reach of the Striker, standing in a normal guard position, the Umpire shall call and signal 'wide ball' as soon as it has passed the line of the Striker's wicket.

The Umpire shall not adjudge a ball as being a wide if:

(a) The Striker, by moving from his guard position, causes the ball to pass out of his reach.

(b) **The Striker moves and thus brings the ball within his reach.**

2 PENALTY

A penalty of one run for a wide shall be scored if no runs are made otherwise.

3 BALL COMING TO REST IN FRONT OF THE STRIKER

If a ball which the Umpire considers to have been delivered comes to rest in front of the line of the Striker's wicket, 'wide' shall not be called. The Striker has a right, without interference from the fielding side, to make one attempt to hit the ball. If the fielding side interfere, the Umpire shall replace the ball where it came to rest and shall order the Fieldsmen to resume the places they occupied in the field before the ball was delivered.

The Umpire shall call and signal 'dead ball' as soon as it is clear that the Striker does not intend to hit the ball, or after the Striker has made one unsuccessful attempt to hit the ball.

4 REVOKING A CALL

The Umpire shall revoke the call if the Striker hits a ball which has been called 'wide'.

5 BALL NOT DEAD

The ball does not become dead on the call of 'wide ball' – see Law 23.4: (The Ball is Not Dead).

6 RUNS RESULTING FROM A WIDE

All runs which are run or result from a wide ball which is not a no ball shall be scored wide balls, or if no runs are made one shall be scored.

7 OUT FROM A WIDE

The Striker shall be out from a wide ball if he breaks Law 35: (Hit Wicket); or Law 39: (Stumped). Either Batsman may be Run Out and shall be out if he breaks Law 33: (Handled the Ball), or Law 37: (Obstructing the Field).

8 BATSMAN GIVEN OUT OFF A WIDE

Should a Batsman be given out off a wide, the penalty

for bowling it shall stand unless runs are otherwise made.

Notes

(a) WIDE BALL NOT COUNTING IN OVER
A wide ball shall not be reckoned as one of the over – see **Law 22.3**: (*No Ball or Wide Ball*).

A No ball must be called and signalled as early as possible after the umpire has noted that **Law 24** has been contravened. The call and signal of Wide ball should, however, be delayed until the ball has passed the line of the striker's wicket. It is better to delay the call until it is clear that the ball is well past the striker's wicket rather than have to revoke a call made too early followed by the striker moving across and making contact with the ball. The call must be loud and distinct enough for all the players to hear. The initial call and signal is intended for the players only; when the ball is dead, and only then, should the umpire repeat the signal to the scorers and obtain an acknowledgment.

Judgment of a Wide

A delivery which is so high over the striker's head as to be out of his reach is rare and will cause no problem for the umpire. It is to be called No ball if it qualifies as a 'fast high full pitch' under **Law 42.9**. Otherwise it is a Wide ball. It is probable that the ball has slipped from the bowler's hand and few bowlers will object to being called for such a delivery. The stature of a batsman, especially with regard to his height and reach, will be an important factor in the judgment of the umpire as to whether or not a ball has passed too high or too wide of the striker for him to be able to reach it with his bat. A tall batsman with long arms will obviously have an advantage in this respect. He is also likely to have a longer stride than that of a small player giving him a wider reach both when standing in a normal guard position and when moving across towards the line of the ball. The striker is not required to move towards the line of the ball. If, in the opinion of bowler's end umpire, the ball passes out of the striker's reach when he is standing in a normal guard position, the umpire should call and signal Wide ball as soon as

126

the ball has passed the line of the striker's wicket. The striker may well move across towards the line of the ball. The umpire must then decide whether the striker brought the ball within his reach. Should the decision be that the ball was not within the striker's reach, despite his movement, the ball will be called wide.

Delivery which is not a Wide

If the striker moves across and brings a wide delivery within his reach, it will not be considered to be a Wide ball. No matter how wide of the wicket a delivery is, it is accepted as a normal delivery, if the striker hits the ball. Similarly if the striker brings the ball within his reach, even if he fails to make any contact, the delivery will not be called a Wide.

The striker cannot create a Wide by moving *away* from a normal guard position, nor by adopting a guard position which was not a normal one, even though the ball passes out of his reach, unless it would have been out of his reach when standing in a normal guard position.

Call and signal of Wide ball

The umpire should use the same technique for calling and signalling Wide ball as that employed for No ball. The call and signal should be made as soon as the umpire is certain that the ball passed out of the striker's reach and has passed the line of the wicket. Having made the call and signal the umpire must watch the ball with his usual concentration until the ball becomes dead. Then, and only then, the umpire should turn to the scorers to repeat the signal followed by the boundary signal, if applicable; he should then wait for the scorers acknowledgment. The Law states five ways in which batsmen may be out off a Wide ball while the ball is in play. Any temptation to signal to the scorer until the ball is dead should be resisted by the umpire who may well fail to observe action upon which he is required to make a decision.

Runs scored off a Wide ball

As with No ball, the one run penalty will count even if a batsman is out. The one run penalty will be awarded if no runs are made otherwise; all runs which are run, or result from a Wide ball, will be scored as wides. If a run out occurs, all runs, except the one being attempted, will be scored as wides.

Should a fielder illegally field a Wide ball, the 5 penalty

runs are added as Wides to any runs scored or, if no other runs accrue, to the one run penalty for the wide delivery, as the 5 penalty runs are not 'made' but 'awarded' for an unfair act.

If the scores are level and a Wide ball is bowled, the same principle applies as that detailed in **Law 24**; the one run penalty is sufficient for the batting side to win the match. Any further action, by either side, will be discounted and the umpire will follow the call of Wide ball by calling Time and removing the bails.

Ball coming to rest in front of striker

If a properly delivered ball comes to rest in front of the line of the striker's wicket, Wide ball is not called or signalled. The striker is allowed one attempt to hit the ball but before he does so the umpire should ensure that all the fielders resume, approximately, the positions that they were in when the ball was delivered. If the non-striker has left his ground at the bowler's end he should be required to return to it and remain there until the striker plays the ball. Should the ball have been picked up by a close fielder, or the bowler, the umpire should quickly intervene and insist that the ball is replaced at the point it came to rest. The striker is allowed just one attempt to hit the ball. If he succeeds, since the ball is hit off the ground, a catch is, of course, invalidated and a boundary 6 cannot be scored. If the attempt is unsuccessful the umpire will at once call and signal Dead ball. The striker may, however, remain in his ground and make no attempt to hit the ball. Should this happen, the umpire is required to call and signal Dead ball.

No ball which is also wide

If No ball is called the delivery is not to be adjudged a Wide. It may be that bowler's end umpire calls and signals Wide ball and, simultaneously, his colleague calls and signals No ball for an encroachment by the wicket-keeper. The call of No ball will prevail and any runs resulting from the delivery will be scored as No balls.

Out off a Wide ball

Surprise is often expressed when a batsman is given out off a Wide ball. Attention was previously drawn to the possibility of a batsman being out by one of five dismissals:

Striker can be dismissed	Either batsman can be out
Hit wicket	Handled the ball
Stumped	Obstructing the field
	Run out

Should either batsman be given out off a Wide ball the penalty of one run is awarded to the batting side, providing no other runs have been made from that delivery.

Field Technique

Emphasis has been given to delaying the call until the ball has passed the line of the striker's wicket. Should the striker make late contact with a ball which has been called wide, the umpire must revoke the call. Better to wait until it is not possible for the ball to be struck.

If the ball comes to rest in front of the striker, the umpire is not required to advise the batsman of the options available to him. In response to any query from the players, the umpire could advise them as to the provision of the Law. It is important that the umpire insists that fielders resume the position they occupied when the ball was delivered and that the non-striker returns to his ground before the striker attempts to play the ball.

A Wide ball does not count in the over. Umpires should exercise the same care, in counting, as that detailed under No ball.

Scoring

Full details of the entries to be made in the score book when Wide ball is signalled are included in Part III pages 213–15.

The striker may be given out Hit Wicket or Stumped. Both dismissals are credited to the bowler.

The penalty of one run or any other runs scored from a Wide ball will be entered in the score book as Wide ball extras. If the striker has made contact with the ball, it cannot be a Wide.

LAW 26 BYE AND LEG-BYE

1 BYES

If the ball, not having been called 'wide' or 'no ball', passes the Striker without touching his bat or person, and any runs are obtained, the Umpire shall signal

'bye' and the run or runs shall be credited as such to the batting side.

2 LEG-BYES

If the ball, not having been called 'wide' or 'no ball', is unintentionally deflected by the Striker's dress or person, except a hand holding the bat, and any runs are obtained the Umpire shall signal 'leg-bye' and the run or runs so scored shall be credited as such to the batting side.

Such leg-byes shall only be scored if, in the opinion of the Umpire, the Striker has:

(a) attempted to play the ball with his bat, or

(b) tried to avoid being hit by the ball.

3 DISALLOWANCE OF LEG-BYES

In the case of a deflection by the Striker's person, other than in 2(a) and (b) above, the Umpire shall call and signal 'dead ball' as soon as one run has been completed or when it is clear that a run is not being attempted or the ball has reached the boundary.

On the call and signal of 'dead ball' the Batsmen shall return to their original ends and no runs shall be allowed.

Byes

Any run scored from a fair delivery which has not been played by the striker nor made contact with any part of his person will be signalled by the umpire and scored as a bye.

Leg Byes

If a fair delivery makes contact with any part of the striker's person, other than the hand(s) holding the bat, the umpire is required to determine whether the deflection was 'unintentional'. This is deemed to be so when the striker either makes a genuine attempt to play the ball with his bat or attempts to avoid being struck by the ball.

There is little difficulty in determining that the striker deliberately deflected the ball if he raises his bat in the air and pushes the ball away with his pad. Difficulty will be experienced if the striker hides his bat behind his pad or stops the movement of his bat before the ball is within his reach. The umpire will be justified in deciding that any subsequent deflection is intentional but the margin is often extremely fine and there is often very little time between the bowler's front foot landing and the impact on the pad, or person.

The action of the striker attempting to avoid being hit by the ball is usually much easier to determine as it will normally be a sharp action by the batsman. There will be occasions, however, when the batsman will attempt to withdraw his bat from the line of the delivery and allow the ball to hit some part of his person. Such an action should not be considered as avoiding being hit by the ball.

Disallowance of attempted leg byes

Should the batsmen attempt a run after the striker has intentionally deflected the ball from a fair delivery or a No ball, they should be allowed to complete one run before the bowler's end umpire calls and signals Dead ball. This sometimes gives the impression that the umpire is reacting to protests by the fielding side but the Law requires the umpire not to intervene until one run has been completed, thus allowing the fielding side a possible opportunity to run out either batsman. Having called and signalled Dead ball the umpire must repeat the signal to the scorers to advise that that run has not been scored and should then ensure that the batsmen return to their original ends.

The umpire must also call and signal Dead ball if, after a deliberate deflection, the ball crosses the boundary. The repetition of the signal to the scorers is vital to ensure they are aware that the boundary should not be scored. The Law also requires the umpire to call and signal Dead ball, after a deliberate deflection, when it is clear that no run is being attempted.

Runs may not be scored from a deliberate deflection

The striker, having deliberately deflected the ball, must not be allowed to gain benefit from doing so. Even though the fielding side are guilty of an act' of illegal fielding, perhaps with the return hitting a helmet placed on the ground, no runs are awarded. Similarly if an attempt to run out either batsman goes for what would normally be overthrows, these are not allowed.

131

The call and signal of Dead ball will nullify all runs unless No ball has been called when the one run penalty will be awarded.

Field Technique
Attention is drawn to the correct signal for leg byes – touching a raised knee with the hand. It is incorrect to also give, as some inexperienced umpires do, the signal for byes.

Scoring
Neither byes nor leg byes can be scored from a No ball or Wide ball.

If the umpire signals No ball and follows with the bye signal he is informing the scorers that the batsman did not make contact with the ball with his bat or the hand holding the bat and any runs are scored as No ball extras.

LAW 27 APPEALS

1 TIME OF APPEALS
The Umpires shall not give a Batsman out unless appealed to by the other side which shall be done prior to the Bowler beginning his run-up or bowling action to deliver the next ball. Under Law 23.1: (g) (The Ball Becomes Dead) the ball is dead on 'over' being called; this does not, however, invalidate an appeal made prior to the first ball of the following over provided 'time' has not been called. See Law 17.1: (Call of Time).

2 AN APPEAL 'HOW'S THAT?
An appeal 'How's That?' shall cover all ways of being out.

3 ANSWERING APPEALS
The Umpire at the Bowler's wicket shall answer appeals before the other Umpire in all cases except those arising out of Law 35: (Hit Wicket) or Law 39: (Stumped) or Law 38: (Run Out) when this occurs at the Striker's wicket.

When either Umpire has given a Batsman not out, the other Umpire shall, within his jurisdiction, answer

the appeal or a further appeal, provided it is made in time in accordance with 1 above (Time of Appeals).

4 CONSULTATION BY UMPIRES
An Umpire may consult with the other Umpire on a point of fact which the latter may have been in a better position to see and shall then give his decision. If, after consultation, there is still doubt remaining the decision shall be in favour of the Batsman.

5 BATSMAN LEAVING HIS WICKET UNDER A MISAPPREHENSION
The Umpires shall intervene if satisfied that a Batsman, not having been given out, has left his wicket under a misapprehension that he has been dismissed.

6 UMPIRE'S DECISION
The Umpire's decision is final. He may alter his decision, provided that such alteration is made promptly.

7 WITHDRAWAL OF AN APPEAL
In exceptional circumstances the Captain of the fielding side may seek permission of the Umpire to withdraw an appeal providing the outgoing Batsman has not left the playing area. If this is allowed, the Umpire shall cancel his decision.

Except for appeals relating to ground, weather and light conditions, this Law covers all the appeals which the umpire is required to answer. On many occasions the batsman will not wait for the fielding side to appeal, or for the umpire's answer, but will accept that he is out and walk from the pitch. Many batsmen, in all grades of cricket, will walk at once if they know they are out. Difficulty can arise when a known and accepted 'walker' waits for the umpire's decision. This must be given on the facts which the umpire has before him and not upon the reputation of the batsman.

The umpire cannot give a batsman out unless there is an appeal from the fielding side. The batsman is fully entitled to stay at the wicket until an appeal is made and answered. An appeal of 'How's that?', or a similar expression, covers all ways of being out which are within the jurisdiction of an umpire.

Answering an appeal
As stated on page 21 it is unnecessary, and undesirable, to qualify the raising of the index finger, either by gesture or spoken word, to signify that the batsman is out in answer to an appeal. Should the verdict be Not out the decision should be given in a completely neutral tone without movement of the head. The umpire should not turn away, nor show any other sign of disapproval. The ball is not necessarily dead and a further appeal may result from subsequent action.

Time of appeals
The Law sets down the time limits within which an appeal can legitimately be made. Provided an appeal is made before the bowler begins his run-up or bowling action for the next delivery, the umpire must answer it. **Law 23** states that the ball shall be considered dead when the umpire calls Over but if the appeal is made before the ball is next brought into play, it should be answered. If, however, an appeal is made after Time has been called the umpire is not to consider nor answer it.

Jurisdiction of each umpire
The Law defines the jurisdiction of each umpire. An appeal to an umpire covers all the ways of being out which are within an umpire's jurisdiction. For instance, although the bowler may make an appeal for LBW which the bowler's end umpire does not consider to be out, he would, if the circumstances required it, give the striker out bowled or caught. In similar circumstances if the appeal had been specific – 'How's that for LBW?' – the umpire would answer 'Not out'. Since there is no advantage to the fielding side in making a specific appeal it is rare for one to be made.

Bowler's end umpire has the responsibility of answering appeals for eight of the ten ways in which a batsman may be dismissed. Both umpires must give decisions on Run Out at their respective ends. Striker's end umpire – and only striker's end umpire – will adjudicate on appeals arising from Hit Wicket or Stumped.

It may happen that a member of the fielding side will apparently direct an appeal to an umpire on a matter which is not within his jurisdiction. Whenever there is an appeal, the umpire who has jurisdiction on the matter should answer it even if a fielder has apparently directed it to the other umpire. Nowadays most appeals are made by many, if not all, the

ach umpire is defined by the Law, ...ire to consult his colleague. When ...ubt, an umpire should not hesitate ...ay have been in a better position to ... emphasis has been placed on the ...pire/scorer team. It is clearly in the ...hat, if there is any uncertainty, an ...rtner before giving a decision, if his ...ition to see what actually happened. ...l consultation between the umpires ...edit to the umpire for having the ...ible to arrive at the correct decision. ...t not be overdone. This would be ...a weakness.

...be unobtrusive, with simple signals ...hould not hesitate to walk across to ...firmation on a point of doubt. Any ...ed that an answer of 'yes' or 'no' can ..., the umpire in whose jurisdiction it ...eal. The Law asserts that if, after ...doubt the decision must be given in

...sult his colleague simply because he is ...n but only when he has been unable ...which his decision is required and if ...en in a better position to see what ...es must be prepared to give decisions ...to transfer responsibility.

There may be .... occasions when an umpire is totally unable to give a decision. The bowler in attempting a sharp return catch may knock the umpire over, thus preventing him from seeing what happened. In this case the umpire would be correct in requesting his colleague to give a decision, if the fielding side make an appeal. The other umpire could do so only if he had been able to see all the details of the incident.

Batsman leaving his wicket under a misapprehension
Due to ignorance of the Law or mistakenly believing he has been fairly dismissed a batsman may leave his wicket without an appeal having been made, or unaware that an appeal has been turned down. Should this happen, the umpire should immediately call and signal Dead ball, if the ball is still in play, and advise the batsman that he is not out. In the extremely unlikely event of the batsman disregarding the umpire's intervention, the batsman should be recorded as Retired out (see **Law 2**).

Umpire may change his decision
Before answering any appeal, the umpire should allow sufficient time to enable consideration to be given to all the facts. No benefit is obtained from an immediate response to an appeal. It may happen, however, that an umpire, even after due consideration, realizes subsequently that he has made a mistake and answered an appeal incorrectly. Should this be the case the umpire must immediately correct the mistake, no matter how uncomfortable the reversal may be for him. Umpires, like players, are not infallible; admission of an error and the subsequent embarrassment needs courage but will, more often than not, earn more respect than it loses.

Withdrawal of an appeal
A number of instances are on record where the Captain of the fielding side has wished to call a batsman back after he has been given out on appeal. The recall often has the best of sporting intentions. It may be that an appeal has been made when the striker has failed to regain his ground after being hurt and the wicket is put down by a fielder. If the umpire did not consider the injury to be a serious one and had not called and signalled Dead ball he would, albeit reluctantly, have to give the batsman out. The fielding Captain may well indicate, in such a circumstance, that he wishes to withdraw the appeal and should be allowed to do so.

On other occasions the Captain may have a doubt as to whether the batsman should have been given out – for instance, a catch taken close to the ground – even though the umpire has no doubt that his decision was correct. It is recommended that whether the wish to withdraw the appeal is a sporting gesture or if the Captain is uncertain that there was doubt about the method of dismissal, the umpire should give serious consideration to the request bearing in mind that the best interests of the game will probably lead him to allow the batsman to continue his innings no matter that he, himself, was not in doubt that the original decision was correct.

The appeal may only be withdrawn providing the batsman has not left the playing area. If the umpire wishes to consult his colleague, he should first ask the batsman to remain where he is since he cannot be recalled once he has crossed the boundary. Only the Captain of the fielding side may seek permission to withdraw the appeal. Permission to do so can only be granted by the umpire who, after due consideration, is prepared to reverse his decision. This in no way undermines the umpire's authority since the final decision rests with him. The umpires would not allow an appeal to be withdrawn if it was considered that the fielding Captain was attempting to gain an advantage by doing so.

Strength of the appeal

The frequency with which most of, if not all, the fielding side appeal has certainly increased. Experienced umpires will be aware that neither the volume of the appeal, nor the number of fielders making the appeal, has any relevance to the way in which it is answered. Occasionally a fielder, particularly the bowler, will make an appeal in an almost quizzical fashion; in this case the lack of volume is irrelevant, although it is reasonable to suppose that the fielder is by no means certain that the appeal will be answered in the affirmative. All appeals must be given due consideration.

Pressure will be exerted on the umpire by persistent appealing, particularly at crucial stages of the match. It is important that the umpire retains his self-control in such situations and gives calm, unhurried decisions to all appeals ignoring any posturing by members of the fielding side. Firmness, fairness and consistency are the qualities needed for a successful umpire to gain and keep the respect of the players.

LAW 28 THE WICKET IS DOWN

1 WICKET DOWN

The wicket is down if:

(a) **Either the ball or the Striker's bat or person completely removes either bail from the top of the stumps. A disturbance of a bail, whether temporary or not, shall not constitute a complete removal, but the wicket is down if a bail in falling lodges between two of the stumps.**

(b) **Any player completely removes with his hand or arm a bail from the top of the stumps, providing that the ball is held in that hand or in the hand of the arm so used.**

(c) **When both bails are off, a stump is struck out of the ground by the ball, or a player strikes or pulls a stump out of the ground, providing that the ball is held in the hand(s) or in the hand of the arm so used.**

2 ONE BAIL OFF

If one bail is off, it shall be sufficient for the purpose of putting the wicket down to remove the remaining bail, or to strike or pull any of the three stumps out of the ground in any of the ways stated in 1 above.

3 ALL THE STUMPS OUT OF THE GROUND

If all the stumps are out of the ground, the fielding side shall be allowed to put back one or more stumps in order to have an opportunity of putting the wicket down.

4 DISPENSING WITH BAILS

If owing to the strength of the wind, it has been agreed to dispense with the bails in accordance with Law 8: Note (a) (Dispensing With Bails) the decision as to when the wicket is down is one for the Umpires to decide on the facts before them. In such circumstances and if the Umpires so decide the wicket shall be held to be down even though a stump has not been struck out of the ground.

Notes

(a) REMAKING THE WICKET

If the wicket is broken while the ball is in play, it is not the Umpire's duty to remake the wicket until the ball has become dead – see **Law 23**: *(Dead Ball). A member of the fielding side, however, may remake the wicket in such circumstances.*

This Law and **Law 29** (Batsman Out of His Ground) set out the conditions for successful appeals under **Law 30** (Bowled); **Law 35** (Hit Wicket); **Law 38** (Run Out) and **Law 39** (Stumped).

The number of ways in which a wicket may be put down suggests possible complications for the umpire but, although the fielding side may sometimes not be certain of the action required to break the wicket, taken stage by stage the requirements should cause no problem.

Breaking the wicket

The wicket is broken if either bail is completely removed from the top of the stumps. A disturbance of the bail is not sufficient, even if the bail is observed to jump clear from the top of the stumps. If the bail lands back in the groove, the wicket has not been broken. Only one bail need be removed; should one bail be off, the wicket may be broken by the removal of the remaining bail. Should a bail lodge between two stumps it has been completely removed from the top of the stumps and the wicket has been broken.

If both bails have been removed, the fielding side may either replace one or both bails in order to break the wicket by the removal of a bail, or the ball, or the hand holding the ball must completely remove a stump from the ground. Note that the fielder must have the ball in the hand which is used to remove the stump. The wicket is not correctly broken if the fielder holds the ball in one hand and removes a stump with the other. Normally the fielder will use both his hands; providing the ball is held in one hand the umpire will regard the wicket as having been correctly broken.

For the fielding side to put the wicket down they must either hit the stumps direct or the ball must be in the possession of the fielder attempting to break the wicket. The fielder may use any part of his hand or arm to break the wicket but must have the ball in the hand or hands so used.

Equally the batsman may put the wicket down if he hits it with his bat, or any part of his person or equipment and displaces one or both bails.

Remaking the wicket

The fielding side may remake the wicket at any time. Providing one bail is placed back on top of the stumps, the wicket can be broken by the removal of that bail. Should all three stumps be out of the ground the fielding side need only replace one stump in order to put the wicket down, providing the ball is held in the hand or hands used to break the wicket.

The umpire should not remake the wicket until the ball has become dead. To do so whilst the ball was still in play would obviously be giving an advantage to the fielding side.

Bails dispensed with

As previously detailed under **Law 8**, the umpires may agree to dispense with the bails when there is continual displacement by a strong wind. Some umpires carry with them a pair of heavy bails, hoping to avoid discarding the bails, as the decision as to when the wicket is put down is very much easier when the bails are in place. Should the umpires be forced to remove the bails, extra vigilance is required to determine whether the fielding side have put the wicket down. The umpires can only make judgment on the facts as they see them. They must judge whether at least one bail would have been removed had the bails been in position. Any firm contact by the ball, or the hand holding the ball, will be sufficient. It is not necessary for the fielding side to remove a stump from the ground in order to break the wicket. There will be occasions when the fielding side will break the wicket on more than one occasion from the same delivery. When the bails are not being used, the fielding side are not required to uproot a stump nor should the umpire consider whether the bails might previously have been removed had they been in use. If one or more stump remains upright in the ground it will be sufficient for a fielder either to hit an upright stump with the ball, or with the ball in hand used, knock a stump with that hand or arm, even though the stump or stumps in the ground could not have supported a bail had they been in use.

An extra difficulty for the umpire is that he may not see any visible evidence, such as the movement of a stump, that contact has been made.

LAW 29 BATSMAN OUT OF HIS GROUND

1 WHEN OUT OF HIS GROUND

A Batsman shall be considered to be out of his ground unless some part of his bat in his hand or of his person is grounded behind the line of the popping crease.

Providing the umpire understands that the popping crease is the back (nearest the stumps) edge of the crease marking he should have little difficulty in determining whether the batsman is in his ground or not.

If the batsman has some part of his person, or bat in hand, **on** the crease marking he is not in his ground. He must have his bat in hand, or some part of his person grounded, behind the inside edge of the marking to be within his ground. Note that only the smallest part of the bat or person need be behind the popping crease and also that the bat must be held in the hand. The batsman cannot gain his ground by throwing his bat into his ground but he may, having dived to make good his ground, do so by placing his hand, or any other part of his person, behind the popping crease.

LAW 30 BOWLED

1 OUT BOWLED

The Striker shall be out bowled if:
(a) His wicket is bowled down, even if the ball first touches his bat or person.
(b) He breaks his wicket by hitting or kicking the ball on to it before the completion of a stroke, or as a result of attempting to guard his wicket. See Law 34.1: (Out – Hit the Ball Twice).

Notes

(a) OUT BOWLED – NOT L.B.W.
The Striker is out Bowled if the ball is deflected on to his wicket even though

141

a decision against him would be justified under **Law 36:** *(Leg Before Wicket).*

This is the first of ten Laws dealing with the ways in which a batsman can be given out by the umpire, after an appeal from the fielding side. A batsman cannot be given out unless an appeal has been made. The decision of the umpire is final although as detailed earlier he may change his mind providing it is done promptly. It is not overstressing the importance of the umpires' responsibility to state that an incorrect decision could ruin a match. Umpires must study the ten Laws until they are thoroughly understood; it is also important to participate in as much field practice as possible, at whatever level, to achieve the level of concentration necessary to carry out all duties with confidence.

Out Bowled
There are very few occasions when umpires are uncertain if a batsman has been bowled. The evidence is usually clear for all to see when a fair ball has been delivered and the wicket has been put down.

Not out Bowled
Two possible complications can arise. The first is a high wind blowing off one or both bails; the other is the ball rebounding from the wicket-keeper's pads, gloves or person and dislodging the bails. In both instances the striker's end umpire is better placed to advise what has happened and should be consulted before a decision is made. As explained under **Law 27** (Appeals) if there is any doubt remaining after consultation the decision must be not out. The umpire at the striker's end is required to concentrate fully on every delivery to ensure that he can give assistance to his partner, should he have any difficulty in determining exactly what has happened. With both umpires giving complete concentration and co-operating with each other, there should seldom be any doubt as to how the wicket was broken.

Ball hit or kicked on to wicket
If the striker plays the ball and then breaks the wicket by hitting

142

or kicking the ball on to the wicket before the completion of his stroke, he will be given out, on appeal, Bowled. He would not, however, be out Bowled, if after playing the ball, he hits or kicks it on to and thereby breaks his wicket *after* completing his stroke. Stroke completion is something that umpires must judge from the actions which they observe. Clearly the striker who has moved forward and then kicks or hits the ball on to the wicket, breaking it, in an attempt to regain his ground in order to avoid being stumped or run out would not be given out Bowled. If, however, he kicks or hits the ball on to his stumps in making a second stroke to protect his wicket, he is deemed not to have completed his stroke and will be given out, on appeal, Bowled.

The striker will be out Bowled if he plays the ball and it continues on to break the wicket without the intervention of any other person. Although the striker would not be out Bowled if the ball rebounds off the wicket-keeper, he might be given out Stumped, or Run Out, in such circumstances, if he was out of his ground when the wicket was broken.

LAW 31 TIMED OUT

1 OUT TIMED OUT

An incoming Batsman shall be out Timed Out if he wilfully takes more than two minutes to come in – the two minutes being timed from the moment a wicket falls until the new batsman steps on to the field of play.

If this is not complied with and if the Umpire is satisfied that the delay was wilful and if an appeal is made, the new Batsman shall be given out by the Umpire at the Bowler's end.

2 TIME TO BE ADDED

The time taken by the Umpires to investigate the cause of the delay shall be added at the normal close of play.

Notes

(a) ENTRY IN SCORE BOOK
The correct entry in the score book when a Batsman is given out under this Law is 'timed out', and the Bowler does not get credit for the wicket.

(b) BATSMEN CROSSING ON THE FIELD OF PLAY
It is an essential duty of the Captains to ensure that the in-going Batsman passes the out-going one before the latter leaves the field of play.

Responsibilities of Captains

The intention of this Law is to avoid time wasting, which is an unfair practice. The onus is placed very heavily upon the Captains, whose obligations include supervising the readiness of their batsmen, so that the outgoing and incoming batsmen cross on the field of play.

A tactful reminder to both Captains, during the pre-match discussion, that they should ensure that time is not wasted can be of considerable value in observance of this Law. The two minute time limit from the fall of the wicket until the incoming batsman appears on to the field of play is ample and should be regarded as a maximum and not as an allowance of two minutes. Once he steps on to the field his innings is considered to have commenced (see also **Law 2**).

Responsibilities of umpires

Both umpires should note the time of the fall of each wicket and also when the incoming batsman steps on to the field of play. If the period of time is longer than two minutes the umpires will take no action unless an appeal is made.

Action required by umpires

If an appeal is made, both umpires should note the time of the appeal and also agree how long has elapsed between the fall of the wicket and the appearance of the new batsman. Should the incoming batsman be on the field of play, and more than two minutes have elapsed, the umpires together will question him to ascertain whether the delay was wilful. It may be necessary to obtain confirmation of the details from the pavilion.

If the incoming batsman has failed to appear after two minutes have elapsed and an appeal is made, the umpires may be required to visit the pavilion to determine the cause of the delay. Again, the umpires are required to use their judgment to determine whether or not the delay was wilful.

Umpires will need all their tact to conduct a quiet and sensible investigation to determine the cause of the delay, without wasting any more time than is absolutely necessary. An injury, illness or some other unavoidable incident will not be interpreted as a wilful act by the batting side to waste time. The responsibility of the Captain, or his deputy, to ensure that the next batsman is ready to begin his innings will be one of the important factors that the umpires will bear in mind. Should they agree that the Law has been transgressed they will have no alternative but to give the incoming batsman out, Timed Out.

Time lost to be added
The time taken to investigate the circumstances of a batsman's delay in appearing on to the field must be added to the time agreed for the close of play on the day the incident occurs. The time to be added will be calculated from the moment of the appeal until either the incoming batsman is given out or until play recommences. If, on the last day of the match, the delay occurs before the last hour of the match, adjusting the time for the match to end will mean that the start of the minimum 20 overs will also be delayed by the same length of time. The adjustment to the finishing time will prevent the batting side from gaining an advantage by deliberate delay.

Field Technique
The responsibility for investigating any delay, after an appeal, must be carried out by **both** umpires. The decision which they reach will be conveyed to the players by the bowler's end umpire. Once the decision has been given and as soon as the umpires and players are in position the bowler's end umpire should call Play.

Scoring
The entry in the How Out column is 'Timed Out' and the bowler does not get credit for the wicket.

LAW 32 CAUGHT

1 OUT CAUGHT
The Striker shall be out Caught if the ball touches his bat or if it touches below the wrist his hand or glove, holding the bat, and is subsequently held by a Fieldsman before it touches the ground.

2 A FAIR CATCH

A catch shall be considered to have been fairly made if:

(a) The Fieldsman is within the field of play throughout the act of making the catch.

  (i) The act of making the catch shall start from the time when the Fieldsman first handles the ball and shall end when he both retains complete control over the further disposal of the ball and remains within the field of play.

  (ii) In order to be within the field of play, the Fieldsman may not touch or ground any part of his person on or over a boundary line. When the boundary is marked by a fence or board the Fieldsman may not ground any part of his person over the boundary fence or board, but may touch or lean over the boundary fence or board in completing the catch.

(b) The ball is hugged to the body of the catcher or accidentally lodges in his dress or, in the case of the Wicket-Keeper, in his pads. However, a Striker may not be caught if a ball lodges in a protective helmet worn by a Fieldsman, in which case the Umpire shall call and signal 'dead ball'. See Law 23: (Dead Ball).

(c) The ball does not touch the ground even though a hand holding it does so in effecting the catch.

(d) A Fieldsman catches the ball after it has been lawfully played a second time by the Striker, but only if the ball has not touched the ground since being first struck.

(e) A Fieldsman catches the ball after it has touched an Umpire, another Fieldsman or the other Batsman. However a Striker may not be caught if a ball has touched a protective helmet worn by a Fieldsman.

(f) The ball is caught off an obstruction within the boundary provided it has not previously been agreed to regard the obstruction as a boundary.

3 SCORING OF RUNS

If a Striker is caught, no runs shall be scored.

Notes

(a) SCORING FROM AN ATTEMPTED CATCH

When a Fieldsman carrying the ball touches or grounds any part of his person on or over a boundary marked by a line, 6 runs shall be scored.

(b) BALL STILL IN PLAY

If a Fieldsman releases the ball before he crosses the boundary, the ball will be considered to be still in play and it may be caught by another Fieldsman. However, if the original Fieldsman returns to the field of play and handles the ball, a catch may not be made.

Completion of a catch

The completion of a catch is defined as the retention of the ball by a member of the fielding side so that he has the power of complete control for its further disposal whilst remaining within the field of play. It is not possible to suggest a period of time during which the fielder must have possession of the ball. When the bowler accepts a fast return, the completion of the catch is almost instantaneous but, on another occasion, a fielder may juggle with the ball for an appreciable length of time before completing the catch. The umpire will assess completion of the catch as the instant the fielder has complete control over the further disposal of the ball in his hand. The fielder's hand may be in contact with the ground providing that the ball did not touch the ground at any time. A fielder who makes a diving catch but has the ball jarred from his grasp by contact with the ground would not be considered to have the ball in his control.

Judgment of a fair catch

Catches by the wicket-keeper standing up to the wicket are always difficult, even for the most experienced of umpires, since the distance between the bat and the wicket-keeper's gloves may not allow the umpire sufficient time to see any deflection. The essential qualities needed to judge how near the bat was to the ball at the one split second of action are complete concentration, good eyesight and hearing. Although good hearing is essential for an umpire, it is possible to be misled by a noise as the striker attempts to play at a ball. Sometimes it will be observed that the ball could not have been in contact with the bat even though there is a distinctive sound. If the bat is seen to be near the ball, any sound at that moment must be given serious consideration, even though the umpire should rely principally on what he observes rather than what he hears.

Catches down the leg side where there is a fine deflection are particularly difficult, as the batsman in playing at the ball may partially obstruct the umpire's view. He should not hesitate to consult his colleague at the striker's end who may have had a better view. The sound of the ball making contact with the striker's pad or clothing can be very similar to that resulting from the ball having very fine contact with the bat. Experience will assist the umpire in distinguishing between the two sounds.

Out Caught

To be out Caught the ball must have made contact with the bat, or the hand holding the bat. If the ball touches only the striker's wrist or any part of the forearm an appeal for Caught should be answered Not out. The modern trend for batting gloves to cover the whole of the wrist does not assist the umpire, a pitch length away, to determine whether the ball made contact on, above, or below the wrist. The umpire should only give the striker out Caught, on appeal, if the ball has touched the bat or hand holding the bat. The ball may also make contact with the striker's person or equipment, either before or after touching the bat or hand holding the bat. Providing the ball did not touch the ground after the first contact, whether it be the striker's equipment or the bat, the striker can be out Caught. The same principle applies with reference to **Law 26** (Bye and Leg Bye). If the ball touches the bat or hand holding the bat, even if contact is first made on the striker's person or equipment, any runs are credited to the striker; contact with the wrist or forearm only may result in leg byes being scored.

Some deflections are so fine that it is almost impossible for the umpire to see them. It is also possible for the sound of contact between bat and ball, particularly if very slight, to be carried away by the wind. If the umpire has not observed any deflection nor has heard any sound he must fearlessly answer an appeal Not out no matter how loud and concerted it may be. Nothing will have been seen or heard that can justify any other decision.

Consultation with colleague

An umpire in doubt as to whether a catch has been taken

cleanly may consult his partner providing his partner was in a better position to see the action. The bowler's end umpire may be prevented from seeing a catch taken close to the ground by a slip fielder or wicket-keeper. The bowler taking a fast return catch may block the line of sight of the bowler's end umpire. Striker's end umpire may have had a clear view of the action and should be consulted on the one point – to ascertain if the ball was taken cleanly. A quiet prearranged signal may be all that is necessary. The bowler's end umpire will give the decision, which must be Not out, should there be any doubt remaining after consultation.

Fielder making catch must remain in field of play

A fielder taking a catch must remain on the field of play from the first moment he is in contact with the ball until the catch is completed. The fielder having caught the ball may realize his momentum will carry him across the boundary and release the ball. Should he do this the ball is still in play and another member of the fielding side may catch or gather the ball. If the original fielder returns to the field and handles the ball, a lawful catch cannot be made either by him or by another fielder. The ball is not dead and play will continue.

If the boundary is marked by a fence or board the fielder may lean against, or over the fence or board, and complete the catch. Although allowed to touch, or lean against, a boundary board or fence a fielder in contact with the ball must not touch the boundary which is marked by a line or rope. If a fielder catches the ball and with ball in hand touches or grounds any part of his person *on or over* a boundary line the striker will not be out Caught and six runs will be awarded. Only if the fielder grounds any part of his person *over* a fence or board will the catch be invalidated and six runs scored. This will obtain even if the fence or board is not upright but should the fence or board be wholly on the ground any fielder in contact with it is clearly grounded on or over the boundary.

On large grounds in higher grades of cricket, the boundary will be anything from 50 to 90 yards from the centre of the ground. Even on smaller playing areas, umpires will often experience difficulty in seeing whether a fielder, running with ball in hand after catching it, has momentarily touched or grounded some part of his foot, or person, on or over the boundary line. The fielder himself may be concentrating solely on making the catch and be completely unaware whether he has stepped on or over the boundary line. Consultation will almost certainly be necessary, as the striker's end umpire may be able to give valuable assistance to his partner. Another member of the fielding side may also have been in a good position to provide information. Any question put should be quite straightforward: 'Was any part of the foot of the fielder on or over the line at any time?' In some cases the sportsmanship and honesty of the catcher will provide the answer and whilst it would be hoped that this will always be the case, as has been pointed out, the fielder may be unaware of his position in relation to the boundary line when taking the catch. Having gathered all information possible, backed by his own observations, the umpire must base his decision on the weight of evidence. If, after considering all the facts, doubt remains, the decision must be Not Out.

Ball lodging in dress or equipment

The striker is out Caught if he has played the ball and it lodges in the dress of a fielder, or the dress or pads of the wicket-keeper. If the ball lodges in the dress or pads of either batsman or the dress of an umpire no catch will be be made as the ball is immediately dead. This also applies if the ball lodges in a protective helmet worn by a fielder, wicket-keeper or batsman.

The ball is still in play if it strikes an umpire, the non-striker or a fielder and the striker will be out if the rebound is caught. If the ball is struck and is deflected off a protective helmet being worn by a fielder and then caught by another fielder, a fair catch has not been made; the ball remains in play. The striker would be out under this Law if having struck the ball it was deflected off the helmet, whether worn or not, of the non-striker and caught by a fielder. He would also be out if the ball is played from his bat on to his own protective helmet and caught by a fielder.

Emphasis has been placed earlier on the importance of the umpires agreeing at the pre-match meeting that any obstruction within the playing area shall be regarded as a boundary; this Law re-emphasizes the wisdom of such an agreement.

A catch will be considered as fair even if the ball touches the striker's person or equipment before or after touching his bat. The striker may also be given out Caught after making a lawful second strike (see **Law 34**). If a fielder, in attempting a catch, deflects the ball on to the wicket of the non-striker who is out of his ground and the ball is subsequently caught by a fielder, the striker will be out, on appeal, Caught, provided the ball has not touched the ground before being held, even though an appeal for running out the non-striker would otherwise have been upheld.

<u>Scoring</u>
No runs will be scored if the striker is out 'Caught'; any runs completed will be disallowed.

The entry in the How Out column is 'Caught' (often abbreviated to 'c' or 'ct') followed by the name of the fielder making the catch. If the fielder is a substitute the entry should be 'Caught sub'.

LAW 33 HANDLED THE BALL

1 OUT HANDLED THE BALL
Either Batsman on appeal shall be out Handled the Ball if he wilfully touches the ball while in play with the hand not holding the bat unless he does so with the consent of the opposite side.

Notes

(a) ENTRY IN SCORE BOOK
The correct entry in the score book when a Batsman is given out under this Law is 'handled the ball', and the Bowler does not get credit for the wicket.

<u>Out Handled the Ball</u>
An appeal against a batsman for handling the ball will always be an embarrassment to the umpire. It is for him to decide if the action was wilful rather than involuntary. Except when requested to do so by the opposing side batsmen should not touch the ball whilst it is still in play unless the hand is holding the bat.

The batsman is entitled to protect himself with his hand(s) if there is a possibility of the ball causing an injury. Such action will always be involuntary and cannot be construed as wilful.

Should either batsman touch the ball whilst it is still in play, even though with the best of intentions, an appeal will place the umpire in a most difficult situation. If the fielding side has not given consent, usually by a courteous word or two, the umpire will have the unpleasant duty of giving the batsman out, Handled the Ball. It is much better if batsmen leave the ball strictly for the fieldsmen to handle and so avoid the subsequent unpleasantness should an appeal be made.

As stated in **Law 2**, an injured batsman can be given out, Handled the Ball, if at any time he or his runner breaches this Law.

Field Technique
If an appeal for Handled the Ball is made it would be incumbent upon the umpires to determine whether the fielding side had granted the batsman permission to pick up the ball. In some cases the umpire will be aware that this was not so, but a question addressed to the Captain of the fielding side might diffuse an embarrassing situation.

Any runs completed before the batsman handles the ball will count. The scorers should be advised if any runs are to be recorded; they will need to be informed of the method of dismissal if a batsman is given out for handling the ball.

Scoring
The entry in the How Out column is 'Handled the Ball'; the bowler does not get credit for the dismissal.

LAW 34 HIT THE BALL TWICE

1 OUT HIT THE BALL TWICE
The Striker, on appeal, shall be out Hit the Ball Twice if, after the ball is struck or is stopped by any part of his person, he wilfully strikes it again with his bat or person except for the sole purpose of guarding his wicket: this he may do with his bat or any part of his person other than his hands, but see Law 37.2: (Obstructing a Ball From Being Caught).

For the purpose of this Law, a hand holding the bat shall be regarded as part of the bat.

2 RETURNING THE BALL TO A FIELDSMAN
The Striker, on appeal, shall be out under this Law, if,

without the consent of the opposite side, he uses his bat or person to return the ball to any of the fielding side.

3 RUNS FROM BALL LAWFULLY STRUCK TWICE
No runs except those which result from an overthrow or penalty, see Law 41: (The Fieldsman), shall be scored from a ball lawfully struck twice.

Notes

(a) ENTRY IN SCORE BOOK
The correct entry in the score book when the Striker is given out under this Law is 'hit the ball twice', and the Bowler does not get credit for the wicket.

(b) RUNS CREDITED TO THE BATSMAN
Any runs awarded under 3 above as a result of an overthrow or penalty shall be credited to the Striker, provided the ball in the first instance has touched the bat, or, if otherwise, as extras.

Out Hit the Ball Twice

Much of the comment added to the previous Law equally applies to this Law. Batsmen will sometimes use their bat or foot to return the ball to a member of the fielding side. If this is done without obtaining permission from the fielding side, and an appeal is made, the umpire has no choice but to give the striker out under this Law. Unless a request is made, which constitutes consent, the striker would be well advised to leave the fieldsmen to gather the ball.

Striker may protect his wicket

The striker is allowed to hit the ball a second time or use any part of his person, other than a hand not holding the bat, to protect his wicket. The umpire must be certain that the striker is hitting the ball for a second time for one purpose only – to guard his wicket. Close observation and concentration will assist the umpire in interpreting the actions and the intention of the striker. After playing the ball with his bat or person, the striker may legally protect his wicket with his bat, or hand holding the bat, or any part of his clothing, equipment or person, except his

153

hands. Although the word 'struck' implies a strike with the bat, in this Law, a second 'stroke' will have been made even if it is with the striker's person or equipment rather than off the bat. The striker may be out Hit the Ball Twice even though he has not at any time hit the ball with his bat.

The striker may cause doubt as to his intentions if he strikes the ball unnecessarily hard on his second attempt to hit the ball, or if he immediately sets off for a run having hit the ball twice. This may be due to the striker's ignorance of the Law but if there is an appeal the umpire can only answer according to what he has observed.

Striker may not obstruct attempted catch

If the striker in lawfully defending his wicket prevents the wicket-keeper or other fielder from attempting a catch, he may be given out, on appeal, for Obstructing the Field, even though legally playing the ball a second time (see **Law 37**).

Runs scored only from overthrows

No runs can be scored except from an award of penalty runs for illegal fielding or from overthrows. Full details as to what constitutes an overthrow are given under **Law 19**. The Law permits the batsmen to score runs from overthrows only. If the batsmen have crossed at the instant of a throw the run in progress will not be allowed but any subsequent run(s) will be scored. The run in progress having been disallowed, the umpire may need to advise the batsmen of the ends at which they should resume (see **Law 18**). If the overthrow crosses the boundary, only four runs would be scored and the batsmen would be required to return to their original ends.

There is no indication in the Law of the umpires' action if the batsmen run unlawfully. It is recommended that umpires treat the incident in the same way as running after an illegal deflection.

No ball is called

The striker will not be penalized if he makes a second stroke in defence of his wicket if No ball has been called, although strictly his wicket is not at risk. The umpires will apply the Law as to the legality of the second stroke, and the restriction on scoring runs, as if the delivery had been a fair one. Nevertheless, the striker will be out on appeal, Hit the Ball Twice, if No ball has been called and the umpire considers that the second stroke was not lawful.

Striker dismissed from a lawful second strike

The striker ·may be given out Bowled if in making a lawful second strike he hits or kicks the ball on to his wicket (**Law 30**). He may also be given out on appeal Caught (**Law 32**), Stumped (**Law 39**) or Hit wicket (**Law 35**). Either batsman may be given out Handled the Ball (**Law 33**), Obstructing the Field (**Law 37**) or Run out (**Law 38**) after the striker has made a lawful second strike.

On appeal, the striker will be out Caught if **either** strike is with the bat and the ball is subsequently held by a fielder in any of the ways described in **Law 32**, providing it has not been grounded at any time since the first strike, whether that was with the bat or not and whether it was an illegal deflection or not.

If the striker makes a lawful second strike, this will not affect decisions on Run Out, Stumped, Handled the Ball or Obstructing the Field except for the special case of obstruction when the striker's lawful attempt to guard his wicket interferes with the action of a wicket-keeper or a fielder attempting to take a catch.

This special case of obstruction is discussed in **Law 37**. Dismissal for Hit Wicket is dealt with under **Law 35**.

Scoring

As stated above, apart from the award of a penalty for No ball or illegal fielding, no runs may be scored from a second strike except runs resulting from an overthrow. Moreover, although the Law allows a second strike in defence of his wicket to be a deliberate deflection by the person, if the **first** strike was off the person of the striker, no runs (other than a No ball penalty) will be allowed unless he attempted to play the ball with his bat or tried to avoid being hit by the ball. The fact that the second strike may have been with the bat does not affect the prohibition on scoring if the first action was an illegal deflection.

If runs are scored, they will be credited to the striker only if the first strike was with the bat. Otherwise they will be recorded as No ball extras or leg byes as the case may be.

The system of signals described in detail in **Law 19** will tell the scorers *how* to record any runs. It is virtually certain that the umpires will need to advise them of the *number* of runs to be recorded.

If the striker is given out under this Law, for making a second stroke which was not in defence of his wicket, the entry in the How Out column of the score book is 'Hit the Ball Twice'. The bowler does not get credit for the wicket.

LAW 35 HIT WICKET

1 OUT HIT WICKET

The Striker shall be out Hit Wicket if, while the ball is in play:

(a) His wicket is broken with any part of his person, dress, or equipment as a result of any action taken by him in preparing to receive or in receiving a delivery, or in setting off for his first run, immediately after playing, or playing at, the ball.

(b) He hits down his wicket whilst lawfully making a second stroke for the purpose of guarding his wicket within the provisions of Law 34.1: (Out Hit the Ball Twice).

Notes

(a) NOT OUT HIT WICKET

A Batsman is not out under this Law should his wicket be broken in any of the ways referred to in 1(a) above if:

(i)   *It occurs while he is in the act of running, other than in setting off for his first run immediately after playing at the ball, or while he is avoiding being run out or stumped.*

(ii)   *The Bowler after starting his run-up or bowling action does not deliver the ball; in which case the Umpire shall immediately call and signal 'dead ball'.*

(iii)   *It occurs whilst he is avoiding a throw-in at any time.*

Striker's end jurisidiction

An appeal for Hit Wicket must be answered by the striker's end umpire. Consultation may be necessary, particularly if the striker's actions have prevented the umpire at the striker's end from seeing how the wicket was put down.

Striker out Hit Wicket

The striker is vulnerable under this Law from the moment the bowler starts his run-up or bowling action until immediately after he has played, or played at, the ball and set off for his first run. 'Any action' by the striker includes his backlift, providing the ball is in play, playing at the ball, any follow through of the bat and any action up to and including setting off for a first run immediately after playing, or playing at, the ball.

If the striker, in using any action to avoid a fairly delivered ball, breaks his wicket with any part of his person, dress or equipment he will be given out on appeal. A striker who falls on his wicket as a result of being struck by the ball will be out on appeal unless it is immediately obvious that the injury is serious and the umpire calls and signals Dead ball.

Within the provisions of **Law 34** the striker has the right to protect his wicket by attempting to stop or divert the ball with his bat or any part of his person (other than the hand), his clothing or equipment but should he break his wicket in doing so, on appeal, he will be out Hit Wicket.

If the striker having hit, or attempted to hit the ball is unbalanced, the striker's end umpire must concentrate on the striker until it is considered that the stroke has been completed. Any inclination to watch what has happened to the ball should be resisted.

Only if the striker breaks his wicket whilst making a stroke or in setting off for a run immediately after the completion of his stroke should he be given out under this Law. Having given full concentration to the striker's actions the umpire should have little difficulty in determining when the stroke has been completed; that is when the striker has full control of himself. Should he then set off for a first run, perhaps due to a misfield, or break his wicket whilst in the process of running or taking any action to avoid being injured or being run out any appeal for Hit Wicket will be unsuccessful. The Law also protects the striker who accidentally breaks his wicket in an attempt to avoid being Stumped, since such action is not adjudged to be part of his stroke.

Not out Hit Wicket

The striker can only be out Hit Wicket when playing at the ball or setting off for the first run. Neither batsman can be out Hit

Wicket if he breaks a wicket whilst running or in avoiding a throw, at any time, or avoiding being run out or stumped.

As previously explained, the ball is in play from the moment the bowler commences his run-up or bowling action and the striker is vulnerable from that moment. If, however, the striker breaks his wicket and the bowler then fails to deliver the ball the striker should not be given out under this Law. One of the umpires must call and signal Dead ball. This will usually be the umpire at the bowler's end.

Hit Wicket off a Wide ball

Hit Wicket is one of the ways in which the striker can be out if the bowler has bowled a Wide ball. Even though the striker may hit his wicket down before the ball passes the line of the stumps, both the penalty for the Wide ball and the dismissal will stand except in two special situations which are most unlikely to occur. If the striker hits his wicket before the ball is delivered, on appeal, and providing the ball is delivered, the striker will be given out at the moment of delivery and any subsequent action is irrelevant. The other exceptional circumstance is when, at the end of a match, nine wickets are down and one run is needed to win. In this case it has been decided that the Hit Wicket dismissal counts and the match is at an end; the penalty for the Wide is not awarded.

Field Technique

Striker's end umpire must give full concentration to the striker until the stroke has been completed resisting any temptation to watch the ball. Only when the stroke has been completed and the striker is balanced or has set off for his first run, should striker's end umpire attempt to locate the ball and watch any ensuing action.

Scoring

The entry in the How Out column in the score book is 'Hit Wicket'. The bowler receives credit for the dismissal.

LAW 36 LEG BEFORE WICKET

1 OUT L.B.W.
The Striker shall be out L.B.W. in the circumstances

set out below:

(a) *Striker Attempting to Play the Ball*
The Striker shall be out L.B.W. if he first inter-cepts with any part of his person, dress or equip-ment a fair ball which would have hit the wicket and which has not previously touched his bat or a hand holding the bat, provided that:

  (i) The ball pitched, in a straight line between wicket and wicket or on the off side of the Striker's wicket, or was intercepted full pitch, and

  (ii) the point of impact is in a straight line between wicket and wicket, even if above the level of the bails.

(b) *Striker Making No Attempt to Play the Ball*
The Striker shall be out L.B.W. even if the ball is intercepted outside the line of the off-stump, if, in the opinion of the Umpire, he has made no genuine attempt to play the ball with his bat, but has intercepted the ball with some part of his person and if the other circumstances set out in (a) above apply.

Without doubt, this is the Law that causes the most controversy. Bowlers are certain every delivery which hits the batsman's pad would have hit the wicket whereas batsmen will rarely accept they were correctly given out LBW. Umpires who are consid-ered to give erratic or hurried decisions will lose the respect of the players.

The Law contains much detail to which the umpire must give full consideration before he can answer any appeal for LBW. Aspiring umpires, having studied the implications of the Law, would benefit from attending net practices, preferably with the assistance of an experienced colleague to offer guidance.

It will be seen that Law is divided into two sections:

1. The striker attempting to play the ball.
2. The striker making no attempt to play the ball.

Both sections can be sub-divided into four basic questions which the umpire must be able to answer honestly and without

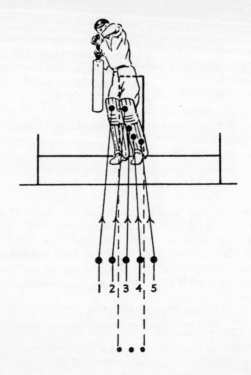

Figure 4

Ball 1: The point of impact on the Striker's person is not in a straight line between wicket and wicket – 'Not out'. But, as the point of impact is outside the line of the off stump, the Striker would be Out if he made no genuine attempt to play the ball – provided that the ball would have hit the wicket.

Ball 2: The ball would have hit the wicket – 'Out'. The Umpire must be satisfied that the ball is not rising sufficiently to pass over the top of the stumps.

Ball 3: The ball would have hit the wicket – 'Out'.

Ball 4: The ball pitched between wicket and wicket and providing the Umpire is satisfied that the break will not cause the ball to pass outside the off stump – 'Out'.

Ball 5: A ball pitching outside the line of the leg stump – 'Not out'.

160

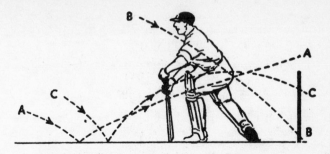

Figure 5   A: Lifting ball passing over the top of the stumps – 'Not out'.
B and C: Dropping balls which will hit the wicket – 'Out'.

doubt. If the answer to all four questions is 'Yes' the striker will be given out providing it was a fair delivery. The striker cannot be out LBW off a No ball. If there is the slightest doubt of the answer to any of the four questions the answer to the appeal must be Not out.

Striker attempting to play the ball

Question 1. Did the ball pitch in a straight line between wicket and wicket, or did it pitch on the off side of the striker's wicket, or was it intercepted full pitch?

As soon as the bowler's front foot has landed the umpire should look down the pitch and pick up, as quickly as possible, the flight of the ball. The earlier the ball is in vision the easier it will be to determine where the ball pitched. If it is intercepted full pitch, then the point of impact must be between wicket and wicket. If, however, the ball pitches, there is need to be certain only that the point at which it pitched was not outside leg stump. To give further consideration to an appeal for LBW, *either* the ball must have pitched, or been intercepted full pitch, between wicket and wicket, *or* it must have pitched outside the line of the off stump. A ball which has pitched on the line of the leg stump has pitched between wicket and wicket but the striker cannot be out LBW to a ball which pitches, or is intercepted full pitch, outside the leg stump.

One difficulty for the umpire is that the leg stump is usually obscured from his vision by the striker. On taking up position at the start of the match the umpire is advised to get a clear mental picture of where the stumps are in relation to any marks on the pitch or any other suitable markers.

> **Question 2.** Was it part of the striker's person, dress or equipment and not the bat, or hand holding the bat, which first intercepted the ball?

If the striker plays at the ball with his bat very close to his pad, particularly when playing forward, difficulty may be experienced in determining whether the *first* point of contact was the bat or the pad. This demands the fullest concentration by the umpire; the slightest snick off the bat or hand holding the bat before, almost immediately, the ball impacts on the pad is sufficient for an appeal for LBW to be answered Not out. The appeal could be successful, however, if the ball first made contact with the pad before hitting the bat, providing all other conditions are met. Judgment by sound alone, or by sight alone, will not always prove reliable. Both senses must be used in conjunction for the umpire to determine what was the *first* interception of the ball.

It can happen that the ball will be deflected from one part of the striker's person, dress or equipment on to another part; perhaps from the front pad on to the back pad. The *first* impact only will be considered for a decision on LBW even though it may be the second impact which prevents the ball from hitting the wicket. Note that the Law uses the term 'any part of his person, dress or equipment'; the striker could be out LBW if he ducks down to avoid a short delivery which does not rise and which hits him somewhere on the body.

> **Question 3.** Was that part of the striker's person, dress or equipment which first intercepted the ball between wicket and wicket at impact, even if above the level of the bails?

Despite answers of 'yes' to the two previous questions, the striker cannot be out LBW unless the part of his person, dress or equipment which was first struck by the ball was between wicket and wicket at the moment it was struck. It is important that judgment is made at the precise moment the ball strikes, remembering that the strip between wicket and wicket is only 9 inches wide. The striker will very often be well outside the 9 inch strip within a split second after the ball has struck him although he was in front of the wicket at the moment of impact, or vice versa. Often the striker will bend his knee away from the wicket after impact. The umpire must strive for complete concentration so that his observation of the striker's position at the moment the ball first made contact is clear, no matter if, after subsequent movement the striker looks round to suggest that he was not between wicket and wicket when struck. If the first point of impact on the striker's person, dress or equipment is high, even above the level of the bails, he may still be out under this Law providing the point of impact was between wicket and wicket and the other conditions for a successful appeal are met.

Question 4. Would the ball have hit the wicket?

The three previous questions are answered by the umpire as a result of his assessment of what he has seen or heard. This last question can only be answered by the umpire's opinion; his prediction as to whether the ball would have hit the wicket had it not been intercepted. A decisive answer must be made. If the umpire has the slightest doubt that the ball would have hit the wicket, not only are the answers to the first three questions irrelevant, but the appeal must be turned down. It is obviously impossible to be certain; indeed there will be many occasions when the bowler and close fielders will express astonishment that a delivery (which did not hit the striker) did not hit the wicket. The opinion must be one made by the umpire alone. He is stationary and in the best position on the field to judge the further travel of the ball and he should have no regard for the strength of the appeal nor the behaviour of the players.

Striker making no attempt to play the ball

Question 1, for a ball that pitches, Questions 2 and 4 remain exactly the same and must still be answered 'yes' for an appeal to be upheld. There is however an important amendment both to Question 3, whether the ball pitches or not, and for the full-pitch interception in Question 1. If the striker does not attempt to play the ball, the interception may be either between wicket and wicket *or outside the line of the off stump*.

So that in addition to

    Was that part of the person, dress or equipment which first

intercepted the ball between wicket and wicket at impact, even if the impact was above the level of the bails?

the umpire must also consider

Was that part of the striker's person, dress or equipment which first intercepted the ball outside the line of the off stump at impact; even if the impact was above the level of the bails?

The criterion here is whether or not the striker made a genuine attempt to play the ball with his bat. The umpire, and only the umpire, will decide the striker's sincerity in attempting to play the ball. If it is considered the striker did not make a genuine attempt to play the ball, he may be out LBW if each of the other three questions are answered 'yes'.

Travelling distance after pitching
The importance of the umpire sighting the ball as soon as possible after it leaves the bowler's hand has been emphasized. Once the ball has pitched it is not possible to assess any movement (swing) there may have been through the air. The period of time for which the ball can be seen after it has pitched and before it impacts on the striker's person is most important. The longer the time the umpire has the ball in view, after it has pitched, the easier it is for him to predict the further flight after impact. Thus a fast delivery will need to be seen for a longer distance than one bowled by a slow bowler.

Striker playing forward
When the striker plays forward, the distance between pitching and impact will be reduced. The bowler's end umpire has the disadvantage that the striker is moving towards him, foreshortening the umpire's line of sight, giving the impression that the striker has moved forward much less than he has. The impact, on the striker's person, will be some distance in front of the wicket. The reduced distance between pitching and impact and consequently the shorter time the ball can be held in sight added to the distance between impact and the wicket makes it extremely difficult for the umpire to predict that the ball would have hit the wicket. Nevertheless, if the striker plays forward he can be given out under this Law providing the umpire is certain,

beyond doubt, that the ball would have gone on to hit the wicket.

The judgment of the umpire will be made more difficult if the ball is swinging or turning off the pitch. A very slight deviation may cause the ball to miss the wicket. Unless the umpire has the ball in view for sufficient time after it has pitched, he cannot predict with certainty the further travel of the ball.

If a full toss impacts on the striker, the prediction of further flight must be based on what the umpire has seen up to the point of impact. He may consider that had there been no interception the ball would have continued on the path on which it was already travelling. The visual evidence up to the point of impact is of paramount importance; what the ball might or might not have done had it pitched has to be speculative with no evidence to assist the umpire to arrive at a conclusion. The nearer to the stumps that the point of impact is, the less significance there will be in this uncertainty as to what might have happened on pitching. For an impact fairly close to the stumps, if the umpire forms the opinion that the ongoing line of the delivery would have caused the ball to hit the wicket, he is in a position to consider an affirmative answer to question number four. On the other hand, if the striker well forward of the crease intercepts the ball full toss, the umpire must of necessity have much greater difficulty in arriving at a firm conclusion that the ball would have hit the wicket. Unless the ball would have pitched close to the stumps, the decision must be Not Out.

Striker playing back
The case of the striker playing back, or not moving forward, to a full toss is less difficult for the umpire who will have more time to judge the movement of the ball through the air. The interception will also be much nearer the wicket than for a forward playing batsman, making it easier for the umpire to predict the further travel.

The striker playing back to a ball that has pitched means, too, that the distance between pitch and impact is likely to be longer. The umpire can then keep the ball, after pitching, in view for a longer period and is consequently able to predict the further travel with greater accuracy. The nearer the stumps the impact on the striker's person, the easier it is for the umpire to decide whether the ball would have hit the wicket.

Rising delivery

Whether the striker is playing forward or not, the ball may be rising sufficiently to pass over the bails. If the ball is rising and hits the striker above bail height (Figure 5), it is reasonable to assess that the ball will pass over the bails. But, if the ball is dropping when it hits the striker, even if the point of impact is well above bail height, the ball could have gone on to hit the wicket but for the interception. The height of the impact on the striker's person is one of the important considerations for the umpire; an inch or two variation of the point of impact can make the difference between the ball hitting or missing the wicket.

Umpire's Technique

As previously stated umpires who are considered to be erratic in their LBW decisions will lose the respect of the players. It is, therefore, important that umpires should study the Law closely and take every opportunity to read other explanations of the subject. Demonstrations with mechanical equipment can greatly enhance the umpire's understanding. Theoretical training and knowledge, however, can only supplement field work where the umpire is alone in making the decision.

Each appeal, however loud, however subdued, or even manifestly absurd must be considered and answered with complete impartiality. Some appeals for LBW, where the facts are obvious, can be dealt with quickly. Many, however, will need a few seconds of reflection before giving a clear and deliberate answer. The best umpires are never caught unawares and take time to answer appeals however loud or concerted.

LAW 37 OBSTRUCTING THE FIELD

1 WILFUL OBSTRUCTION
Either Batsman, on appeal, shall be out Obstructing the Field if he wilfully obstructs the opposite side by word or action.

2 OBSTRUCTING A BALL FROM BEING CAUGHT
The Striker, on appeal, shall be out should wilful obstruction by either Batsman prevent a catch being made.

This shall apply even though the Striker causes the

166 NO Ball vin obstricy calch
NSmker obstricts catch — he is out,
nt striker.

obstruction in lawfully guarding his wicket under the provisions of Law 34. See Law 34.1: (Out Hit the Ball Twice).

Notes

(a) ACCIDENTAL OBSTRUCTION
The Umpires must decide whether the obstruction was wilful or not. The accidental interception of a throw-in by a Batsman while running does not break this Law.

(b) ENTRY IN SCORE BOOK
The correct entry in the score book when a Batsman is given out under this Law is 'obstructing the field', and the bowler does not get credit for the wicket.

Although appeals under this Law are the responsibility of the bowler's end umpire, his partner at the striker's end may often be in a better position to see an act of obstruction. Consultation will often be justified and necessary.

Was the obstruction wilful?
The dominant word used in this Law is 'wilfully'. Umpires are required to differentiate between accidental or involuntary obstruction, and wilful obstruction of the fielding side by either batsman. Although accidental obstructions can easily occur, fortunately for the game, wilful obstruction by batsmen is infrequent. Umpires will, however, have to give serious consideration to obstruction by a batsman if this appears to the fielding side to be unfair and an appeal is made.

Physical obstruction can take different forms, including a batsman running into a fielder. The batsman who shouts or comments as a fielder is about to take a catch is an example of obstruction by word rather than deed. Decisions as to the wilfulness of an obstruction must be based not only on close observation of the incident, supplemented if necessary by consultation between the umpires, but also on common sense. Too hasty a decision may lead to the wrong conclusion. The umpire must have no doubt that what the batsman did, or what he said, was a deliberate attempt to hinder the fielding side unfairly.

A batsman accidentally deflecting a ball from a throw-in will not be considered to be wilfully obstructing the field. The ball will remain in play; any further runs scored will be allowed; the batsmen will remain vulnerable to any subsequent dismissal. Players often regard the taking of further runs in this situation as unfair. While for the batsmen to refrain from running accords with the highest ethics of the game, it is not mandatory in Law.

The striker may also be given out under this Law if, in lawfully guarding his wicket, his second strike interferes with action of the wicket-keeper or of a fielder attempting to take a fair catch. The obstruction may not in this case be wilful, but an otherwise legitimate attempt to defend his stumps. Nevertheless, the Law makes it clear, that wilful or not, this is to be considered as obstructing a catch and the striker must suffer the penalty.

Which batsman is out

In most cases, of course, whichever batsman was responsible for the action will be the one who is out on appeal, if the umpire considers the obstruction was wilful. If, however, a batsman wilfully prevents a lawful catch being made, the striker will be given out, whether he caused the obstruction himself or whether it was the non-striker who did.

This is a particular case when an injured batsman, who is not taking strike, may be given out. He is to stand where he does not interfere with play, but if he brings himself into the game he must suffer the penalty for any transgression of the Law (**Law 2**). An obstruction of the fielding side is one way in which he may bring himself into the game. If there is an appeal, the umpires will have to give consideration to the wilfulness of the action. If it is wilful, then he will be given out. His runner is also vulnerable under this Law.

Scoring

The method of dismissal may not be clear to the scorers, the more so if the striker is given out, although the non-striker caused the obstruction. The entry of runs is by no means straightforward. In the case of the striker being dismissed because an obstruction prevented a catch being taken, no runs will be allowed. In all other cases, any runs completed before the incident are to be counted. It is therefore essential that the umpires ensure that the scorers are fully aware of what occurred.

The entry in the How Out column in the score book is 'Obstructing the Field'; the bowler does not get credit for the wicket.

LAW 38 RUN OUT

1 OUT RUN OUT
Either Batsman shall be out Run Out if in running or at any time while the ball is in play – except in the circumstances described in Law 39: (Stumped) – he is out of his ground and his wicket is put down by the opposite side. If, however, a Batsman in running makes good his ground he shall not be out Run Out if he subsequently leaves his ground, in order to avoid injury, and the wicket is put down.

2 'NO BALL' CALLED
If a 'no ball' has been called, the Striker shall not be given Run Out unless he attempts to run.

3 WHICH BATSMAN IS OUT
If the Batsmen have crossed in running, he who runs for the wicket which is put down shall be out; if they have not crossed, he who has left the wicket which is put down shall be out. If a Batsman remains in his ground or returns to his ground and the other Batsman joins him there, the latter shall be out if his wicket is put down.

4 SCORING OF RUNS
If a Batsman is run out, only that run which is being attempted shall not be scored. If however an injured Striker himself is run out, no runs shall be scored. See Law 2.7: (Transgression of the Laws by Injured Batsman or Runner).

Notes

(a) BALL PLAYED ON TO OPPOSITE WICKET
If the ball is played on to the opposite wicket neither Batsman is liable to be Run Out unless the ball has been touched by a Fieldsman before the wicket is broken.

(b) ENTRY IN SCORE BOOK
The correct entry in the score book when the Striker is given out under this

169

Law is 'run out', and the Bowler does not get credit for the wicket.

(c) RUN OUT OFF A FIELDSMAN'S HELMET
If, having been played by a Batsman, or having come off his person, the ball rebounds directly from a Fieldsman's helmet on to the stumps, with either Batsman out of his ground, the Batsman shall be 'Not Out'.

Both this Law and the next one (Stumped) deal with a batsman being dismissed because, with the ball in play, he is out of his ground when the wicket is fairly put down by the fielding side. It is therefore essential that umpires have a clear understanding of what is meant both by 'the wicket is put down' (**Law 28**) and by 'out of his ground' (**Law 29**). For 'the wicket is down', the main points are that a fielder can throw the wicket down with the ball, he can put it down with the ball in his hand, or even with his arm, provided that he has the ball in the hand of that arm. He cannot legally put the wicket down with one hand, with the ball in the other hand. There are, however, many other detailed points in this Law which should be re-examined.

To be 'in his ground' the batsman must have some part of his person, or his bat in hand, grounded behind the line of the popping crease, that is behind the back edge of the popping crease marking. Allied to this is understanding of what is *his ground*. It is *his ground* if either he is in that ground, or he is nearer to it than the other batsman is, although this simple definition does not quite cover all the points. These are discussed in detail, together with the batsmen crossing, under the Law on scoring (**Law 18**). That discussion should be revisited.

Avoiding injury
It is not sufficient for a batsman merely to make good his ground. In order to avoid the risk of being run out he must stay within his ground until the ball is dead. There is one exception. If he has left his ground to avoid injury, and the wicket is fairly put down while he is thus temporarily out of his ground, he will not be run out. Perhaps he jumped in the air, fearing to be hit on the ankle; perhaps, with only his bat grounded behind the line, he ducked sharply to avoid the throw-in and in this movement raised his bat off the ground. It will be for the umpire

170

Figure 6 (*Top*) The batsmen have crossed and A running for wicket is 'Run out'. (*Lower*) The batsmen have not crossed and B leaving wicket is 'Run out'.

alone to decide that his action, whatever form it takes, is a genuine attempt to avoid injury. On many occasions it will be obvious that this was the case; on other occasions the umpire must use his common sense and experience in making the judgment. He would be wise to consult his colleague.

Which batsman is out

A batsman is out under this Law if, while the ball is in play, he is out of *his ground* and the wicket is fairly put down by the fielding side at *his end*. This definition avoids the difficulties associated with 'he that runs for the wicket' and 'he that has left the wicket'. Except in the special case of an injured striker, discussed below, the crucial point is whether or not the batsmen had crossed in running, at the moment when the wicket was put down. Figure 6 above shows the provisions in the Law, covering which batsman is out if they are running and a wicket is put down by the fielding side. In the upper diagram, they have crossed and the wicket is put down at A's end. In the lower diagram, the batsmen have not crossed and now it is B's end where the wicket is put down.

It would be helpful to study again the discussion about 'Batsmen Crossing' in **Law 18**. It will be remembered that if one batsman stays within his crease then no crossing can take place. If for example the striker is within his ground at the wicket-keeper's end, and the non-striker joins him there, there has been no crossing. If the wicket is put down at the bowler's end, it will be the non-striker who is out. If, however, the striker stands outside his crease and the non-striker passes him there, then the batsmen 'have crossed in running' even though the striker was not physically running. Now, if the wicket is put down at the bowler's end, it will be the striker who is out. He will be deemed to be the one who is running for that end, because that is now *his end*. If both batsmen arrive at the same end, then whichever made good the ground first is the one who can claim it as *his end*. If both batsmen are in the same ground, and one of them then leaves it, then the ground at the other end will become *his ground*. It will also be remembered that 'shoulder to shoulder' is taken to be 'not yet crossed'.

Injured striker

The injured striker may be out of his ground playing at the ball and not able to return to his ground. He may start to run in spite of his injury. Whatever the reason, if he is out of his ground, **Law 2** makes it clear that should the wicket be put down at the wicket-keeper's end, the injured striker is the one who will be run out, irrespective of the position of his runner or of the non-striker. The wicket-keeper's end is always *his ground*. If he remains within it, or returns to it after playing at the ball, before the wicket is put down, then he will not himself be run out. In that case, the runner and non-striker are alternately at risk at that end, as they cross.

Conversely, for an injured striker, the bowler's end is never *his end*. If the wicket is put down at the bowler's end, then only the positions of the runner and the non-striker need be considered in adjudicating on an appeal for a possible run out. See **Law 2**.

The new batsman will go to the end at which the wicket was put down. There is often confusion when there is a runner as well as two batsmen and the umpire must be ready to direct the batsmen to the correct ends.

No Ball

While the striker cannot in any circumstances be stumped if No ball has been called, he may be run out from a No ball, but only if he is attempting a run. If running has already taken place, then the question does not arise. If the wicket is put down at the striker's end and there is an appeal, when there has been no running since the striker played at the ball, it will be for the umpire to decide whether he is out of his ground to attempt a run, or not. If the striker is attempting to run, the wicket-keeper may run him out, with or without the intervention of another fielder. A fielder could also run him out directly.

If he is out of his ground in playing at the ball, but for any reason has not returned to his ground, and if the umpire judges that he is not attempting a run, then he cannot be run out if No ball is called. In the case of an injured striker, it should be noted that whenever the runner is out of his ground he is deemed to be attempting a run. Consequently, while the injured striker himself will not be liable to be run out if No ball has been called, his runner will be. The call of No ball will not affect run out in the case of the non-striker.

Helmets

If the ball rebounds from a helmet worn by a batsman, either the striker or the non-striker, this will have no effect on a decision for run out.

If the ball rebounds from a helmet worn by a fielder then the ball is still in play. Nevertheless, should it rebound directly on to the stumps, neither batsman is liable to be run out from this breaking of the wicket. The batsman would only be liable to be run out if, after hitting the fielder's helmet, the wicket was put down by the further action of one of the fielding side.

If the ball strikes a fielder's helmet placed on the ground, then the ball becomes automatically dead. This is dealt with in greater detail under **Law 41**. If, of course, the ball lodges in a batsman's helmet or a fielder's helmet, the ball will be automatically dead and no dismissal will be valid.

Ball played on to the opposite wicket

Many players still believe that if the striker plays the ball directly back down the pitch to break the wicket at the bowler's end, then the non-striker will automatically be run out on appeal if he is out of his ground. While it is true that the non-striker may be run out in these circumstances, an appeal will be upheld only if a member of the fielding side made contact with the ball after it left the striker's bat and before it broke the wicket.

Run out before the ball is delivered

Law 24 (No Ball) deals with attempts by the bowler to run out either the striker or the non-striker before the ball is delivered. Once the bowler has started his run-up, the ball is in play. Consequently either batsman is at risk of being run out. The Law sets out three different circumstances

1 The bowler attempts to run out the non-striker before delivering the ball
If the non-striker leaves his ground before the bowler has delivered the ball, then the bowler may stop before delivery and put down the non-striker's wicket in any of the recognized ways. In order for such an attempt to be valid, however, it must be made before the bowler completes his delivery action. If he goes right through the delivery swing before attempting to break the wicket, the umpire will call and signal Dead ball, and any appeal will not be upheld. If the attempt to run out the non-striker fails, the batsmen are entitled to run. The umpire does not call No ball but any runs accruing are to be scored as No ball extras. The ball does not count as one of the over.

Over the years a convention has become established that the bowler must warn the backing up non-striker before taking action against him. This is commendably within the spirit of the game but has no more status than a convention. It is not mandatory in Law. If the non-striker is out of his ground when the wicket is properly put down, and there is an appeal, the umpire must give the decision Out, whether or not a warning has been given.

2 The bowler attempts to run out the striker before delivering the ball
If the striker is out of his ground before the ball is delivered, the bowler is entitled to throw the ball at the striker's wicket in an attempt to run him out. Such a throw is not to be distinguished from any other throw in delivering the ball. Whether the bowler stops in mid run or action and throws, or whether he throws the ball in his delivery stride, either umpire – but usually the striker's end umpire – will instantly call and signal No ball. All the normal consequences of a No ball call will follow. The striker cannot be run out unless the umpire adjudges that he is attempting a run; there will another ball in the over and a penalty of one run, unless the batsmen score runs in some other way, which, if the striker is not given out, they are entitled to do.

3 Both batsmen attempt to run before the bowler delivers the ball
Such an attempt is specifically cited as unfair in **Law 42**. The bowler is entitled to try to run out either batsman, as set out

above. If he does not make such an attempt, then as soon as the batsmen cross, the umpire at the bowler's end will call and signal Dead ball. No run will be allowed. The batsmen must return to their original ends.

Field Technique

To judge a run out, the umpire must be in a position to see both that the wicket was fairly put down by the fielding side and simultaneously that the batsman was or was not within his ground. For the bowler's end umpire this means moving rapidly away from his position behind the stumps. In any case he must do this if the batsmen run, to check the completion of each run at his end. He must do everything in his power to move into a position from which he can clearly see the crease, the batsman, the ball and the breaking of the wicket. This will be sideways on to the creases, as far away from the stumps as possible, and in general on the side to which the ball has been played. If he is on the other side of the wicket then his view may be impeded by a fielder standing with the stumps between himself and the fielder throwing in the ball. The striker's end umpire is already square on to the creases, but cannot move to the other side of the stumps, so may be unsighted by a fielder, or the wicket-keeper. He must be prepared to move aside, in order to see the breaking of the wicket and the crease. If in spite of his best endeavours either umpire is unsighted, his colleague may be in a position to see whether or not the wicket was fairly broken.

It will not always be possible to move into the perfect position for observation, but having reached the best position available to him the umpire must apply the greatest concentration at the crucial moment. He must particularly try to have his head still at that instant. The beginner umpire may find difficulty in watching everything involved in the action, without concentrating too much on one feature. The experienced umpire will form a contained picture of the action and make his decision accordingly. Beside being in the best position he can, the most important thing is for the umpire to stay calm and controlled, however fast and excited the action and however heavy the pressure.

If an injured striker has a runner, then of course the runner may be run out. The umpires must ensure that as well as the wicket and the creases, they can also see the runner, who is likely to be running at some distance from the wicket. The umpire must nevertheless be able to see whether or not he is within his ground at the breaking of the wicket. He must of course also be checking for short runs. The bowler's end umpire must now move, not necessarily to the side where the ball has been played, but to the side of the wicket opposite to that on which the runner is running. The striker's end umpire will position himself and the runner on opposite sides of the wicket from the start.

If the striker plays the ball straight back, so that there is a possibility of the non-striker being run out, the umpire at that end must anticipate the bowler or fielder deflecting the ball on to the non-striker's wicket. He will not have time to move far during this split second action, but must give himself the best chance of seeing the facts in adjudicating on the appeal.

He must equally be aware of the position of the non-striker during the bowler's run-up. The umpire must be ready for an appeal if the bowler makes an attempt to run out the non-striker before delivering the ball. His prime duty, however, is first to watch the placing of the bowler's feet in his delivery stride, then to follow the subsequent events during the flight of the ball and thereafter as the striker receives it. He must not divert his attention from these vital matters by dwelling too long on where the non-striker may be.

Both umpires must watch the batsmen in running, so that if a run out is likely at one end, the umpire at the other end knows whether or not the batsmen had crossed at the instant that the wicket was put down.

Scoring

The entry of Run Out in the How Out column of the score book is straightforward. The bowler does not get credit for the wicket. Although it is not essential to do so, advanced scorers will wish to show in the bowling analysis where the run out occurred, and the runs, if any, from the delivery. There will be no runs if an injured striker himself is run out; otherwise, all completed runs will be counted except the one being attempted.

The case of an attempt to run out the non-striker before delivering the ball is a difficult one for scorers. No ball will not be called, but any runs accruing will be scored as No ball extras. The umpires must ensure that they know what has happened. The ball has been neither delivered nor received, yet a wicket may fall, or runs accrue from it. Many scorers will make a side note to explain the circumstances. It is essential, in any case, that the umpires inform the scorers of the detail of what those circumstances are.

LAW 39 STUMPED

1 OUT STUMPED

The Striker shall be out Stumped if, in receiving the ball, not being a no ball, he is out of his ground otherwise than in attempting a run and the wicket is put down by the Wicket-Keeper without the intervention of another Fieldsman.

2 ACTION BY THE WICKET-KEEPER

The Wicket-Keeper may take the ball in front of the wicket in an attempt to Stump the Striker only if the ball has touched the bat or person of the Striker.

Notes

(a) BALL REBOUNDING FROM WICKET-KEEPER'S PERSON
The Striker may be out Stumped if in the circumstances stated in 1. above, the wicket is broken by a ball rebounding from the Wicket-Keeper's person or equipment other than a protective helmet or is kicked or thrown by the Wicket-Keeper on to the wicket.

This Law is similar to the previous one, Run Out, in that a batsman may be dismissed on appeal because, with the ball in play, he is out of his ground when the wicket is fairly put down by the fielding side. There are however important differences.

Special conditions for stumping
Only the striker can be given out Stumped. He must not be attempting a run. The delivery must not be a No ball. The wicket must be put down by the keeper without the intervention of any other fielder.

Attempting a run
If the wicket is put down and there is an appeal, the umpire will have to decide whether or not any movement by the striker

constitutes an attempt to run. If he decides that there *was* an attempt to run, then the striker cannot be given out Stumped. He might in these circumstances be run out.

No ball and Wide ball
If No ball is called, the striker cannot be given out Stumped in any circumstances. He will not be given Run Out either, unless he is attempting a run. It is often when there is the prospect of a stumping that the wicket-keeper will come too far forward, in his anxiety to take the ball and break the wicket before the striker can return to his ground. The striker's end umpire must of course always be vigilant for a possible No ball if the wicket-keeper does not remain behind the stumps. He is allowed to come in front before the ball reaches the wicket, only if it has first touched the bat or person of the striker, or the striker attempts a run. In the latter case, of course, the striker could not be given out Stumped, but Run Out might be considered

The call of Wide ball does not affect a decision for stumping.

The wicket is put down
The striker cannot be out Stumped if the wicket is put down by the action of a fielder, or by the wicket-keeper after the intervention of a fielder. In such circumstances a decision of Run Out may be justified.

The wicket-keeper can put down the wicket in any of the recognized ways. It is also allowable for the wicket to be broken by the ball rebounding from the wicket-keeper's pads, or any other part of his person, other than his helmet.

If the wicket is broken by the ball rebounding from the wicket-keeper's helmet, then the ball is still in play, but the striker cannot be given out Stumped, nor, for that matter, can he be run out from that breaking of the wicket.

Injured striker
If an injured striker has a runner, and the wicket is put down in the circumstances which could justify a decision of Stumped, there are two possibilities. The striker himself may be out of his ground. In that case, he will himself be out Stumped.

If the injured striker is in his ground, but the runner is not, then the striker will be out for the transgression by his runner, but the method of dismissal will be Run Out.

Unlike Run Out, a stumping dismissal will be credited to the bowler. There can of course be no runs from that delivery, other than a penalty for a Wide ball, if applicable.

It will be essential that the scorers know whether the dismissal is Run Out or Stumped. There will occasions when this will not be clear to them. There will be a particular difficulty for them in deciding which it is, if there is an injured striker with a runner. The umpires must ensure that they know what has occurred.

LAW 40 THE WICKET-KEEPER

1 POSITION OF WICKET-KEEPER

The Wicket-Keeper shall remain wholly behind the wicket until a ball delivered by the Bowler touches the bat or person of the Striker, or passes the wicket, or until the Striker attempts a run.

In the event of the Wicket-Keeper contravening this Law, the Umpire at the Striker's end shall call and signal 'no ball' at the instant of delivery or as soon as possible thereafter.

2 RESTRICTION ON ACTIONS OF THE WICKET-KEEPER

If the Wicket-Keeper interferes with the Striker's right to play the ball and to guard his wicket, the Striker shall not be out, except under Laws 33: (Handled the Ball), 34: (Hit the Ball Twice), 37: (Obstructing the Field), 38: (Run Out).

3 INTERFERENCE WITH THE WICKET-KEEPER BY THE STRIKER

If in the legitimate defence of his wicket, the Striker interferes with the Wicket-Keeper, he shall not be out, except as provided for in Law 37.2: (Obstructing a Ball From Being Caught).

Position and movement of wicket-keeper
The position of a wicket-keeper standing back to a fast or medium fast bowler will cause no concern. When the wicket-keeper is standing up to the stumps it is essential for the striker's end umpire to keep him under close observation.

The wicket-keeper must remain wholly behind the wicket from the moment the ball comes into play until the striker has touched the ball with his bat, person or equipment; or attempts a run; or until the ball passes the wicket. The intention of this Law is to safeguard the striker's right to receive and play at a delivery without any interference by a member of the fielding side. While there may be little interference if the wicket-keeper has the tips of his gloves, or the peak of his cap, in front of the line of the wicket as the bowler starts his run up, it is not for the umpire to determine whether any encroachment however slight causes interference, nor whether the wicket-keeper has thereby gained any advantage. If the wicket-keeper does not remain wholly behind the line of the stumps from the moment the ball comes into play until released from this restriction in one of the three ways stated above, then he has contravened this Law. The striker's end umpire must call and signal No ball at the moment of delivery or, if the infringement occurs later, as soon as possible thereafter.

Once the striker has touched the ball, the wicket-keeper may move in front of the stumps in an attempt to take a catch or effect a stumping. There will be little difficulty in determining if the striker has set off for a run, which would enable the wicket-keeper to move in front of the wicket in an attempt to run out one of the batsmen.

Protection of striker's right to play the ball
The Law protects the striker's right to play the ball without interference. Should the wicket-keeper physically interfere with the striker's right to play the ball, he will obviously have contravened this Law and the striker's end umpire should call and signal No ball. The striker can then only be dismissed (**Law 24.10**) if he Handles the Ball; Obstructs the Field; Hits the Ball Twice or is Run Out whilst attempting a run.

Striker's right to play the ball
It must be appreciated, however, that this right to play the ball does not extend indefinitely, either in time or in space. Except in the specific case of a ball coming to rest in front of the striker (see **Law 25**), it is restricted to the reasonable limits of playing the ball from a normal guard position. While the striker must not be denied the right to move over to play a delivery that

would otherwise have been Wide, nor should he be prohibited from attempting to play the finest of late cuts or to 'follow the ball round' on the leg side, once the ball has passed beyond these limits, his right to play it should be considered at an end.

Striker may obstruct wicket-keeper

The striker is entitled to protect his wicket with a second stroke of his bat or person, even if in doing so he obstructs the wicket-keeper from picking up the ball. If, however, the striker, lawfully defending his wicket, interferes with the wicket-keeper who is attempting to take a catch, on appeal the striker should be given out Obstructing the Field. (**Law 37**).

Wicket-keeper wearing pads and gloves

The traditional right of the wicket-keeper to wear pads and gloves is valid only when he is clearly discharging the traditional role of the wicket-keeper. There have been instances in recent years of the wicket-keeper, in the final stages of a close match, standing as a leg side fielder before the ball is delivered. It is of course accepted that the wicket-keeper will often chase the ball during the course of play, but if the umpire considers that, standing in this position before delivery, the wicket-keeper is not able to 'keep wicket' as normally understood, then he becomes only a fieldsman. If he fields the ball with his gloves or pads the 5 run penalty for illegal fielding will be awarded. He will also have to be counted in the tally of fielders, in assessing whether there are more than two behind the line of the popping crease at the instant of delivery.

LAW 41 THE FIELDSMAN

1 FIELDING THE BALL

The Fieldsman may stop the ball with any part of his person, but if he wilfully stops it otherwise, 5 runs shall be added to the run or runs already scored; if no run has been scored 5 penalty runs shall be awarded. The run in progress shall count provided that the Batsmen have crossed at the instant of the act. If the ball has been struck, the penalty shall be added to the score of the Striker, but otherwise to the score of byes, leg-byes, no balls or wides as the case may be.

2 LIMITATION OF ON-SIDE FIELDSMEN

The number of on-side Fieldsmen behind the popping crease at the instant of the Bowler's delivery shall not exceed two. In the event of infringement by the fielding side the Umpire at the Striker's end shall call and signal 'no ball' at the instant of delivery or as soon as possible thereafter.

3 POSITION OF FIELDSMEN

Whilst the ball is in play and until the ball has made contact with the bat or the Striker's person or has passed his bat, no Fieldsman, other than the Bowler, may stand on or have any part of his person extended over the pitch (measuring 22 yards/20.12m. × 10 feet/ 3.05m.). In the event of a Fieldsman contravening this Law, the Umpire at the Bowler's end shall call and signal 'no ball' at the instant of delivery or as soon as possible thereafter. See Law 40.1: (Position of Wicket-Keeper).

4 FIELDSMEN'S PROTECTIVE HELMETS

Protective helmets, when not in use by members of the fielding side, shall only be placed, if above the surface, on the ground behind the Wicket-Keeper. In the event of the ball, when in play, striking a helmet whilst in this position, five penalty runs shall be awarded, as laid down in Law 41.1 and Note (a).

Notes

(a) BATSMEN CHANGING ENDS
The 5 runs referred to in 1 above are a penalty and the Batsmen do not change ends solely by reason of this penalty.

Illegal fielding

Fielders must not be allowed to stop the ball by any unfair means without incurring a penalty. Should any fielder transgress, a penalty of 5 runs is awarded to the batting side. The ball is automatically dead, but the umpire is advised to call and signal Dead ball.

The use of any discarded piece of clothing to stop the ball is considered to be unfair, even if the fielder has pushed off a hat or cap whilst running after the ball. If the return touches the discarded piece of clothing, the penalty should be awarded. Wicket-keepers often discard one glove when running to field the ball; should another fielder put the glove on his hand and collect the return in the glove this, too, is regarded as unfair fielding. If a fielder's hat or cap is blown from his head, as he runs after the ball, and the return touches the hat or cap, this is not to be regarded as a transgression as the hat or cap has not been discarded wilfully. Should the ball make contact with a fielder's protective helmet which has been placed on the ground behind the wicket-keeper, the 5 penalty runs will be awarded.

Umpires should be vigilant at all times and require a fielder who drops any discarded clothing inside the field of play to pick up any such item and, wherever possible, deposit it over the boundary line.

Recording of penalty runs

If the striker played the ball with his bat he is credited with the 5 penalty runs plus any runs scored. If the ball was not struck the 5 penalty runs will be recorded as byes, leg-byes, no balls or wides as appropriate. If the delivery has been called No ball or Wide ball and no runs are scored, the 5 penalty runs are added to the penalty for the unfair delivery so that six runs are scored in total.

Any runs completed before the act of illegal fielding took place will be added to the penalty. Umpires should note the position of the batsmen at the moment of the illegal act and award the run in progress, providing the batsmen have crossed. The scorers must be informed of the number of runs scored as well as being given any appropriate signal.

If the batsmen have crossed when the act of illegal fielding takes place they will remain at the end to which they were running or had reached. An even number of runs scored would normally require the batsmen to resume at their original ends. In the case of the award of 5 penalty runs, this does not apply; the batsmen do not change ends.

On-side fieldsmen

The Law restricts the number of fielders allowed to stand on the on-side of the pitch, behind the line of the popping crease, at the moment the ball is delivered. Should there be more than two, striker's end umpire should call and signal No ball. The position taken by the wicket-keeper is disregarded in this context.

Note that if there are two fielders on the on side behind the striker and a third fielder is straddling the line of the popping crease the Law is being infringed. The striker's end umpire should be prepared to move to the off side of the pitch, having advised the Captain of the fielding side, the striker and his colleague, if a fielder behind him may be responsible for the Law being infringed. It is possible for a fielder to move, while the bowler is running up, into a position which will cause an infringement. If at the moment of delivery there are more than two fieldsmen behind the popping crease on the on-side No ball must be called and signalled.

It is possible that the striker's end umpire, having failed to notice the infringement, will not call and signal No ball. Should this happen the delivery will be treated as a fair one even though either the striker or the bowler's end umpire is aware of the infringement.

Fieldsmen on, or over, the pitch

Law 40 (The Wicket-keeper) imposes a limitation on the wicket-keeper's movements. He must remain wholly behind the wicket until the ball touches the bat or person of the striker, the ball passes the wicket or the striker attempts a run. The intention of **Law 40** is to give the striker a right to play the ball and guard his wicket without being obstructed by the wicket-keeper. The striker also has a right to play the ball and guard his wicket free from any obstruction by another fielder. The Law prohibits a fielder from standing on or having any part of his person extended over the pitch until the ball has made contact with the bat or striker's person, or has passed the bat. **Law 7** defines the area of the pitch which is not necessarily the cut strip.

It is the bowler's end umpire's responsibility to watch for any encroachment of a fielder on the pitch. The inexperienced umpire, aware that he is required to watch both feet of the bowler in the delivery stride, observe the flight of the ball and concentrate on the action at the striker's end may wonder how it is also possible to watch for encroachment by a fielder, particularly if there is a ring of close fielders. The work load of the bowler's end umpire does seem to be formidable, but in practice, and with experience, the umpire will develop a

184

technique and rhythm which will enable him to discharge all his duties without feeling under undue pressure.

Shadows on pitch
Some players believe that a fielder's shadow on the pitch infringes this Law. This is not true, but if the umpire considers that the striker is incommoded by such a shadow, he will be justified in asking the fielding Captain to ensure that the fielder remains still until the striker has received the ball (see also **Law 42**).

Scoring
The 5 run penalty is added to a penalty for a No ball or Wide ball, or to any runs scored by the batsmen, including the one in progress if they have crossed at the moment of the infringement.

LAW 42 UNFAIR PLAY

1 RESPONSIBILITY OF CAPTAINS
The Captains are responsible at all times for ensuring that play is conducted within the spirit of the game as well as within the Laws.

2 RESPONSIBILITY OF UMPIRES
The Umpires are the sole judges of fair and unfair play.

3 INTERVENTION BY THE UMPIRE
The Umpires shall intervene without appeal by calling and signalling 'dead ball' in the case of unfair play, but should not otherwise interfere with the progress of the game except as required to do so by the Laws.

4 LIFTING THE SEAM
A Player shall not lift the seam of the ball for any reason. Should this be done, the Umpires shall change the ball for one of similar condition to that in use prior to the contravention. See Note (a).

5 CHANGING THE CONDITION OF THE BALL
Any member of the fielding side may polish the ball provided that such polishing wastes no time and that no artificial substance is used. No one shall rub the

ball on the ground or use any artificial substance or take any other action to alter the condition of the ball.

In the event of a contravention of this Law, the Umpires, after consultation, shall change the ball for one of similar condition to that in use prior to the contravention.

This Law does not prevent a member of the fielding side from drying a wet ball, or removing mud from the ball. See Note (b).

6 INCOMMODING THE STRIKER
An Umpire is justified in intervening under this Law and shall call and signal 'dead ball' if, in his opinion, any Player of the fielding side incommodes the Striker by any noise or action while he is receiving the ball.

7 OBSTRUCTION OF A BATSMAN IN RUNNING
It shall be considered unfair if any Fieldsman wilfully obstructs a Batsman in running. In these circumstances the Umpire shall call and signal 'dead ball' and allow any completed runs and the run in progress or alternatively any boundary scored.

8 THE BOWLING OF FAST SHORT PITCHED BALLS
The bowling of fast short pitched balls is unfair if, in the opinion of the Umpire at the Bowler's end, it constitutes an attempt to intimidate the Striker. See Note (d).

Umpires shall consider intimidation to be the deliberate bowling of fast short pitched balls which by their length, height and direction are intended or likely to inflict physical injury on the Striker. The relative skill of the Striker shall also be taken into consideration.

In the event of such unfair bowling, the Umpire at the Bowler's end shall adopt the following procedure:

(a) In the first instance the Umpire shall call and signal 'no ball', caution the Bowler and inform the other Umpire, the Captain of the fielding side and the Batsmen of what has occurred.

(b) If this caution is ineffective, he shall repeat the above procedure and indicate to the Bowler that this is a final warning.

186

In October 1998 Law 42.9 and text (p.194) become

9 THE BOWLING OF HIGH FULL PITCHES

Any high full pitched ball (regardless of its pace) which passes or would have passed above waist height of the Batsman standing upright at the crease shall be called and signalled 'No Ball' by the Umpire at the Bowler's end.

In the event of a Bowler bowling a 'fast' high full pitched ball (i.e. a "beamer"), the Umpire at the Bowler's end shall adopt the procedure of caution, final warning, action against the Bowler and reporting as set out in 42.8 above.

However if the Umpire at the Bowler's end considers that such a 'fast' high full pitch has been bowled 'deliberately' at the Batsman he shall call and signal 'No Ball' and direct the Captain of the fielding side to take the Bowler off forthwith without adopting the procedure of caution and final warning.

High full pitches

The Law clearly defines high full pitches. There are three 'levels' of transgression. The umpire must call and signal No ball every time, at whatever level, even if the delivery might otherwise be deemed a Wide ball. They are:

- a high full pitch (a No ball penalty only)
- a fast high full pitch
- a fast high full pitch deliberately bowled at the batsman.

At the *first* fast high full pitch, the umpire must begin the procedure of caution, final warning, action against the bowler and reporting, including the call and signal of No ball. At each repetition, the procedure is to be taken to the next stage. The criterion for judging a ball fast is how much time the striker has to deal with this potentially lethal delivery. The threshold for a young, inexperienced batsman will be lower than for a skilled one.

For a fast high full pitch bowled at the striker deliberately, the penalty not merely of No ball but also of instant suspension, without any warnings, is a serious one. Umpires must not hesitate to direct the captain to impose this sanction if it is warranted. They must play their part in eradicating this dangerous bowling from the game.

(c) **Both the above caution and final warning shall continue to apply even though the Bowler may later change ends.**

(d) **Should the above warnings prove ineffective the Umpire at the Bowler's end shall:**

   (i) **At the first repetition call and signal 'no ball' and when the ball is dead direct the Captain to take the Bowler off forthwith and to complete the over with another Bowler, provided that the Bowler does not bowl two overs or part thereof consecutively. See Law 22.7: (Bowler Incapacitated or Suspended during an Over).**

   (ii) **Not allow the Bowler, thus taken off, to bowl again in the same innings.**

   (iii) **Report the occurrence to the Captain of the batting side as soon as the Players leave the field for an interval.**

   (iv) **Report the occurrence to the Executive of the fielding side and to any governing body responsible for the match who shall take any further action which is considered to be appropriate against the Bowler concerned.**

9 THE BOWLING OF FAST HIGH FULL PITCHES

The bowling of fast high full pitches is unfair.

A fast high full pitched ball shall be defined as a ball that passes, or would have passed, on the full above waist height of a Batsman standing upright at the crease. Should a Bowler bowl a fast high full pitched ball, either Umpire shall call and signal 'No Ball' and adopt the procedure of caution, final warning, action against the Bowler and reporting as set out in Law 42.8.

10 TIME WASTING

Any form of time wasting is unfair.

(a) **In the event of the Captain of the fielding side wasting time or allowing any member of his side to waste time, the Umpire at the Bowler's end shall adopt the following procedure:**

(i) In the first instance he shall caution the Captain of the fielding side and inform the other Umpire of what has occurred.

(ii) If this caution is ineffective he shall repeat the above procedure and indicate to the Captain that this is a final warning.

(iii) The Umpire shall report the occurrence to the Captain of the batting side as soon as the Players leave the field for an interval.

(iv) Should the above procedure prove ineffective the Umpire shall report the occurrence to the Executive of the fielding side and to any governing body responsible for that match who shall take appropriate action against the Captain and the Players concerned.

(b) In the event of a Bowler taking unnecessarily long to bowl an over the Umpire at the Bowler's end shall adopt the procedures, other than the calling of 'no ball', of caution, final warning, action against the Bowler and reporting as set out in 8. above.

(c) In the event of a Batsman wasting time (see Note (e)) other than in the manner described in Law 31: (Timed Out), the Umpire at the Bowler's end shall adopt the following procedure:

(i) In the first instance he shall caution the Batsman and inform the other Umpire at once, and the Captain of the batting side, as soon as the Players leave the field for an interval, of what has occurred.

(ii) If this proves ineffective, he shall repeat the caution, indicate to the Batsman that this is a final warning and inform the other Umpire.

(iii) The Umpire shall report the occurrence to both Captains as soon as the Players leave the field for an interval.

(iv) Should the above procedure prove ineffective, the Umpire shall report the occurrence to the Executive of the batting side and to any governing body responsible for that match who shall take appropriate action against the Player concerned.

11 PLAYERS DAMAGING THE PITCH

The Umpires shall intervene and prevent Players from causing damage to the pitch which may assist the Bowlers of either side. See Note (c).

(a) In the event of any member of the fielding side damaging the pitch the Umpire shall follow the procedure of caution, final warning and reporting as set out in 10 (a) above.

(b) In the event of a Bowler contravening this Law by running down the pitch after delivering the ball, the Umpire at the Bowler's end shall first caution the Bowler. If this caution is ineffective the Umpire shall adopt the procedures, other than the calling of 'no ball', of final warning, action against the Bowler and reporting as set out in 8. above.

(c) In the event of a Batsman damaging the pitch the Umpire at the Bowler's end shall follow the procedures of caution, final warning and reporting as set out in 10 (c) above.

12 BATSMEN UNFAIRLY STEALING A RUN

Any attempt by the Batsman to steal a run during the Bowler's run-up is unfair. Unless the Bowler attempts to run out either Batsmen – see Law 24.4: (Bowler Throwing At Striker's Wicket Before Delivery) and Law 24.5: (Bowler Attempting to Run Out Non-Striker Before Delivery) – the Umpire shall call and signal 'dead ball' as soon as the Batsmen cross in any such attempt to run. The Batsmen shall then return to their original wickets.

13 PLAYER'S CONDUCT

In the event of a Player failing to comply with the instructions of an Umpire, criticizing his decisions by word or action, or showing dissent, or generally behaving in a manner which might bring the game into disrepute, the Umpire concerned shall in the first place report the matter to the other Umpire and to the Player's Captain requesting the latter to take action. If

this proves ineffective, the Umpire shall report the incident as soon as possible to the Executive of the Player's team and to any Governing Body responsible for the match, who shall take any further action which is considered appropriate against the Player or Players concerned.

Notes

(a) THE CONDITION OF THE BALL
Umpires shall make frequent and irregular inspections of the condition of the ball.

(b) DRYING OF A WET BALL
A wet ball may be dried on a towel or with sawdust.

(c) DANGER AREA
The danger area on the pitch, which must be protected from damage by a Bowler, shall be regarded by the Umpires as the area contained by an imaginary line 4 feet / 1.22m. from the popping crease, and parallel to it, and within two imaginary and parallel lines drawn down the pitch from points on that line 1 foot / 30.48cm. on either side of the middle stump.

(d) FAST SHORT PITCHED BALLS
As a guide, a fast short pitched ball is one which pitches short and passes, or would have passed, above the shoulder height of the Striker standing in a normal batting stance at the crease.

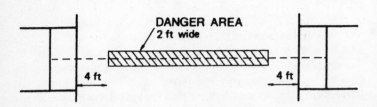

Figure 7   The danger area (see text page 196)

(e) TIME WASTING BY BATSMEN
Other than in exceptional circumstances, the Batsman should always be ready to take strike when the Bowler is ready to start his run-up.

Responsibility for ensuring play is conducted fairly and in the correct spirit

The Captains are responsible for the behaviour of their players and it is their duty to ensure that the game is conducted within the traditional spirit of the game as well as within the Laws.

The umpires are required to control the game with absolute fairness and impartiality. Should there be any instances of unfair play the umpires are required to act without appeal from either side. It is important to remember that umpires should not interrupt the flow of the game, and the enjoyment of the players, without good cause unless required to do so by the Laws. An officious, over-assertive umpire can not only spoil the game but also seriously endanger the respect in which umpires are held. The umpires' role can best be carried out quietly but firmly. An umpire should not enter into the game unless required to do so, and then without any officiousness.

Following an instance of unfair play, without any appeal from the players, the umpire should call and signal Dead ball and, with his colleague, advise the Captain of the reason for the intervention. The Captain would be expected to take the appropriate action to prevent any repetition of the incident.

That the umpires are the sole judges of fair and unfair play is given due importance by being part of both **Laws 3 and 42**. It is a joint responsibility, requiring umpires to consult on most occasions when an instance of unfair play occurs. If consultation is not necessary, the umpire taking action must keep his colleague fully informed both of the reason for the intervention and the action taken.

Changing the condition of the ball

It is essential that umpires inspect the ball frequently and at irregular intervals to ensure members of the fielding side are not tampering with the ball in an attempt to gain an unfair advantage. The condition of the ball can be altered in a number of different ways. Recent events and reports suggest that it has been endemic in most grades of cricket for many years.

The bowler, or other members of the fielding side, will sometimes attempt to raise the seam of the ball by running a finger nail, or thin object, around the seam. Umpires should inspect the ball if it suddenly begins to deviate off the seam although this may be due to the skill of the bowler rather than any unfair action. It is unwise to carry out inspections at regular intervals as it is possible for the fielding side to flatten the seam before offering it for inspection.

The fielding side should not be allowed to roughen one side of the ball deliberately, either by use of an implement or by rubbing on the ground, in the hope that the bowler will be able to make the ball swing.

Both umpires should watch how members of the fielding side handle the ball as it is transferred back to the bowler, in an attempt to observe any illegal tampering with the condition of the ball. The striker's end umpire is best placed to note any apparent unfair action by the bowler as he walks back to his mark. The umpires should confer immediately any suspicion is aroused and the condition of the ball should be checked.

Cleaning and drying the ball

The fielding side are allowed to polish the ball or to dry it with a towel or sawdust providing time is not being wasted and no artificial substance is used to enhance the shine of the ball; Perspiration is not an artificial substance but lip salve, hair oil, grease and sun lotions most certainly are. Any mud clinging to the ball may also be removed either with a finger nail or the ball being wiped on wet grass. Such action must be closely supervised by the umpire. Removing mud from the ball requires a very different action from that used to raise the seam. No member of the fielding side should be allowed to rub the ball in a bare patch of earth even if claiming to be removing mud from the ball.

Should either umpire detect any sudden change to the condition of the ball he should immediately draw it to the attention of his colleague. Together they would inform the Captain of the fielding side of the unfair act. The ball should be changed to one of similar condition before the transgression took place. The batsmen should be advised of the change.

Striker's right to play without interference

The striker is entitled to play the ball and to guard his wicket without any interference by noise or action, by the fielding side. If the umpire considers any noise or movement might be a cause of distraction to the striker the umpire should immediately call and signal Dead ball and advise the Captain of the fielding side of the reason for his action.

No fielder may stand with any part of his person on or over the pitch. It may be, however, that late in the day the shadow of one or more of the fieldsmen lies across the pitch at the striker's end. This is not unfair providing the fielder, or fieldsmen, remain perfectly still as the striker receives a delivery. Should a fielder, and thus his shadow, move before the striker has played at the ball, the umpire should call and signal Dead ball and anticipate that the Captain will take action to prevent any recurrence. If the Captain does not take the appropriate action, the bowler's end umpire should request him to do so.

Wilful obstruction of the batsman whilst running

A fielder running towards the ball will not always be aware of the position of a running batsman. A collision between a batsman and a member of the fielding side is not necessarily the result of an unfair action. It may be necessary for the umpires to consult to determine whether the action by the fielder was wilful. If it is determined that the act was unfair the umpire should not allow the fielding side to gain any advantage either by dismissing the batsman or preventing a run being scored. Except when a boundary is scored, the run in progress will be allowed, even if the batsmen have not crossed. The batsmen will be directed to, and remain at, the ends to which they were running. The scorers should be advised of the number of runs to be recorded.

Fast, short pitched deliveries

Great concern has been expressed at the increase in the use of fast, short pitched balls which it is argued are always an attempt to intimidate the batsman. Despite calls for such deliveries to be made illegal the cricketing authorities acknowledge that a fast, short pitched delivery is an acceptable tactic for a bowler to employ and require the umpire to determine when the use of such deliveries becomes intimidatory.

Intimidation is defined as a likelihood or deliberate intention of inflicting physical injury on the striker. There is no difficulty in assessing that a fast delivery is deliberately pitched short nor that the striker is in some physical danger if the ball is travelling towards his head. The umpire will often find it extremely difficult to assess the intention of the bowler particularly if the striker shows a relish for short pitched bowling. The relative skill of the striker is one of the factors which the umpire must take into consideration. The body language of the bowler may be of assistance to the umpire in determining the bowler's intention. The striker's reaction to fast, short pitched bowling will also give guidance to the umpire as to whether he should take action against the bowler.

The skill of the striker is not always reflected in his place in the batting order. Some lower order batsmen are quite prepared to attempt to hook short pitched deliveries and refuse to be intimidated whilst others, who bat higher up the order, show little liking for such deliveries.

Although, over the years, regulations have been introduced into Test and First Class cricket to limit the number of fast, short pitched balls which may be bowled in an over, the Law is so framed that one delivery, which the umpire considers to be intimidatory, is unfair. The umpire should not hesitate, having called No ball on each occasion, to **caution** the bowler, give him a **final warning**, request **action** and subsequently make a **report**. A Note to the Law defines, as a guide to umpires, a fast, short pitched ball as one which passes above shoulder height of the striker when standing in his normal batting stance.

Fast, high full pitches
Whereas the umpire is required to make a judgment relating to fast, short pitched balls, the Law insists that the bowling of a **fast**, high full pitch will **always** be deemed to be unfair. The umpire must, having called and signalled No ball give the bowler a **caution** on the first occasion followed by a **final warning**. If further fast high full pitches are bowled, he must take **action** against the bowler. Note that either umpire may call and signal No ball for this offence. The Law makes no mention of the line of the delivery nor of any possible injury resulting to the striker. Any fast, high pitched delivery, no matter whether it be directed at the striker or wide of him, should be regarded as unfair and the appropriate action taken.

Any caution applies throughout the innings

If an umpire administers a caution or final warning to a bowler, he must advise the Captain of the fielding side that he has done so in the expectation that the Captain will carry out the duty imposed upon him by the Laws of the game. He must also inform the batsmen and, most importantly, his colleague. Any caution given to a bowler continues throughout the innings no matter from which end the bowler is operating. Thus it is important for both umpires to be aware of any caution or final warning administered.

Time wasting

Any manner of time wasting is detrimental to the game and is unfair. Captains and players have a variety of ways in which the time can be deliberately and unfairly wasted in attempting to gain a tactical advantage. **Law 42.10** gives wide powers to the umpires to control this form of unfairness by any of the players and they should not hesitate to intervene as soon as any instance of time wasting is apparent. A quiet word to any offender may be sufficient to ensure the game progresses with little time being wasted but if the practice continues, the umpires should consult and take the joint action required by the Law.

The Captain of the fielding side might arrange for the bowlers to walk back to their positions at the slowest possible pace. Fieldsmen can cross, between overs, very slowly after being positioned to ensure they have a lengthy distance to cover. They can also waste time by throwing the ball to one another, perhaps retaining it for a short time under the pretext of polishing the ball, before returning it to the bowler who can add to the time wasted by waiting until he receives the ball before moving back to the start of his run up. Captains can be very meticulous in field placing before the start of an over and also hold up play by moving fielders during an over. They may have good reason for this but if the intention is to waste time the umpires must take action. The caution, final warning, action and report procedures will be used against a bowler who takes unnecessarily long to bowl an over. The caution and final warning will continue to apply even though the bowler may change ends. Should the final warning be ineffective, the Captain will be requested to take the bowler off forthwith and, except for the calling and signalling of

No ball, the procedure as set out for the bowling of fast, short pitched balls will be followed.

The Law reminds the Captains of their responsibility for the behaviour of their players and the conduct of their play. Umpires have a right to expect Captains to put a stop at once to sharp practices. There are many ways in which players can slow down play and the umpires should not hesitate to use the caution, final warning and report procedure against any player.

Other than when a new batsman delays starting his innings, which may result in him being Timed Out (**Law 31**) action should be taken against batsmen guilty of wasting time. Periods of unnecessary beating of the pitch with the bat; lengthy mid-pitch conferences; standing clear of his wicket when the bowler is ready to start his run-up; the removal and replacement of pads and many other delaying tactics are examples of unfair, time wasting practices. The caution, final warning and report procedure should be used against the batsmen. It will be noted that the umpires are not empowered to take action against members of the batting side.

Damage to the pitch and Danger Area

The pitch can be unfairly damaged by fieldsmen, bowlers or batsmen. The danger area which the umpires *must* protect from damage is shown in Figure 7 (see p. 190). Although the defined danger area must be protected umpires should take action to prevent damage to any part of the pitch which they consider might assist the bowlers of either side.

Any member of the fielding side can unfairly damage the pitch when crossing from one side to the other. Even though the damage may be claimed to be accidental, umpires should use the caution, final warning and report procedure if any fielder does damage the pitch.

Umpires are responsible for the protection of the danger area. It is not possible for the umpire to watch the bowler's feet, after the delivery stride has been completed as his full concentration must be on the flight of the ball. The umpire will, however, be aware if a bowler is running straight down the pitch and an examination of the pitch may show some marking in, or near, the danger area. Often, the bowler will take note of the umpire's examination of the pitch and will alter his follow through to avoid damaging the danger area. It must be re-stated that, even if the pitch is damaged outside the limits of the danger area and the umpires consider the damage may assist the bowlers of either side the bowler must at once be cautioned. The caution, final warning, action and report procedure will be applied to bowlers who damage the pitch. The sanction against the bowler – being taken off for the rest of the innings – is severe, but, it must be recognized that damage to the pitch is unfair. The umpire's responsibility is to prevent it. Prevention may not always be possible. It may well be that the procedure of caution, final warning and action allows damage which cannot be repaired to have taken place on three occasions. Umpires will be failing in their duty to control the game fairly if immediate action is not taken against all forms of pitch damage.

It is possible for the bowler to follow through so straight as to obstruct the umpire's view but yet cause no damage to the pitch. The umpire should point out to the bowler the difficulty he is experiencing in following the flight of the ball and of seeing the action at the other end of the pitch. The bowler should also be informed that he is likely to cause some damage to the pitch, which would result in a caution being administered if he continues straight down the pitch when following through. The bowler should see the wisdom of moving away from the pitch as soon as possible in his follow through.

The caution, final warning and report procedure should be followed against any batsmen who damage the pitch. Batsmen are allowed to beat the pitch with their bats, provided no damage to the pitch is caused. This is not likely to occur early in an innings but, towards the end of an innings, batsmen may well attempt to enlarge small areas of damage by the use of their bats. Batsmen may also deliberately run down the middle of the pitch with the intent of scuffing the surface. Umpires should closely observe batsmen towards the end of innings both when they are running and also when the striker moves out of his ground, after playing the ball, even though not attempting a run.

Batsmen unfairly stealing a run
The ball is in play when the bowler starts his run-up but the Law states that an attempt by the batsmen to steal a run during the bowler's run up is an unfair act. Unless a run out is attempted the bowler's end umpire will call and signal Dead ball as soon as the

batsmen have crossed and check that the batsmen return to their original ends. If during the unfair attempt to steal a run, the bowler throws at the striker's wicket, either umpire will call and signal No ball although it is unlikely that bowler's end umpire will be aware that the ball has been thrown. If the bowler throws at the non-striker's wicket, neither umpire will call and signal No ball but any resulting runs will be scored as no balls. Bowler's end umpire will have to make this clear to the scorers (see also **Law 38**).

Player's conduct

The Law, in detailing offences uses the term 'criticizing the umpire's decision by word or action'. Umpires have always used their sound common sense in dealing with the odd hasty word or action made through excitement. Slight misdemeanours are best resolved by a quiet word of caution on the field but anything other than a trivial offence must be firmly dealt with. Both umpires will approach the Captain concerned and request him to take appropriate action. In the event of the Captain failing to put a stop to bad behaviour, the umpires will, as soon as possible, make a report to the team's Executive. Written reports from both umpires should be made to the Governing Body responsible for the match, who are compelled under the Laws of the game to take action against the offending player or players concerned.

Protective clothing

Law 2 imposes an obligation on a runner to wear the same external protective equipment as the injured batsman is wearing. It is interesting that although batsmen and wicket-keepers have worn gloves and pads for well over 100 years, the Laws have never specified or granted permission for the wearing of protective clothing or equipment. It has become traditional, over the years, that only the wicket-keeper and batsmen may wear gloves and pads, but this has now been extended to other forms of protective clothing and equipment. Nevertheless, fieldsmen, other than the wicket-keeper, should not be allowed to wear gloves or bandages unless permission has been given by the Captain of the batting side. Bowlers must not be allowed bandages or plasters on the hand delivering the ball unless the opposing Captain agrees. The batsmen at the wicket are deputies for their Captain. It is possible for a wrist watch, even if innocently worn, to reflect a flash of light which can be disconcerting for the striker. The umpire should ask the bowler to remove a wrist watch before he begins bowling.

Umpires should be prepared to intervene if they consider time is being wasted by members of the fielding side putting on and taking off items of protective padding/clothing.

Responsibility of the umpires

In dealing with unfair play, or the action of players which might be to the disadvantage of the opposing side, the umpires must be on their guard to avoid being in any way offensive or dictatorial. The game must be firmly controlled, and the success of the umpire will depend upon a manner which commands respect, ensures safety and enables the game to flow according to the Laws. It is possible for the umpires to use their considerable powers with courtesy and dignity. A caution should be delivered quietly with carefully selected words which will impress the offending player without attempting to make him look foolish, thus creating bitterness or resentment. Above all, umpires must avoid sarcasm.

Fortunately for the game, instances of direct refusal to accept the umpire's instructions or decisions are extremely rare. Unfortunately, the traditional teaching of young cricketers that immediate acceptance of the umpire's decision is an indispensable part of their cricket character seems to have lapsed. It seems that in the schools and youth sections of clubs young cricketers have acquired a much more questioning attitude towards the Laws. Rather than playing in the spirit of the game and its Laws there is a penchant now to find a way round them. Criticism of the umpire's decision by words or action; the public showing of dissent; bad language and undisciplined behaviour have all grown into the game. Young cricketers have always attempted to imitate the great players and now do more so than ever due to the influence of television close-ups and playbacks. Captains and players in the top grades of cricket should be aware of their responsibilities in setting an example in behaviour. If the character of the game is not to be changed completely, firmness in umpiring at all levels is now more essential than ever. If firm and impartial control of the game and insistence that it is played according to the Laws, result in temporary unpopularity, umpires from Test match to village green must be prepared to accept the disapproval, knowing that such control and insistence best serve the interests of the game.

Part III Scoring

Law 4 provides for the appointment of scorers and details their joint duties with the umpires. The Law and its definitions must be closely studied.

Scorers are required in order that the correct totals of the two sides can be ascertained, and the result determined under **Law 21**. However, a well-kept score book also provides a wealth of additional information and for this purpose there should be one scorer from each side. He, or she, should be someone familiar with that side, able to recognize individual players at a glance. When only one scorer is available, the responsibility for the accuracy of the score is increased, and every possible check must be made throughout the match.

Methods of scoring are largely matters of convention based on practical experience. The more closely scorers follow the same method, the easier it is for two scorers to check each other's books, or for one scorer to take over from another in the middle of an innings.

BEFORE THE GAME

The home team scorer should seek out the visiting scorer and together they should meet the umpires and discuss such matters as:

> Hours of play and intervals
> Watch or clock to be followed
> Whether 6 or 8 ball overs to be bowled
> The signal for the start of the last hour 20 overs period
> Any local agreement as to boundary allowances
> Any agreement on the use of new balls

The rules of any relevant Competition, so far as these concern scorers, including:

- Restrictions on the time or number of overs available to the batting side
- Restriction on the number of overs allowed to any one bowler
- How the result is to be determined if play is stopped by ground, weather or light conditions.

This last is particularly important if it refers to, say, the first ten overs of each innings. The scorers must be prepared, at the end of the innings, to show what the scores were at the various early stages and how many men were out at each stage.

The scorers should also note the names of the two umpires and which side has won the toss.

EQUIPMENT

Besides his score book, a scorer should have with him:

Several pencils with pencil-sharpener
or
Fine-point ball pens
Rubber
Watch
Up-to-date copy of the official Laws and of the Rules of the Competition
Note paper, should a note have to be sent to the umpires.
For acknowledging signals, something reflective which the umpires can see against the background of the score-box: even a newspaper will serve the purpose

THE SCORE BOOK

There are many types of score books/score sheets but, in principle, the object is the same.

The score book has two main parts. They are quite distinct and a sample is shown. (see pages 206, 207) The essential part, usually the left-hand or upper part, is the 'batting sheet' (Figure 8) where the basic facts are recorded on which the result will depend. For this purpose there are spaces for the name, score and method of dismissal of each of the eleven players of the batting side; and for extras (or sundries); byes; leg-byes; Wides; and No balls. The sheet also provides for entering the total runs scored at the fall of each wicket, and in some cases at the end of each over.

The second main part is the 'Bowling Analysis' (Figure 9) which is not necessary for determining the result but provides a check for the accuracy of the batting sheet. The main purpose of the analysis is to record the detailed bowling performances of the bowlers and it is essential if their averages are to be taken out at the end of the season.

A third part is a printed list of all numbers from 1 to 300 (or more). These are ticked off as the batting side's running total rises.

There are usually spaces at the top and bottom of the pages for the title of the match; the name of the batting side; and, sometimes, the winner of the toss; the names of the umpires and scorers; these details should be completed before the start of the match.

The story of the innings is shown between the two examples on pages 206–7 and 210–11.

MAIN CAUSES OF INACCURACIES

Errors in scoring may arise because of:

> Lack of knowledge of the Laws relevant to scoring
> Failure on the part of the umpires to keep the scorers informed on points about which there may be doubt
> Bad signalling by umpires or failure on their part to insist on acknowledgment of signals
> Inaccurate entries
> Lack of constant checks within the score book
> Lack of constant checks with one's partner.

Errors do little harm if found and put right at once, and it cannot be too strongly emphasized that constant checking will show up most errors in time for them to be put right.

Law 4 instructs that if two scorers have been appointed they shall frequently check the total to ensure that the score sheets agree. If this instruction is carried out regularly, cases of disagreement regarding the scores and results of matches should not occur.

At any one time, the total runs scored by all batsmen, plus all runs scored as No balls or Wides, must equal the total runs conceded by all bowlers. At the same time, the total runs conceded by all bowlers plus byes and leg-byes must equal the running total. This check should be carried out by each scorer at the end of each over and at the fall of each wicket. At the same time, the scorers should check with each other to see that the two books agree.

The umpires are responsible for satisfying themselves as to the correctness of the scores throughout and at the conclusion of the match, (**Law 3.14**). They also have the responsibility of making any decisions about the correctness of the scores (**Law 21.6**).

THE MORE IMPORTANT LAWS AFFECTING SCORING

Scorers should be versed in all the Laws with their interpretations, but some are of special importance to them.

Law 2: If a substitute fielder makes a catch, the entry in the score sheet is 'Caught sub'. If a striker is dismissed by the wicket-keeper because his *runner* is out of his ground, he is 'Run out' and not 'Stumped'.

Law 3: Scorers must know all the official signals given to them by the umpires. They must acknowledge promptly when an umpire signals to them.

The signals for No ball and Wide are made twice, once while the ball is in play, for the benefit of the players, a second time when the ball is dead, for the benefit of the scorers. It is only the second signal which should be acknowledged.

Scorers must appreciate that, if after runs have been taken off a No ball the bye signal is given, it is to tell them that the striker did not hit the ball. The runs go down as No balls, not as byes.

Law 19 and Law 26: Scorers must never assume that the umpire has failed to signal when he should have done so. For example, when the batsmen run and there is no signal, the scorers must never guess that the runs were byes, but must credit them to the striker. The scorers must record the decision of the umpire even if they have good reason to think that it was a mistaken one. For example, the scorers must enter the actual runs completed if no boundary is signalled, although they could see that the ball had actually reached it.

If, however, the batsmen have run one or three and then walked back to their original ends without any signal having been given to the scorers, the run or runs may have been disallowed or a boundary scored. If the umpires have failed to give any instruction, the scorers may, and indeed should, ask the umpires for guidance.

Scorers may always seek the umpires' guidance but should not interrupt play to do so.

Laws 16 and 17: When play ends or is interrupted by ground, weather, or light conditions, the scorers should note who bowled the last ball, and who is to be the striker for the next ball.

Law 17: Scorers should be alert to time any interruptions during the last hour of play and to assist if requested, but the umpires will make the final decision.

Law 18: Scorers must be completely conversant with the definition of a run and the disallowance in the case of short runs, a catch or a run out.

Law 19: If 5 runs have been completed before the instant the ball reaches the boundary, all 5 count. Overthrow boundary allowances are added to the runs completed, plus the one in progress, if the batsmen have crossed, at the instant of the throw.

Law 20: If 7 runs have been made before Lost ball is called, all 7 count.

If less than 7 have been made, 6 runs are scored. All runs scored off lost balls are credited to the striker unless the umpire signals otherwise.

Law 22: If the umpire inadvertently allows 7 or more balls in an over, all balls bowled should be recorded. If the umpire only allows 5, only 5 should be shown. If he repeatedly makes the same mistake in counting, the scorers should draw his attention to this, although the other umpire should have already done so. In either case this is one complete over.

Law 22: When a bowler is taken off, a thick vertical line in the analysis will indicate the end of his spell.

Laws 24 and 25: are dealt with in detail later.

Law 30: If the striker 'plays on', i.e. the ball hits the bat

A SIMPLE SCORE SHEET

HOME SIDE ..... WESSEX ..... CRICKET CLUB V ..... NORTHSHIRE ..... C. CLUB

VISITORS

..... FIRST ..... INNINGS OF ..... WESSEX ..... PLAYED AT ..... SUMMER GROUND ..... ON ..... 8 JUNE 19 96

BATSMEN	TIME IN	TIME OUT	RUNS SCORED	SCORING RATE 50	100	150	HOW OUT	BOWLER	TOTAL
1 T. STOKES			2.2.3.14				BOWLED	BROWN	12
2 W. BALL			4.1.2.2.4.4.				CT. COX	BROWN	17
3 G. HARRIS			4.1				HIT WKT	WHITE	5
4 C. WEST			2.4.1.2.4.1.2				ST. COX	GREEN	16
5 S. PEARCE			1.3.1.4.3.2.1.1				BOWLED	GREEN	16
6 T. CLARKE			1.4.3.1.2				BOWLED	BLACK	11
7 P. MORRIS							ST. COX	GREEN	0
8 B. JARVIS			4.4.2				NOT OUT		10
9 R. FOWLER			2.1.1.4.4				CT. BLACK	GREEN	12
10 H. BROWN			2.1				BOWLED	GREEN	3
11 D. SMITH			4.4.2				RUN OUT		10

NO BALLS 2 1
WIDES 1 1
BYES 4
LEG BYES

EXTRAS	3
	2
TOTAL	4
	1
	121

FOR 10 WICKETS

RUNS AT THE FALL OF EACH WICKET AND NO. OF OUTGOING BATSMAN

1	2	3	4	5	6	7	8	9	10
20	29	37	62	81	85	90	106	111	121
1	3	2	4	6	7	5	9	10	11

Figure 8   Batting sheet

Figure 9 Bowling analysis

BOWLERS	1	2	3(B)	4(C)	5	6	7	8	9	NO BALLS	WIDES	BALLS B'WLD	OVERS	MDNS	RUNS	WKTS	AV'GE
1 J.WHITE (A) (J)	∔2·· 0-3	·2· 3 0-8	⊙2· 0-10	W 1-14	2∔− 1-22					1	1	38	6	1	22	1	22
2 T.BROWN	∔·· 0-4	·0· 0-6	··W 1-10	∔∔· 1-15	∔· W2 2-23	3(b)0 2-29				1	1	43	7	–	34	2	17
3 M.GREEN (E)	·· W 0-0	·1· 2 1-3	2⊙· 1-7	W 2-11	W 2 3-4	∔ W 4-22	W 2 (H) 5-32			1	1	41	6.4	1	32	5	6.4
4 F.BLACK (F)	⊙3 W 0-7	∔3· 1-14	·4· 1-19	·2· 1-24	·2· 1-29					1	1	31	5	–	29	1	29
												BYES 4			117		
											LEG BYES	0			121		

NOTES

(A) White opens with a Wide - no runs taken.

(B) White bowled a No Ball which was not hit. Batsmen ran 2. These runs count against the Bowler and it is not a Maiden over.

(C) Harris was out 'Hit Wicket' - the Bowler is given credit for the wicket.

(D) Brown bowled a No Ball which was not hit and Batsmen did not run

(E) The fact that a 'boundary - 4 byes' occurred does not prevent this from being a Maiden over

(F) Batsman hit 3 off a No Ball. The Umpire correctly allowed an extra ball.

(G) Batsman was stumped off a Wide. Penalty of one run correctly entered.

(H) Smith was run out attempting a third run but was correctly credited with two runs.

(J) Figures denote the Bowler's analysis progressively.

(K) Runs are crossed off in blocks. ▢ a single, ◿ 3 runs. Horizontal lines show that a block begun at the end of one line continues at the start of the next line.

Figure 9 Bowling analysis

207

The two score sheets on pages 206, 207 and 210, 211 both show the innings set out below. The first version is a basic record.

The second version includes some refinements which are becoming very common practice.

▷ All the deliveries faced by a batsman are shown as part of his innings. In this case they are set out in a horizontal line. To save space, sequences of dots can be shown in vertical pairs. That is ··2˙3··1 would be :2˙3:˙1. and so on. The number of balls in the bowling is then balanced against those in the batting. Notice that although the wides are shown against the batsmen where they occur, they are not counted in the total of balls received.

▷ Extras are separated out into 'bowling extras' (No balls and Wides) and 'fielding extras' (Byes and Leg byes). This facilitates checking since bowling extras are shown against the bowler in the analysis, fielding extras are not.

▷ Captain and Wicket Keeper are marked * and † respectively.

▷ Underlining is used to show that the batsmen are not at the ends which would be expected from the number of runs scored off that delivery.

Neither version shows any times for length of innings. These and many other details can be added by the more experienced scorer.

Wessex CC v Northshire CC. Played at Summer Ground: 8 June 1996

Only those deliveries on which there was some incident are listed. The letters A to K (A to M for the second version) correspond to those in the notes.

Notice that the method shown is not the only way of crossing off runs in blocks (K). Some scorers use horizontal lines for the blocks and then extend the line into the margin to show a carry over into the next line.

OVER	BOWLER	DELIVERY	INCIDENT
1	J. White	1st ball	**A** Wide Ball signalled; batsmen do not run
		4th ball	Batsmen run 2; no signal
2	T. Brown	5th ball	Umpire signals Boundary 4
3	J. White	4th ball	Batsmen run 2; no signal
		5th ball	Batsmen run 3; no signal
4	T. Brown	1st ball	Batsmen run 1; no signal
		4th ball	Batsmen run 1; no signal
5	J. White	4th ball	**B** Batsmen run 2; Umpire signals No Ball and Bye
6	T. Brown	2nd ball	Umpire signals Boundary 4
		6th ball	T. Stokes out – Bowled; replaced by G. Harris
7	J. White	1st ball	Batsmen run 2; no signal
		2nd ball	Batsmen run 2; no signal
8	T. Brown	3rd ball	Umpire signals Boundary 4
		4th ball	Batsmen run 1; no signal
9	J. White	1st ball	**C** G. Harris out – Hit Wicket; replaced by C. West (Capt)
10	T. Brown	1st ball	Umpire signals Boundary 4
		2nd ball	Umpire signals Boundary 4
		6th ball	W. Ball out – Caught P. Cox; replaced by S. Pearce

OVER	BOWLER	DELIVERY	INCIDENT
11	J. White	1st ball	Batsmen run 2; no signal
		2nd ball	Umpire signals Boundary 4
		3rd ball	Batsmen run 1; no signal
		4th ball	Batsmen run 1; no signal
12	T. Brown	1st ball	Batsmen run 3; no signal
		3rd ball	Batsmen run 2; no signal
		4th ball	**D** Batsmen do not run; Umpire signals No Ball
13	M. Green	1st ball	**E** Umpire signals Bye and Boundary 4
14	T. Brown	1st ball	Umpire signals Boundary 4
		6th ball	Batsmen run 1; no signal
15	M. Green	1st ball	Batsmen run 2; no signal
		3rd ball	C. West out – Stumped Cox; replaced by T. Clarke
		6th ball	Batsmen run 1; no signal
16	F. Black	3rd ball	Umpire signals Boundary 4
		5th ball	**F** Batsmen run 3; Umpire signals No Ball
17	M. Green	1st ball	Batsmen run 1; no signal
		2nd ball	Batsmen run 1; no signal
		3rd ball	Batsmen run 2; no signal
18	F. Black	1st ball	Umpire signals Boundary 4
		2nd ball	Batsmen run 3; no signal
		3rd ball	T. Clarke out – Bowled; replaced by P. Morris (Keeper)
19	M. Green	1st ball	Batsmen run 2; no signal
		2nd ball	Batsmen run 1; no signal
		3rd ball	**G** P. Morris out – Stumped; Umpire signals Wide ball
			Morris replaced by B. Jarvis
20	F. Black	1st ball	Batsmen run 1; no signal
		4th ball	Umpire signals Boundary 4
21	M. Green	1st ball	S. Pearce out – bowled; replaced by R. Fowler
		2nd ball	Batsmen run 2; no signal
		3rd ball	Batsmen run 1; no signal
22	F. Black	1st ball	Batsmen run 1; no signal
		2nd ball	Umpire signals Boundary 4
23	M. Green	1st ball	Umpire signals Boundary 4
		2nd ball	Umpire signals Boundary 4
		4th ball	R. Fowler out – Caught F. Black; replaced by H. Brown
			L Batsmen had crossed before catch, so Jarvis faces
24	F. Black	1st ball	Batsmen run 2; no signal
		2nd ball	Batsmen run 1; no signal
		3rd ball	Batsmen run 2; no signal
25	M. Green	1st ball	H. Brown out – Bowled; replaced by D. Smith
		2nd ball	Umpire signals Boundary 4
		3rd ball	Umpire signals Boundary 4
		4th ball	**H** D. Smith out – Run out at the bowler's end, going for 3rd run. (**M**)

THE SAME INNINGS – SHOWING MORE DETAIL

WESSEX CRICKET CLUB V NORTHSHIRE C. CLUB

HOME SIDE / VISITORS

FIRST INNINGS OF WESSEX PLAYED AT SUMMER GROUND ON 8 JUNE 1996

	BATSMEN	BALLS	RUNS SCORED	SCORING RATE 50	100	150	HOW OUT	BOWLER	TOTAL
1	T. STOKES	20	+ · · 2 · · · · · · 2 3 1 · · · 4 · · · W				BOWLED	BROWN	12
2	W. BALL	31	· · · 4 · · · 1 · · ⊙ · · 2 2 · · · · · 4 4 · · W				CT. COX†	BROWN	17
3	G. HARRIS	5	· · 4 1 W				HIT WKT	WHITE	5
4	C. WEST*	25	· · · · · 2 4 1 · · · 2 0 · · · 4 · · · · 1 2 · W				ST. COX†	GREEN	16
5	S. PEARCE	17	1 3 · · · · · · · · 1 4 3 2 1 1 W				BOWLED	GREEN	16
6	T. CLARKE	14	· · 1 · · 4 ③ 1 2 · · · W				BOWLED	BLACK	11
7	P. MORRIS†	3	· · W				ST. COX†	GREEN	0
8	B. JARVIS	23	· · · · · · 4 · · · · · 4 · · · · · · 2 · · ·				NOT OUT		10
9	R. FOWLER	7	2 1 1 4 4 · W				CT. BLACK	GREEN	12
10	H. BROWN	3	2 1 W				BOWLED	GREEN	3
11	D. SMITH	3	4 4 2				RUN OUT		10

TOTAL BALLS RECEIVED 151

NO BALLS	21	3	BOWLING EXTRAS	5
WIDES	11	2		
BYES	4	4	FIELDING EXTRAS	4
LEG BYES		–		
			TOTAL FOR 10 WICKETS	121

RUNS AT THE FALL OF EACH WICKET AND NO. OF OUTGOING BATSMAN

1	2	3	4	5	6	7	8	9	10
20	29	37	62	81	85	90	106	111	121
1	3	2	4	6	7	5	9	10	11

(K)

0	1	2	3	4	5	6	7	8	9
10	1	2	3	4	5	6	7	8	9
20	1	2	3	4	5	6	7	8	9
30	1	2	3	4	5	6	7	8	9
40	1	2	3	4	5	6	7	8	9
50	1	2	3	4	5	6	7	8	9
60	1	2	3	4	5	6	7	8	9
70	1	2	3	4	5	6	7	8	9
80	1	2	3	4	5	6	7	8	9
90	1	2	3	4	5	6	7	8	9
100	1	2	3	4	5	6	7	8	9
110	1	2	3	4	5	6	7	8	9
120	1	2	3	4	5	6	7	8	9
130	1	2	3	4	5	6	7	8	9
140	1	2	3	4	5	6	7	8	9
150	1	2	3	4	5	6	7	8	9
160	1	2	3	4	5	6	7	8	9
170	1	2	3	4	5	6	7	8	9
180	1	2	3	4	5	6	7	8	9
190	1	2	3	4	5	6	7	8	9
200	1	2	3	4	5	6	7	8	9
210	1	2	3	4	5	6	7	8	9
220	1	2	3	4	5	6	7	8	9
230	1	2	3	4	5	6	7	8	9
240	1	2	3	4	5	6	7	8	9
250	1	2	3	4	5	6	7	8	9
260	1	2	3	4	5	6	7	8	9
270	1	2	3	4	5	6	7	8	9
280	1	2	3	4	5	6	7	8	9
290	1	2	3	4	5	6	7	8	9
300	1	2	3	4	5	6	7	8	9
310	1	2	3	4	5	6	7	8	9
320	1	2	3	4	5	6	7	8	9
330	1	2	3	4	5	6	7	8	9
340	1	2	3	4	5	6	7	8	9
350	1	2	3	4	5	6	7	8	9
360	1	2	3	4	5	6	7	8	9
370	1	2	3	4	5	6	7	8	9

Figure 10 Batting sheet

BOWLERS	1	2	3	4	5	6	7	8	9	NO BALLS	WIDES	BALLS B'WLD	OVERS	MDNS	RUNS	WKTS	AV'GE
1 J.WHITE (A)	· · 2 ·	2 3	⊙ ·	2 2	M	2 · 4 ·				L	1	38	6	1	22	1	22
(J)	0-3	0-8	0-10	0-14	1-14	1-22											
2 T.BROWN	· 4 ·	· 4 ·	· 4 w	· · 4 4	· 4 · w 2	3 ⊙ 4 ·	· · · 1 2 3 4			ł	1	43	7	—	34	2	17
	0-4	0-6	1-10	1-15	2-23	2-29	2-34										
3 M.GREEN (E)	M 2 · w	· — 1 2	· — 1 2	2 (⊙) 4	w 2 4(L) w	w 4 w w	w 2 (H)				1	41	6.4	1	32	5	6·4
(F)	0-0	1-3	1-7	2-11	3-14	4-22	5-32										
4 F.BLACK (F)	③ 4 · w	4 3	· 4 ·	· 4 ·	2 · 2	· · ·				ł		31	5	—	29	1	29
	0-7	1-14	1-19	1-22	1-29						1						
										3	2	153	2 BYES	2	117	9	r.o.
											WIDES 2		LEG BYES		4	1	
												151			121		10

NOTES

(A) White opens with a Wide - no runs taken.

(B) White bowled a No Ball which was not hit. Batsmen ran 2. These runs count against the Bowler and it is not a Maiden over.

(C) Harris was out 'Hit Wicket' - the Bowler is given credit for the wicket.

(D) Brown bowled a No Ball which was not hit and Batsmen did not run

(E) The fact that a 'boundary - 4 byes' occurred does not prevent this from being a Maiden over

(F) Batsmen hit 3 off a No Ball. The Umpire correctly allowed an extra ball

(G) Batsman was stumped off a Wide. Penalty of one run correctly entered.

(H) Smith was run out attempting a third run but was correctly credited with two runs.

(J) Figures denote the Bowler's analysis progressively.

(K) Runs are crossed off in blocks. ⧄ a single, ⧅ 3 runs. Horizontal lines show that a block begun at the end of one line continues at the start of the next line.

(L) The w is underlined since, although there were no runs (Fowler was Caught), the batsmen have changed ends.

(M) Underlining shows that Smith is at the howler's end and although he scored 2

Figure 11 Bowling analysis

211

before hitting the wicket, his dismissal should be entered as Bowled.

Law 32: If a batsman is caught no run is scored under any circumstances.

Law 37: The runs already scored before the dismissal count, except where the obstruction prevents the striker from being caught.

Law 38: The run in progress does not count, but runs made before the run out will count.

Law 39: The difference between being stumped and run out by the wicket-keeper without the intervention of a fielder, depends on whether or not, in the opinion of the umpire, the striker was attempting to run. The striker may be stumped even if he has hit the ball. If in doubt ask the umpire at the first available opportunity.

Law 41: The 5 runs penalty is in addition to the runs already scored, so that, if the batsmen have already run one, 6 runs must be credited to the striker (or to extras if the umpires so signal). The umpire will normally advise you in such cases. (See **Part II:** pages 123 and 128)

Law 42: Where a bowler has been taken off, as directed by the umpires, the scorers should draw a horizontal line along the blank spaces of the analysis to indicate that he may not bowl again in the innings.

Signals The scorers must recognize the umpire's signals and acknowledge them promptly.

MAKING ENTRIES IN THE SCORE BOOK

The learner is advised to practise scoring while watching at two or three matches before undertaking the responsibility of being an official in the score-box.

In the following notes, the term 'entry in the analysis', unless otherwise qualified, means entry in the space provided for recording the details of each over. This space is usually square, allowing for six symbols representing the six balls of an over to be entered in a block formation. In some books the space is an elongated rectangle in which a single line of symbols is entered.

Runs off the bat are entered by placing the appropriate figure against the striker's name in the score sheet and the same very small figure in the analysis. Other runs are recorded as dots.

Byes and leg-byes are entered in the special spaces provided in the score sheet and by putting a dot in the analysis.

The entry of no balls and wides in the score sheet and analysis can be somewhat intricate and is dealt with separately in the next section.

If there is nothing to record, a dot is put in the analysis to assist in counting the balls in the over.

Whenever runs are credited to the striker or to extras they should also be marked off in the running total. It facilitates the search for errors if the running total is not marked off run by run, but by using one line to cover two numbers when two runs have been scored, and so on.

When a batsman is out the method of dismissal is entered in the score sheet in the column headed 'How out'. The name of the bowler is added in the next column, except when the bowler is not entitled to claim credit for the wicket. If the bowler *is* entitled to credit, a small 'w' is entered in the analysis instead of a dot. If the bowler is *not* entitled many scorers put 'R' in the analysis instead of a dot. This shows the ball at which the wicket fell and the fact that the bowler does not get credit for the wicket. As soon as these entries are made, the batsman's total is added up and entered in the 'Total runs' column of the batting sheet. The total runs for the side at the fall of the wicket is then entered in the space provided.

By convention a maiden over is a complete over in which no runs are conceded by a bowler. Even if no runs are scored off the bat, the over must not be considered a maiden over if it contains a No ball or a Wide, but a maiden over may contain byes or leg-byes. When a maiden over has been bowled, the scorer links the dots together to form the letter 'M' or, if the bowler has taken a wicket, the letter 'W'.

THE ENTRY OF NO BALLS AND WIDES IN THE SCORE BOOK

The general symbols used for analysis entries are 'O' for no ball and '+' for wide, with secondary additions as indicated in the following table:

No balls	Batting sheet Entry	Analysis Entry
1 No run taken	1 N.B.	○
2 'bye' signalled (striker did not hit the ball) 1, 2, 3, or 4 runs scored	1, 2, 3, or 4 N.B.s	○ with 1 dot or 2 or 3 or 4 dots
3 'bye' not signalled (striker has hit the ball) 1, 2, 3 or 4 runs scored	1, 2, 3, or 4 runs to the striker	① or ② or ③ or ④
4 A batsman out off a No ball Striker out – Hit the Ball Twice.	1 N.B.	○
Either batsman out: Handled the Ball.	*	†
Obstructing the Field.	*	†
or Run Out.	*	†

* Insert, as in (1), (2) or (3) above, the number of runs completed before the occurrence.

† Insert 'O' with dots or figures corresponding to the penalty or the number of runs completed before the occurrence.

5 Before delivery, the bowler tries to run out the striker. This is treated as an ordinary No ball.

6 Runs are scored due to an unsuccessful attempt by the bowler to run out the non-striker. These are scored as No balls even though No ball has not been called. The ball does not count as one of the balls in the over.

No balls	Batting sheet Entry	Analysis Entry
7 No ball is called and signalled, but the bowler does not release the ball. The umpire will revoke the call and no entry is made in the book.		

Wides	Batting sheet Entry	Analysis Entry
1 Ball not played.		
No run taken	1 W	+
Batsmen run one only.	1 W	+
Batsmen run 2 or 3	2 or 3 W	+ or +
Batsmen run 4 or ball reaches boundary.	4 W	+
2 Ball played with the bat. Umpire revokes call; entries are made for whatever else happens, just as if call had not been made.		
3 Batsman out off a wide.		
Hit wicket or stumped.	1 W	+^{W}
Any other method of dismissal	*	†
* Insert as wides the penalty of 1, or the number of runs completed before the occurrence.		
† Insert + with dots corresponding to the number of runs completed before the occurrence.		

Scorers must specially note that the penalty of one run for a No ball or Wide is never entered in addition to any runs made by the batsmen or to a boundary allowance. However, the penalty stands, and indeed may be the winning run, even if a batsman is out, e.g. when the striker is stumped off a wide. Scorers must also note that neither No balls nor Wides count as balls in the over. Should they occur, the scorer will have to fit more than six symbols into the space for the over in the analysis.

All runs struck by the bat, all runs scored as Wides and (whatever the reason for the penalty) all runs scored as No balls, are runs conceded by the bowler.

OTHER ENTRIES

There is often a small space under each box in the analysis. This should be used to show either:

    1   The runs conceded by that bowler in that over,

or 2   The total runs conceded by him in that innings up to the end of that over.

The second of these is to be preferred as it makes it easy to keep checking the total conceded by all bowlers with the total hit by all batsmen, plus all runs scored as Wides or No balls.

Space may be provided for the score at the fall of each wicket. If the first wicket to fall is that of the number 2 batsman when the total is, say, 26, the entry for score at fall of first wicket will be '26' (for the score) and '2' for the number of the batsman. Spaces may also be provided for the times when each batsman's innings begins and ends. These should be entered up with care, and it must be remembered that, although a batsman's innings commences when he steps on to the field, there could be some delay in time before he takes guard.

TOTALLING THE SCORE AND COMPLETING THE ANALYSIS

At the end of an innings, the scorer must complete his score sheet by adding up the 'Total Runs' column and agreeing the total for the innings with his colleague.

The scorers will next extract the final bowling summary of each bowler in the section of the analysis sheet head 'Total of Overs; Maidens; Runs; Wides; No balls and Wickets'.

The numbers of No balls and Wides to be entered in this summary are taken from the totals in the special spaces provided for recording each infringement. The numbers so entered in the summary should agree with the total numbers of the general symbols 'O' and '+' in the 'over' spaces, and not with the entries in the score sheet. For example: if a bowler has bowled only one No ball, he appears in the summary as having bowled one No ball; even though it appears in the score sheet as 4 No ball extras or as 4 runs to the striker. Finally, the number of runs conceded by each bowler, including, of course, runs scored as No balls or Wides, should be summated and byes and leg-byes then added to provide a grand total, which should equal the batting side's score.

FINAL POINTS

OVERS

Where a new ball may be taken after 85 overs and the fielding Captain delays it until, say, 90 overs have been bowled, he cannot take the third new ball until at least 175 overs have been bowled because the fielding side must bowl at least 85 overs with the second new ball before being entitled to another change. But if the new ball is taken in the course of an over, the whole of that over counts as one of the next 85.

Where the score-board has a space for the number of overs, it is better to show the number of completed overs, for example when the 24th over is in progress, the board should show 23.

TIMINGS

Expert scorers make a point of entering the times of various happenings in the score book. This provides a picture of the progress of play and is particularly useful should an account of the match have to be written up later. Where the score book does not make provision for this, the following suggestions could be adopted –

Time of the fall of each wicket – enter against the batsman's name in the 'How Out' column.

Minutes taken by individual batsmen to complete their 50 or 100 – enter in margin against the batsman's name.

TABLE OF WAYS OF BEING OUT

Method	Umpire with first jurisdiction	Does Bowler Get Credit?	Possible off a 'No Ball'?	Possible off a 'Wide Ball'?
Bowled	Bowler's end	Yes	No	No
Caught	Bowler's end	Yes	No	No
Handled the Ball	Bowler's end	No	Yes	Yes
Hit Ball Twice	Bowler's end	No	Yes	No
Hit Wicket	Striker's end	Yes	No	Yes
L.B.W.	Bowler's end	Yes	No	No
Obstructing the Field	Bowler's end	No	Yes	Yes
Run Out	Depends on the end	No	Yes	Yes
Stumped	Striker's end	Yes	No	Yes
Retired, out	Bowler's end umpire should inform the scorers	No	Yes	
Timed out	Bowler's end umpire should inform the scorers	No		Yes

Minutes taken for side to reach 50, 100, 150 etc. – enter in margin at top or bottom of page.

Times of start and end of intervals for meals, or stoppages for ground, weather or light – enter on the margin of the analysis sheet.

ADVANCED SCORING

Expert scorers, who find the usual type of score book inadequate for the provision of all the information their teams require, may use score sheets of their own design, or one of the several advanced score sheets now on the market. Scorers experienced in club or League cricket will have no difficulty in understanding one of these.

The basic score sheet illustrated on pp. 206 and 207 contains the essentials. Most established scorers will also record against each batsman the balls faced by him. This technique is illustrated by the second score sheet (recording the same innings) on pp. 210 and 211. There are many more additional items of interesting information which the really experienced scorer can include when recording the match.

Correspondence courses and classes, both giving full information on such items, are run by the Association.

SCORE CHARTS

These are a refinement and the average scorer will not find the time to provide them. There is no objection to very experienced scorers undertaking this additional task, but it must not be done at the expense of the fundamental and necessary duties of a scorer.

Index

The relevant law number for each entry is set in bold and parenthesis after the page number

225